IMAGES
of America

WEST DEPTFORD

I0807093

On the Cover: Workers prepare soup in the soup kitchen at the Sanitarium Playground of New Jersey, Inc., located in West Deptford Township. The sanitarium began during the 1876 cholera epidemic in Philadelphia when a group of charity-minded citizens and businesses wanted to prevent suffering and disease and alleviate sickness by providing city children with an opportunity to spend time in the fresh country air. At one time, Soupy Island served 840 fifty ounce cans of soup, 6,000 pints of milk, 35 to 40 cases of graham crackers, and 30 cases of saltine crackers during its summer operating season. (Courtesy of the Sanitarium Playground of New Jersey, Inc.)

IMAGES
of America

WEST DEPTFORD

April Maska and Noreen Mikulski

ARCADIA
PUBLISHING

ISBN 978-0-7385-7602-2

Published by Arcadia Publishing
Charleston, South Carolina

Printed in the United States of America

Library of Congress Control Number: 2011923875

For all general information, please contact Arcadia Publishing:
Telephone 843-853-2070
Fax 843-853-0044
E-mail sales@arcadiapublishing.com
For customer service and orders:
Toll-Free 1-888-313-2665

Visit us on the Internet at www.arcadiapublishing.com

This book is dedicated to the people of West Deptford Township, past, present, and future, and with lots of love to our families.

Contents

ACKNOWLEDGMENTS

For us, this book is so much more than pictures and text printed on pages that are bound between a front and back cover. This book is a true labor of love and a dream realized. As with many dreams, the idea of preserving West Deptford's rich history began small—over lunch in the teachers' room at Oakview Elementary School. But thanks to support from our wonderful families, dear colleagues, and friends, the dream grew. The West Deptford Historical Association was formed. Pictures and artifacts were soon collected, prized family treasures were donated and displayed, and stories long forgotten were remembered and shared, so that, at long last, the people of West Deptford would receive this book.

As with any accomplishment, one does not reach true success alone. And that is why we need to send our heartfelt thanks to all that have helped make our dream come true.

First and foremost, we want to thank the West Deptford Township Committee, Mayor Anna Docimo and committeepersons Len Daws, John Cobb, Hugh Garrison, and Donna Symborski, for all of your support. We would also like to thank the Gloucester County Historical Society for sharing collections and knowledge with us. Many thanks go to the West Deptford Free Public Library for providing us with a "home." Thank you, Karen Boucher, for doing anything we ask and always doing it with a smile. Thank you, Joseph R. Jackson, our tech guy, for all of the scanning and rescanning that made this book a success. To Nancy Conover-Huebshman, Ruth Wariger, Theresa Holovachuk, and Grace M. Janson, words are not enough for all of the behind-the-scenes work that you wonderful ladies accomplished. Special thanks go to William W. Phifer Sr. and family and Sharon Phifer-Rattay for helping launch the historical association. To all members of the West Deptford Historical Association, past and present, thank you! A big thank you goes to all who shared your piece of history to make this book. April would like to thank her fabulous husband, Pat; her daughter, Aimee; and extended family for being the president and supporters of her fan club and being there whenever she needs them. You are my rock, and I love you all. Noreen would like to thank her huge family, especially her daughter, Sarah; her son, Cameron; and her husband, Chris, for their never-ending patience, support, and love.

Unless otherwise noted, all images are from the collection of the West Deptford Historical Association.

INTRODUCTION

West Deptford Township was not officially incorporated until 1871, when it broke away from the much larger Deptford Township. Its history, however, begins much earlier. Early pioneers navigated what is now called Woodbury Creek, looking for plots of land that were not already occupied. Although they feared encounters with the Mantas tribe (Lenni Lenape), their search for a home outweighed their fears. The small territory that these pioneers first came to was known as the Wilkins property and fell within the borders of the current West Deptford Township. Some of the names of these early pioneer families, such as Wilkins, Bender, Budd, Rambo, Lodge, Leonard, Platt, and Low, can still be found in the township today.

Prior to the start of the Revolutionary War, these early pioneers struggled just to find shelter and provisions. Despite these hardships, the small plots of land grew into small family farms. Farm life took a back seat when the Revolutionary War came to the area. While the British occupied Philadelphia, the whole defense of the Delaware River depended on the success of Fort Mercer. It was on October 22, 1777, that Count Von Donop and the Hessian troops attacked Fort Mercer by land while the British Fleet attempted to destroy the fort from the Delaware River. The battle lasted less than an hour with the Hessians retreating, leaving the wounded behind. Their leader, Count Von Donop, was carried to the Whitall mansion and rowed across Woodbury Creek to the Low house on Jobstown Road, where he died three days later.

As the war ended, the people within township lines went back to their family farms unaware of the changes that were about to take place. By the 1840s, railroads, the newest mode of transportation, were transforming the nation. The first railroads in this area were built between Camden and Woodbury and extended to Kings Highway and ran the length of the township. The Swedesboro Railroad, which travels from Woodbury to Swedesboro, was built in 1869 and had two stations within township borders—one was the Parkville Station and the other was the Odgen Station. In 1874, the Delaware River Railroad laid rails and had stations in Thoroughfare, Leonard's Farm, and Paradise. Local farmers were then able to export their goods to other areas of the country.

By 1893, another new technology began to leave its mark on the landscape. Thomas-Houston Electric Company began to crisscross the area with its trolley lines. Lines now ran through what is currently the Sunoco Refinery, across Crown Point Road, and continued to Colonial Avenue in Colonial Manor. Many of the trolley lines became obsolete during the 1940s when Public Service Transportation replaced trolleys with buses. Most of the tracks from the old trolley lines can no longer be found, as the steel was deemed too valuable and was removed during World War II to help with the war effort.

As railroads and trolleys brought more people to the area, it was decided that a large area of Deptford Township should be dissolved, and West Deptford Township was born. Through an act of legislation approved on March 1, 1871, the boundaries separating the townships of Deptford and West Deptford were drawn. Then in 1878, the eastern boundary line was moved to leave the whole village of Westville in Deptford Township. And in 1902, the borough of National Park was removed from West Deptford Township.

By the early 1900s, the Industrial Revolution was underway and changed the tiny farming community, one small neighborhood at a time. Verga and Colonial Manor, the unique areas found within the northern section of the township, attracted families who came to open small family businesses, to travel via the trolley lines to and from work, and to build homes. By the 1950s, Greenfields and Greenfields Village, located in the southern end of the township, continued the established farming tradition but, at the same time, attracted families who were looking to build homes and raise families in a newly established suburbia. Central to the township is the Thorofare section (often spelled Thoroughfare in the early accounts of the area). Named because it was exactly that, a thoroughfare between Woodbury and Paulsboro, it is now the heart of the township. It is the home of the township government, library, community center, and recreational parks.

Wherever you have been in this unique section of Gloucester County, you have encountered a community of people that believes in West Deptford Township. It all started with a meeting on March 21, 1871, at the Thoroughfare No. 3 School with one town clerk and three town committeemen who dreamed of making a thriving community into a prosperous township. Today, although the buildings have changed, the mission has not. The people of West Deptford are still passionate about the township, are filled with West Deptford pride, and continue the tradition of excellence established by its forefathers.

One

Centennial

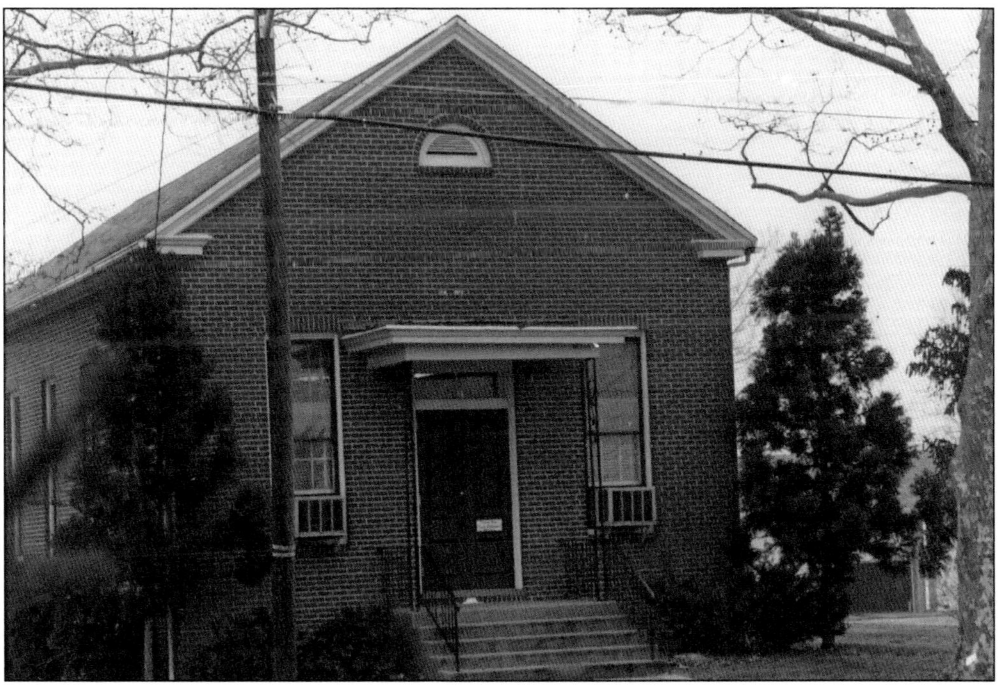

On March 21, 1871, the first township meeting was held at the Thoroughfare No. 3 School. It was not until March 3, 1874, that the township voted to construct a new building for less than $2,500, which included furnishings, horse sheds, and hitching posts. On March 2, 1875, the first town meeting was held in the new town hall. Pictured here is the original West Deptford Town Hall. Today, 140 years after the township's incorporation, the town hall remains as a reminder of how much the township has thrived and is a symbol of pride felt by residents.

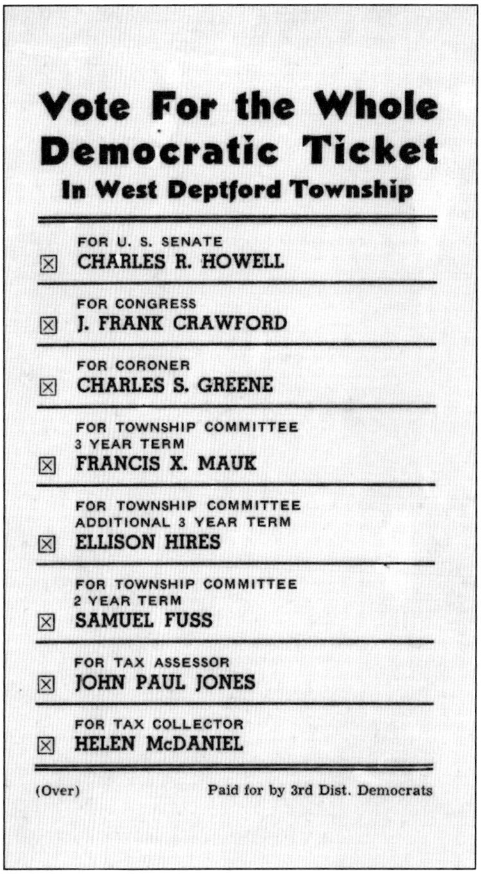

Over the years, the township building has been home to both Democrats and Republicans. Shown are election ballots for both parties. No matter the party, elected officials have always been dedicated to the betterment of the township and its residents. (Both, courtesy of the West Deptford Historical Association.)

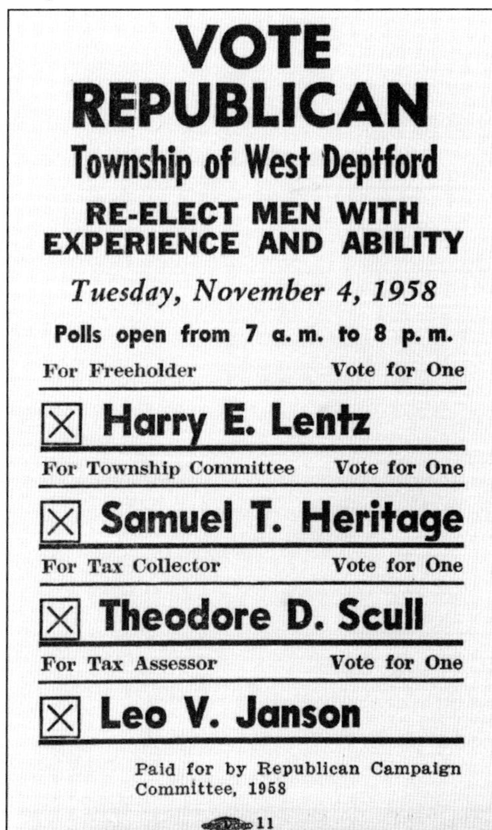

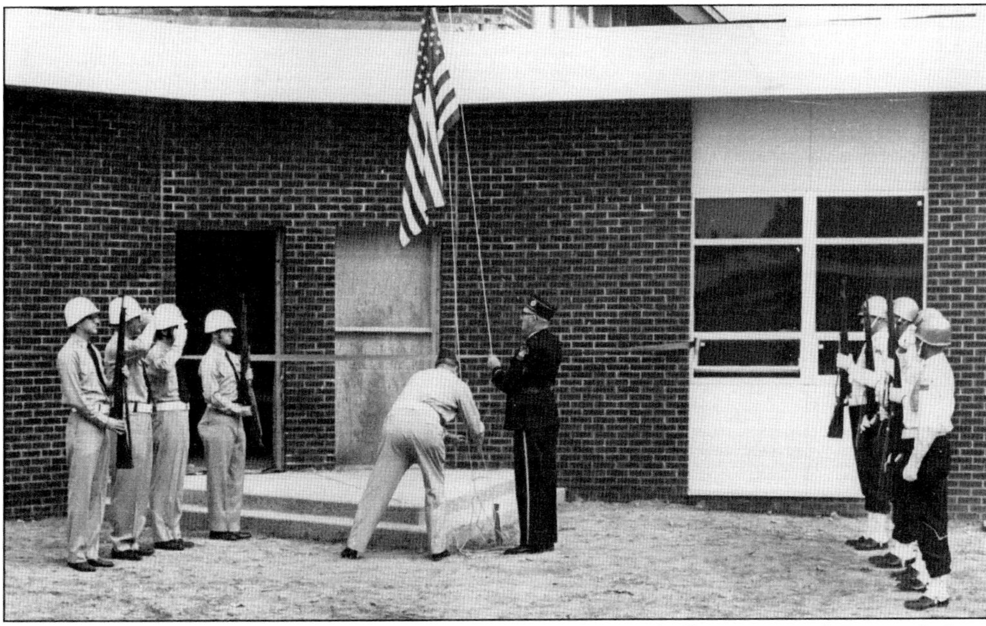

After outgrowing the original township building, a new town hall was erected. Pictured above is the flag raising that was held during the opening ceremony on March 6, 1971. The cost of the new town hall was approximately $600,000 and was erected directly across from the original township building at the intersection of Crown Point and Grove Roads.

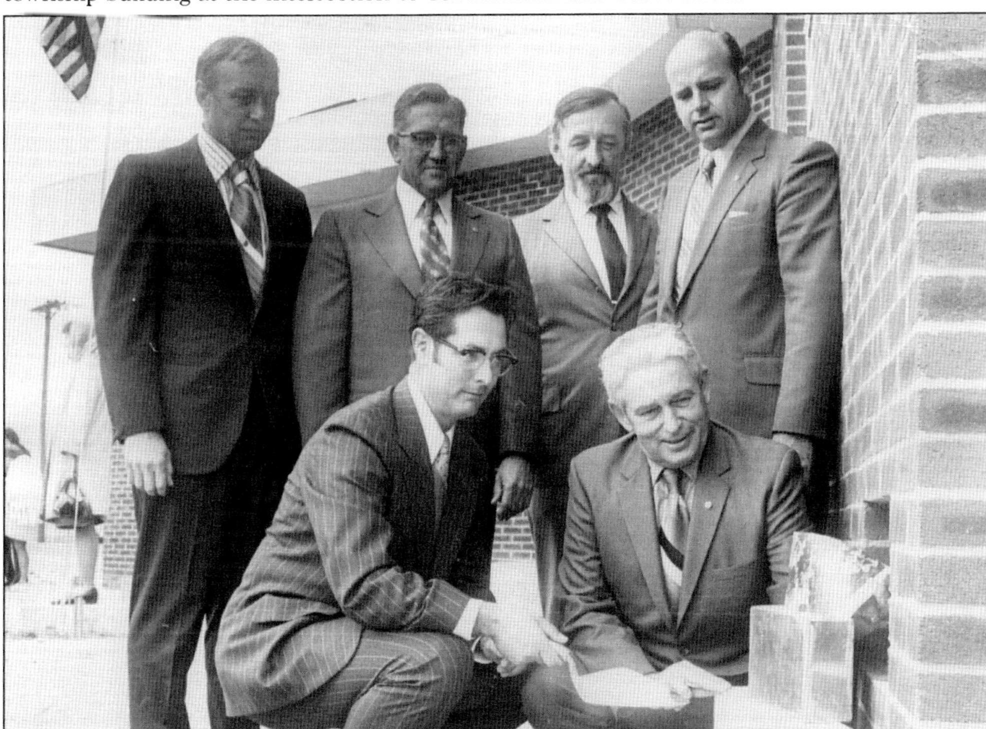

During the opening ceremony, township officials placed the cornerstone into the new municipal building. This ceremony coincided with the township's 100th anniversary celebration.

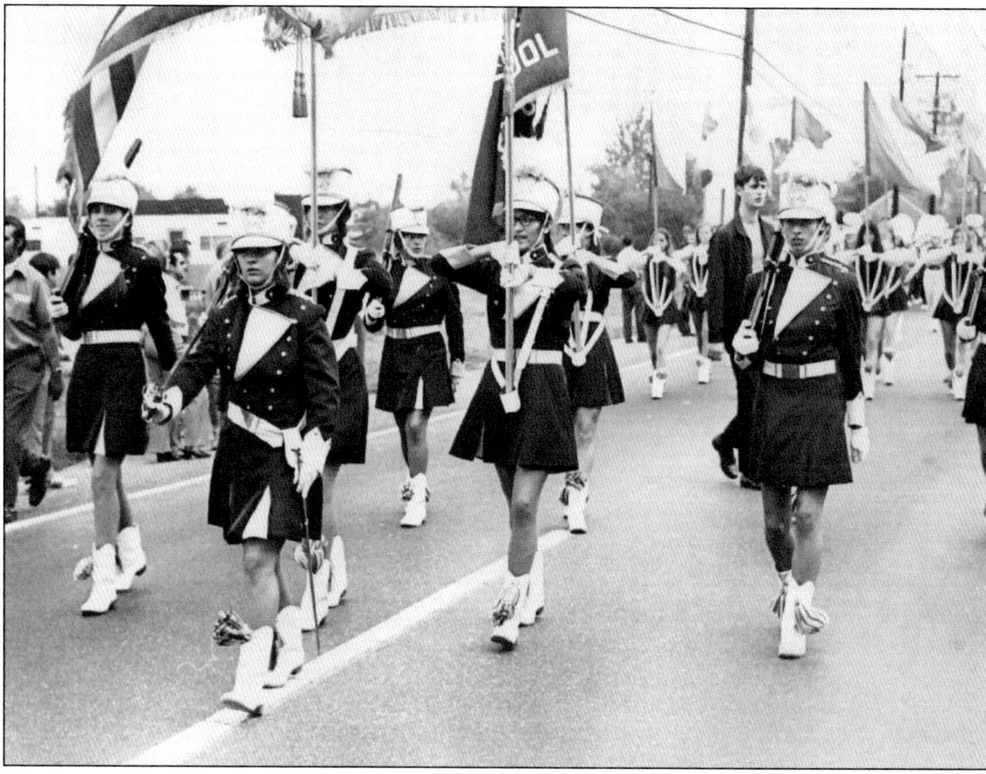

Members of the West Deptford Township Marching Band and Colonial Twirlers, sponsored by Colonial Manor American Legion Post 100, marched in the West Deptford Centennial Parade.

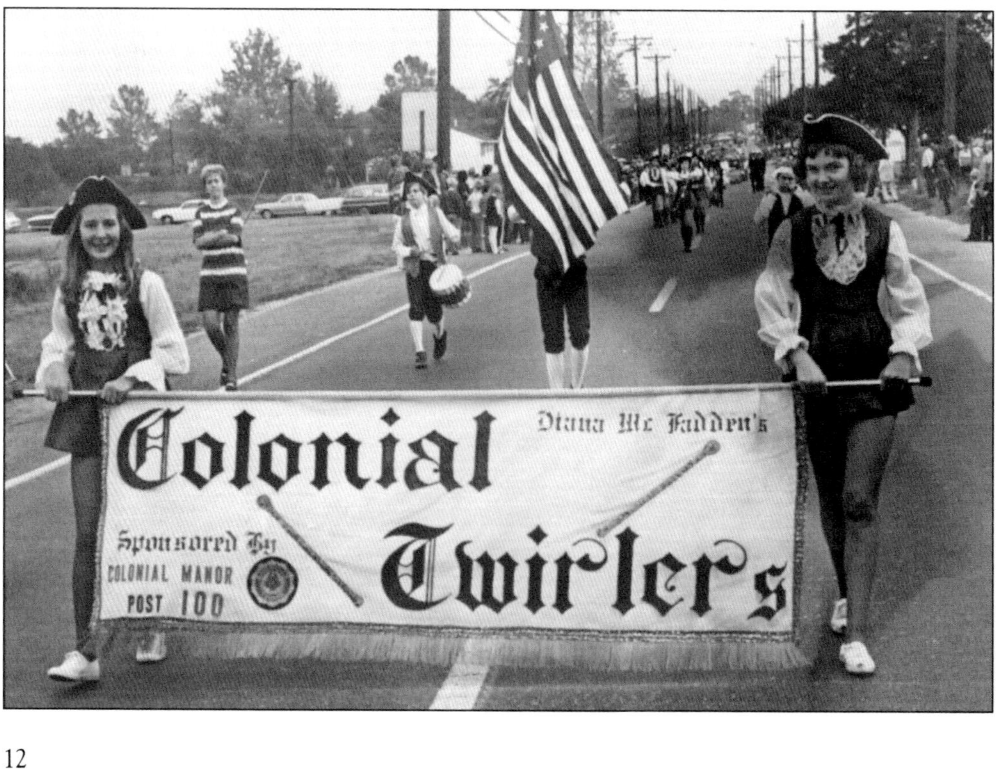

Children of all ages helped celebrate the township's centennial. Even future police officers joined in on the fun.

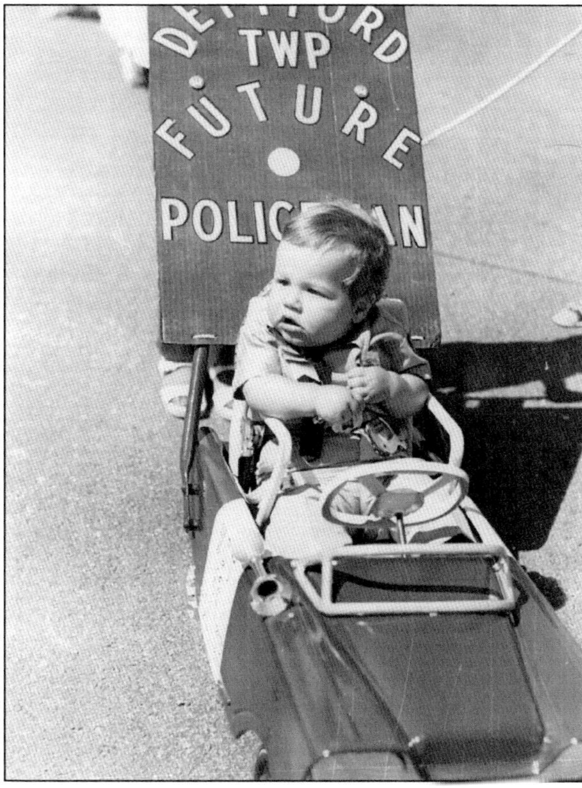

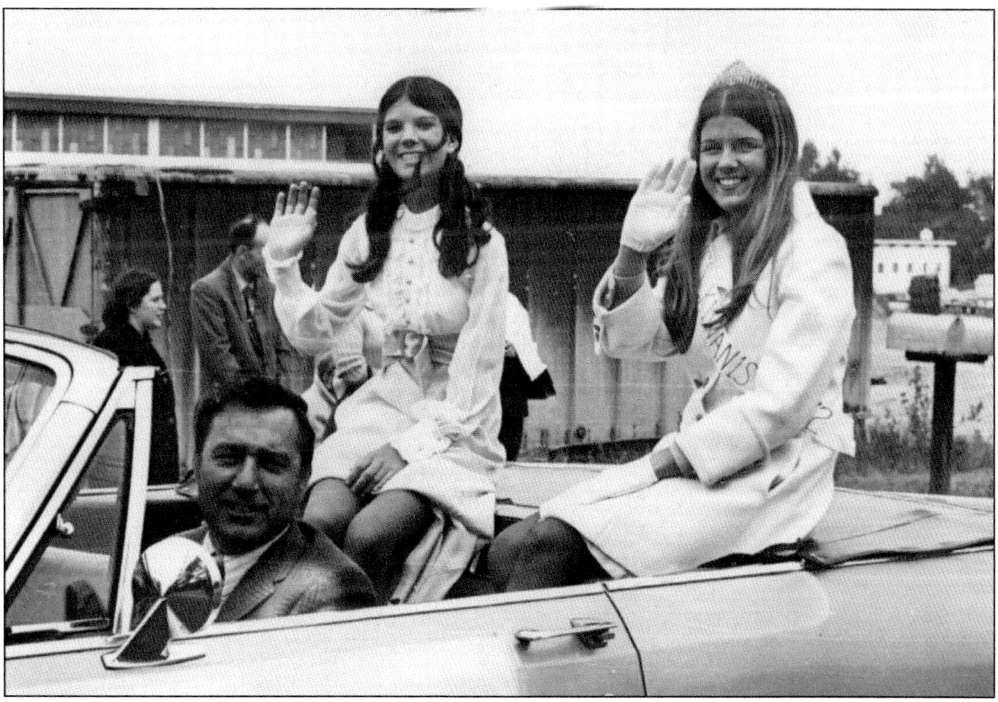

Pictured in the Miss Kiwanis car during the celebration are Robin Wagner (left) and Arlene St. Petery.

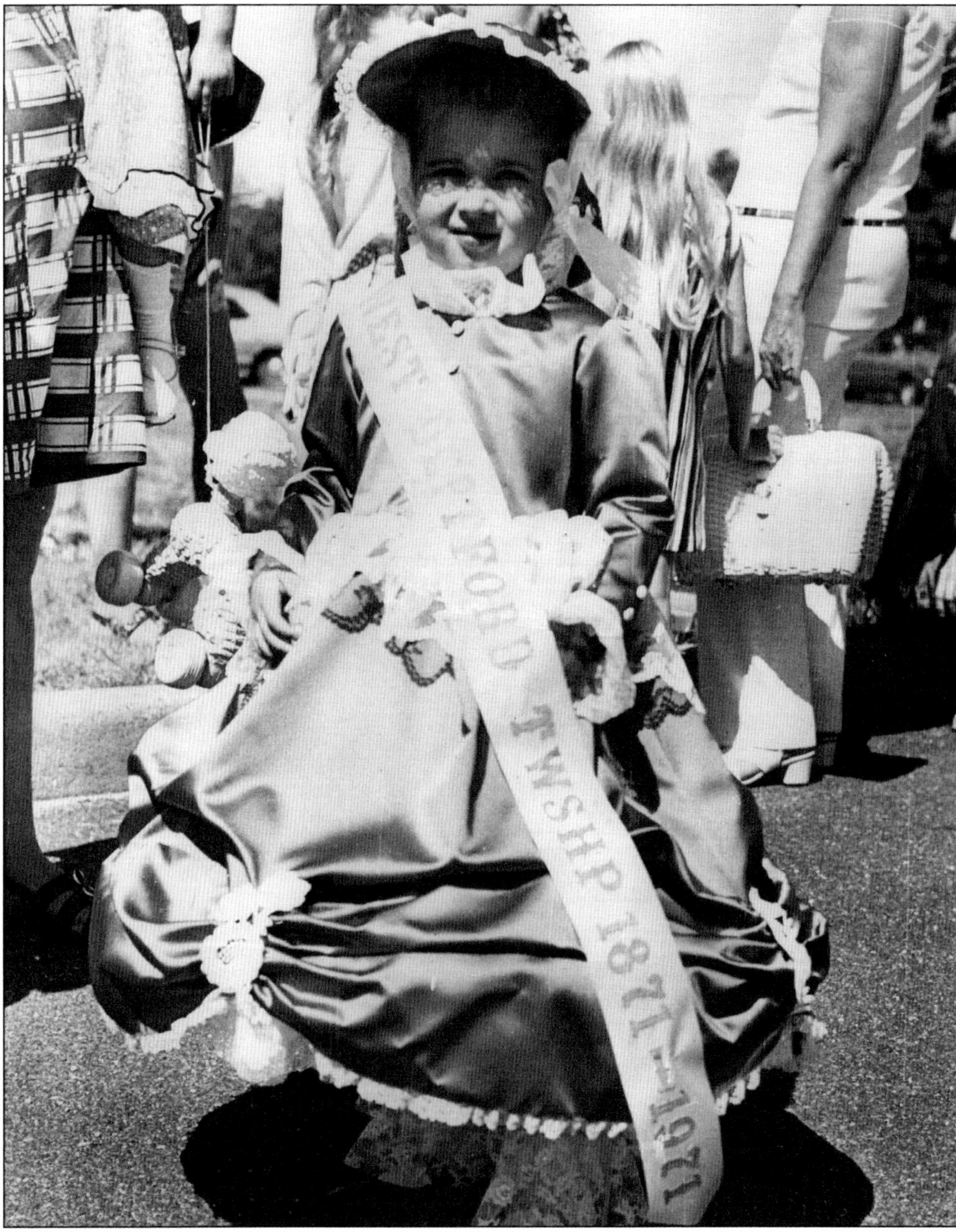

Getting into the true spirit of the centennial celebration, Miss West Deptford Township 1871–1971 portrays the look of an early pioneer in her traditional costume.

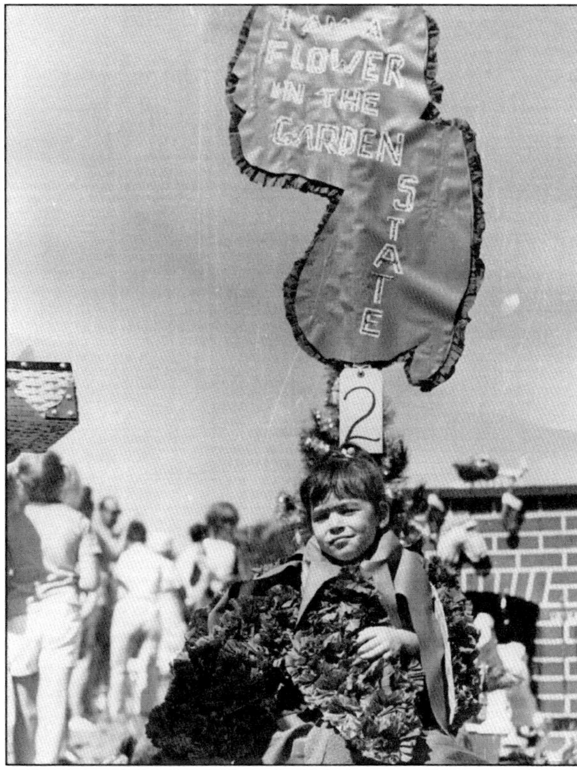

Pictured at right, a true flower of the Garden State blooms while parading through town during the centennial parade. Pictured below, parade watchers got a glimpse into the future as a Miss West Deptford 1984 hopeful passed by in her rendition of fashions to come. (Both, courtesy of the West Deptford Historical Association.)

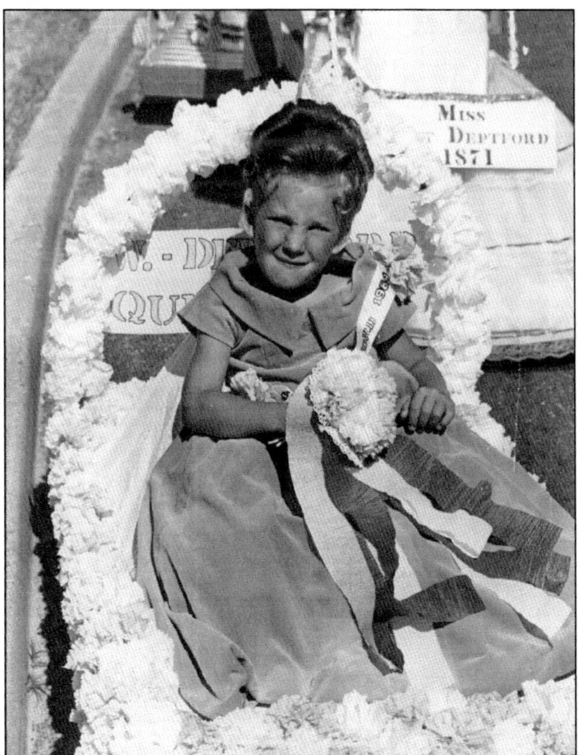

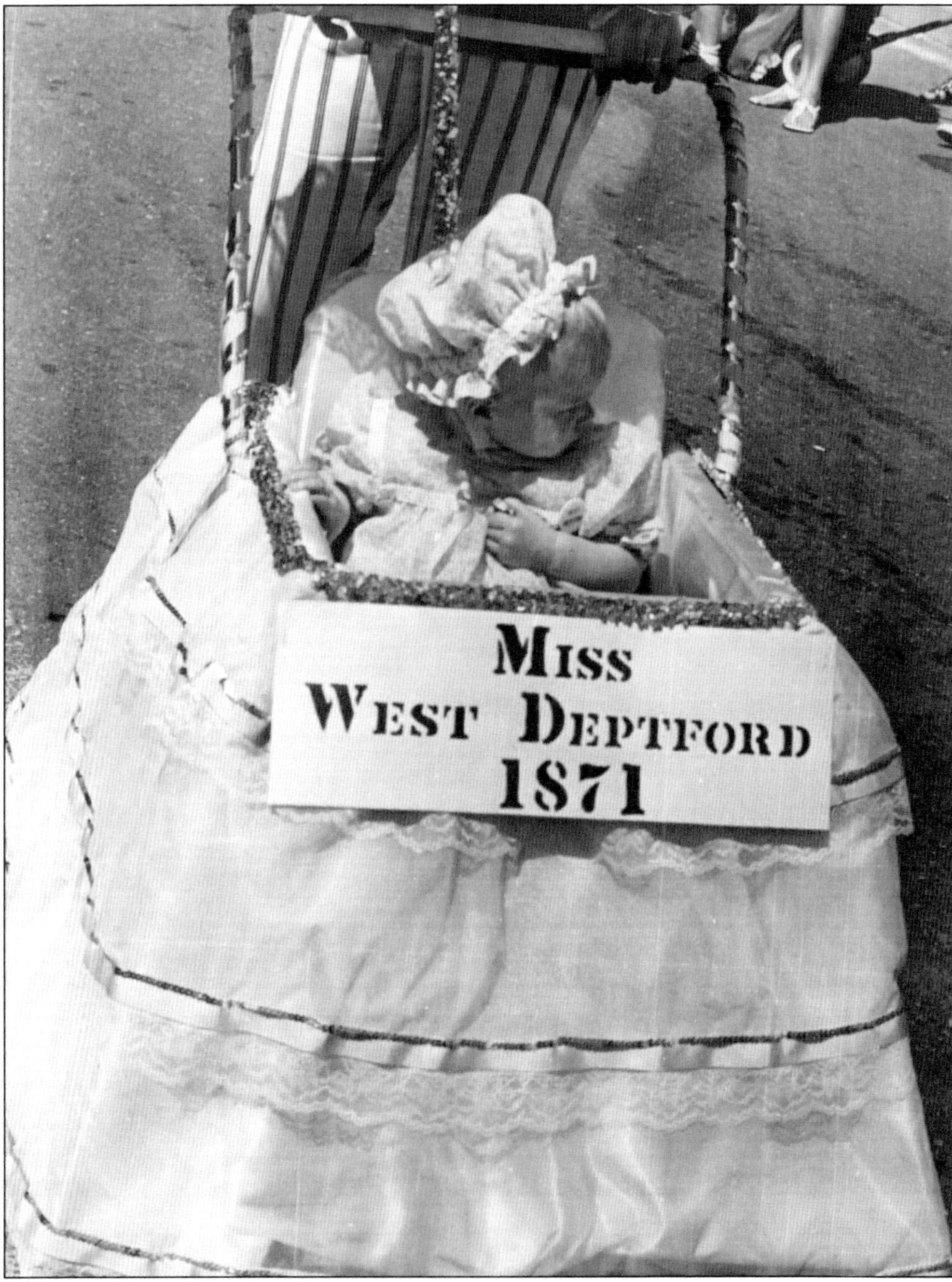

Even the youngest of residents participated in the centennial celebration. Pictured here, Miss West Deptford 1871 strolls down the parade route celebrating 100 years of growth and prosperity.

Two

Family Farms and Local Businesses

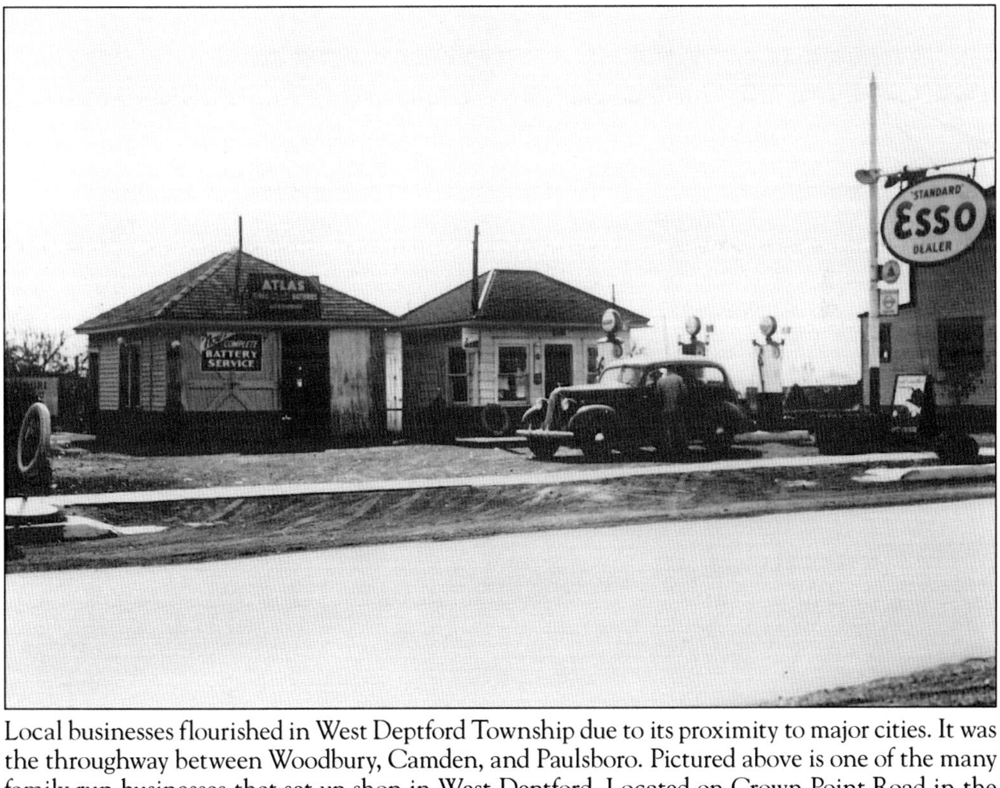

Local businesses flourished in West Deptford Township due to its proximity to major cities. It was the throughway between Woodbury, Camden, and Paulsboro. Pictured above is one of the many family-run businesses that set up shop in West Deptford. Located on Crown Point Road in the Verga section of the township was Rase's Gas Station. This gas station serviced local residences, pumping Esso gasoline. (Courtesy Edna Rase.)

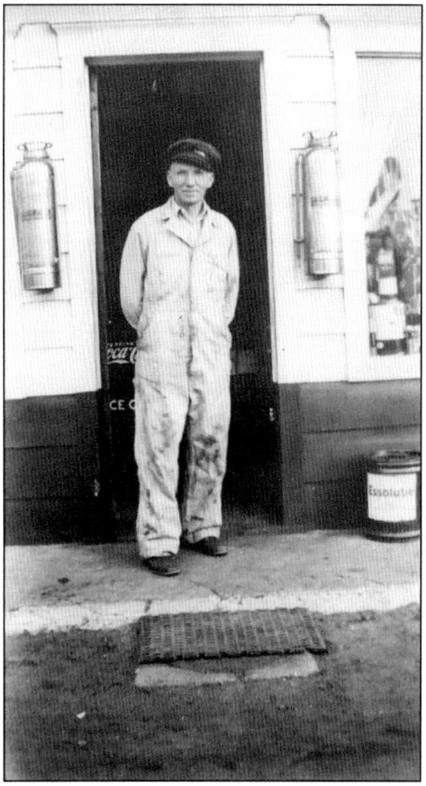

Local proprietary Otto Rase stands outside of Rase's Gas Station. He took pride in servicing the vehicles of his valued customers. (Courtesy of Edna Rose.)

The Rase home, located at 1353 Crown Point Road, Verga, was situated next to the gas station. The home still stands today and is currently a private residence. (Courtesy of Edna Rose.)

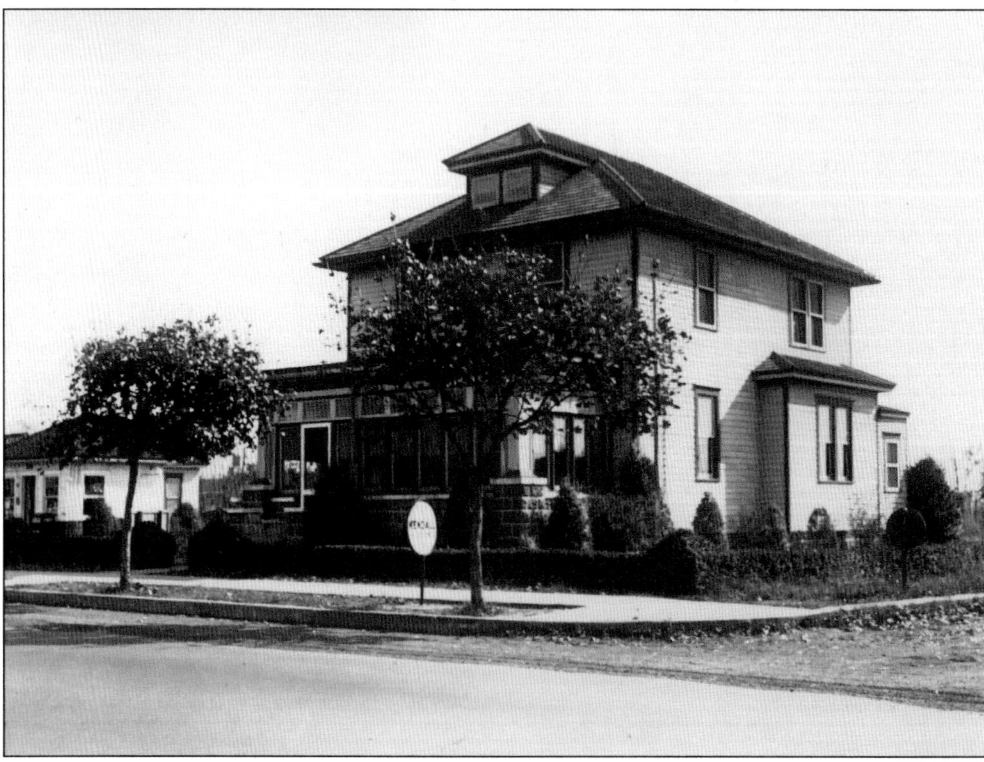

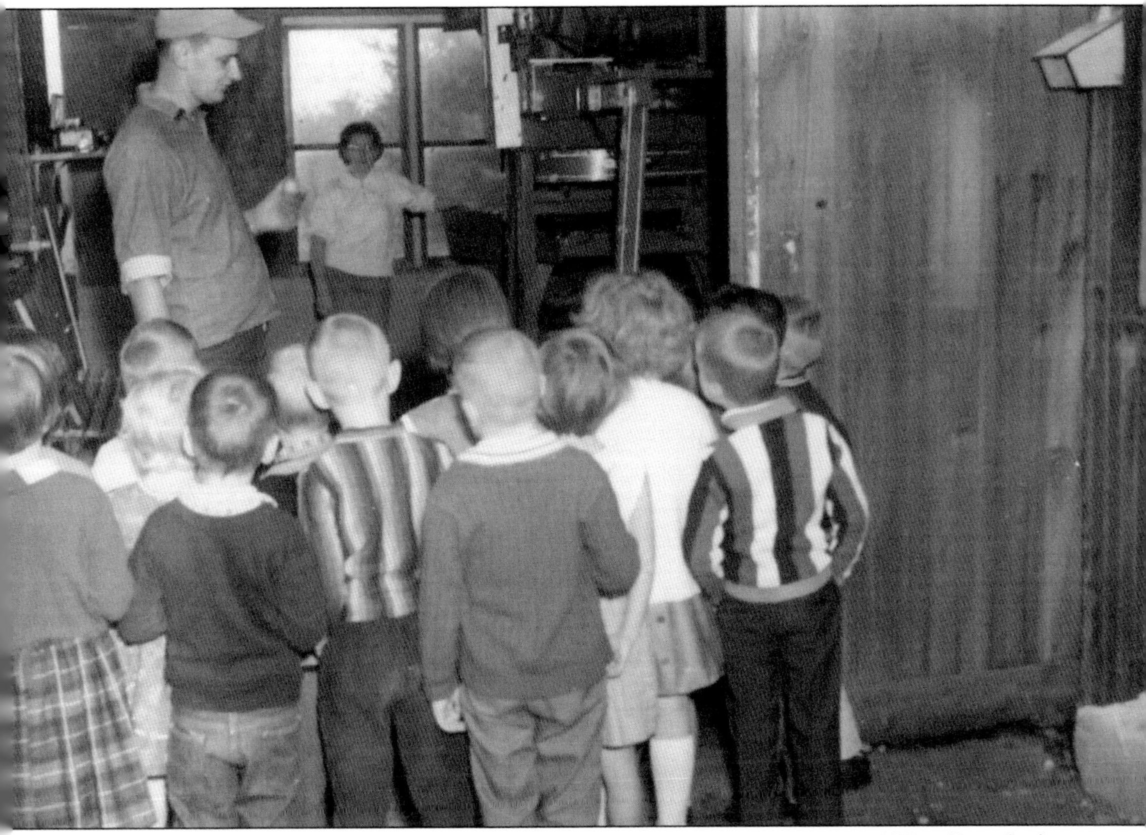

The Phifer farm is located on Kings Highway in the Mantua Grove section of West Deptford. Established by Howard and Ella (Allen) Phifer, the farm was purchased from the Stetser family. In the 1800s, the farmhouse was once a tollhouse and collected tolls from the bridge from Mount Royal into the area that is now West Deptford Township. The cider mill began in the 1950s when Howard and Ella's son Bill Phifer planted apple trees as a hobby. That hobby turned into a thriving business for the Phifer family. Bill Phifer delighted in allowing local schoolchildren to tour the cider mill. He is shown explaining how apple cider is pressed to students from Mantua Grove School. (Courtesy of the Phifer family.)

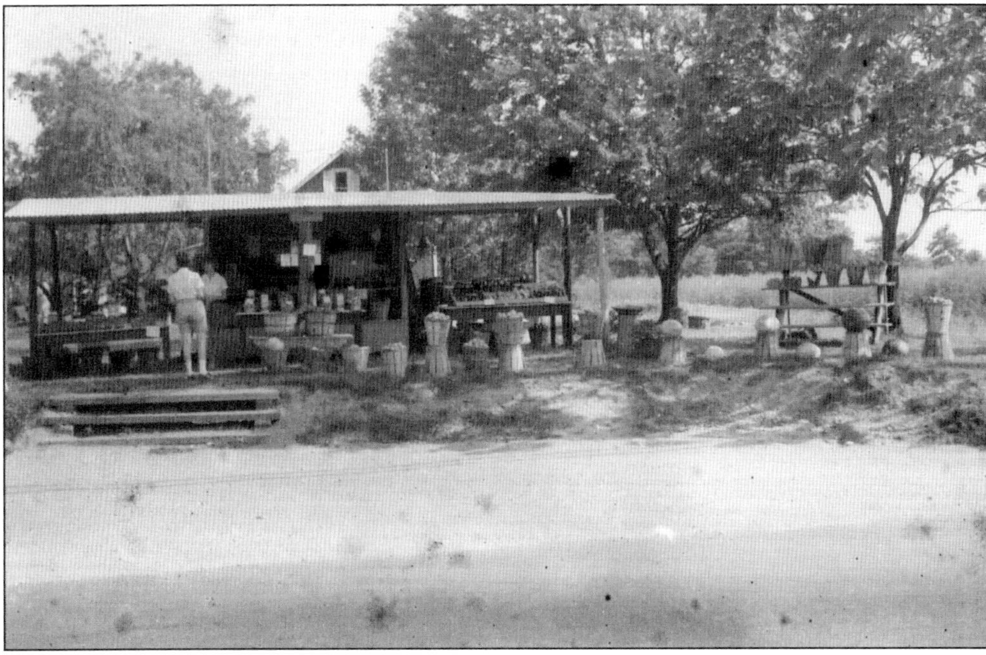

Pictured above is the Phifer's cider mill roadside stand. The roadside stand featured fall produce, mums, pumpkins, and baked goods. The market was not built until 1969. Pictured below are local children looking for the perfect pumpkin. (Both, courtesy of the Phifer family.)

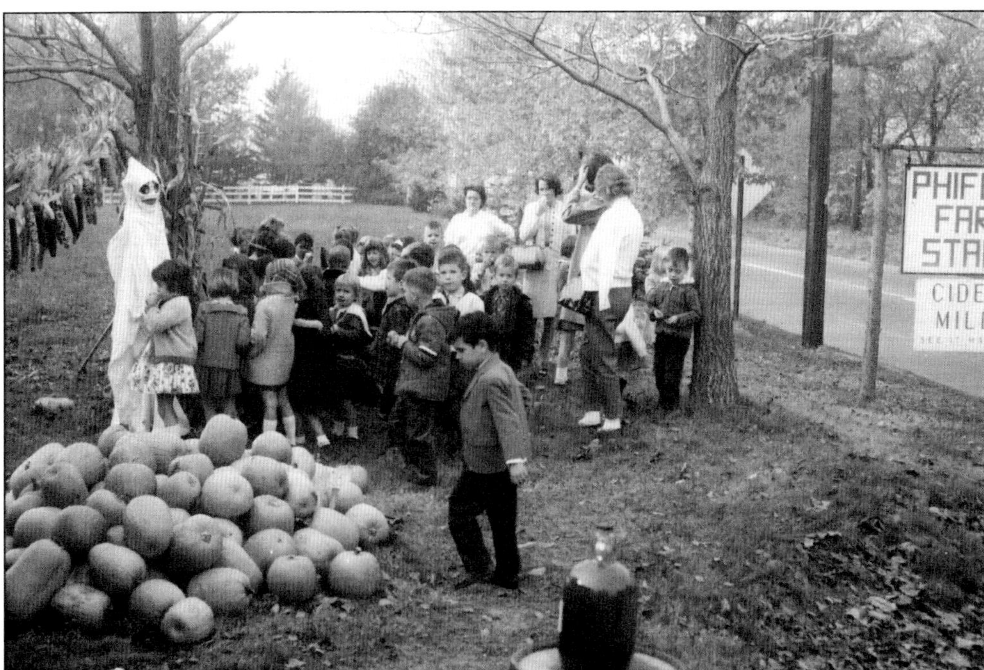

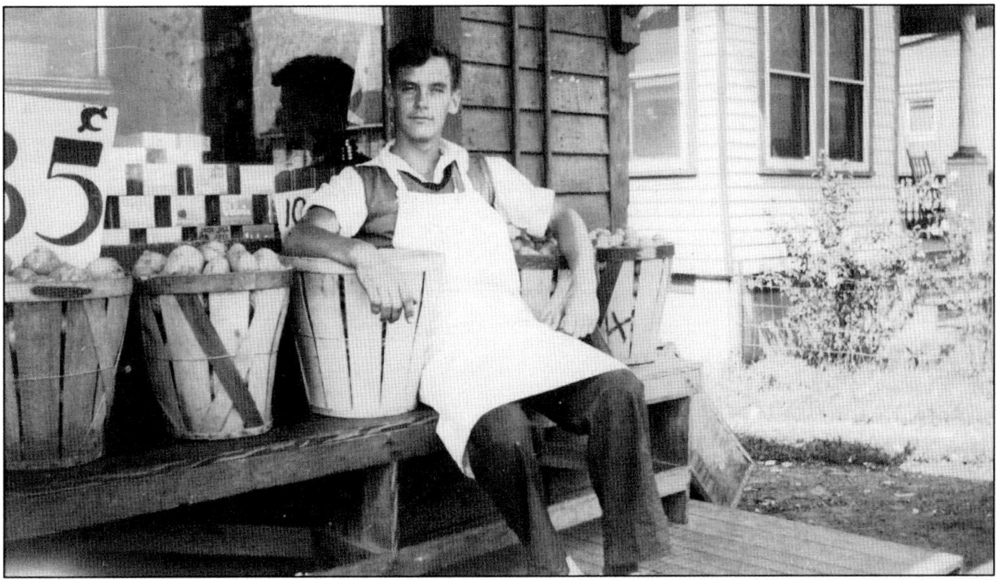

Pictured here is a young Roger Nicolai working at Etherington's Grocery Store, located on old Crown Point Road. His father, A.C. Nicolai, was the proprietor of Verga Service Station, also located in Verga. This receipt from Verga Service Station showcases typical services rendered during the 1920s for car repair. A.C. Nicolai charged this customer $110 for a new motor and $10 for installing the motor. Bill Press was the mechanic for the station. (Both, courtesy of Florence Kappeler.)

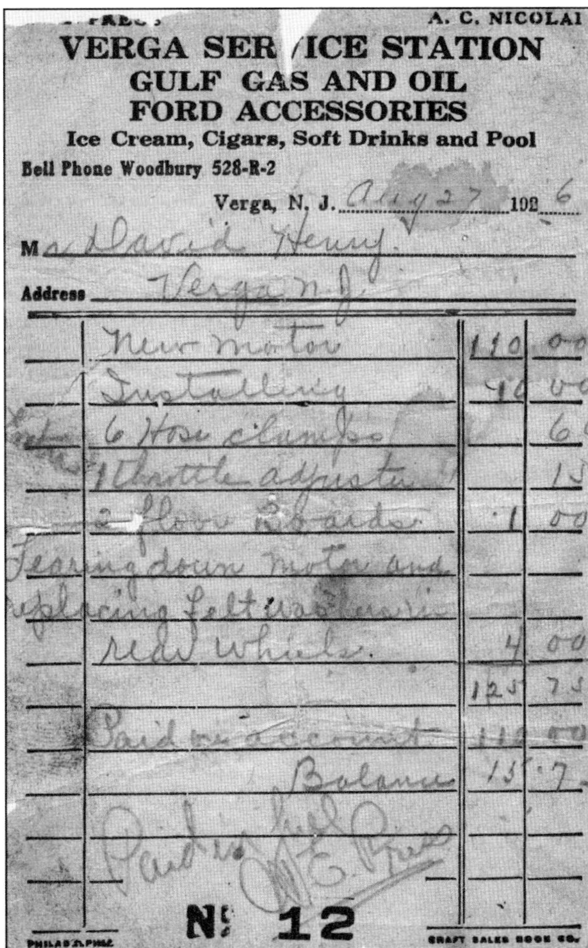

A. C. NICOLAI

VERGA SERVICE STATION
GULF GAS AND OIL
FORD ACCESSORIES
Ice Cream, Cigars, Soft Drinks and Pool
Bell Phone Woodbury 528-R-2

Verga, N. J. Aug 27 1926

Mr David Henry
Address Verga N.J.

New motor	110	00
Installing	10	00
6 Hose clamps		60
Throttle adjuster		15
2 floor boards	1	00
Tearing down motor and replacing felt washers in rear wheels	4	00
	125	75
Paid on account	110	00
Balance	15	75

Paid in full

No. 12

PHILA., PHILA. CRAFT SALES BOOK CO.

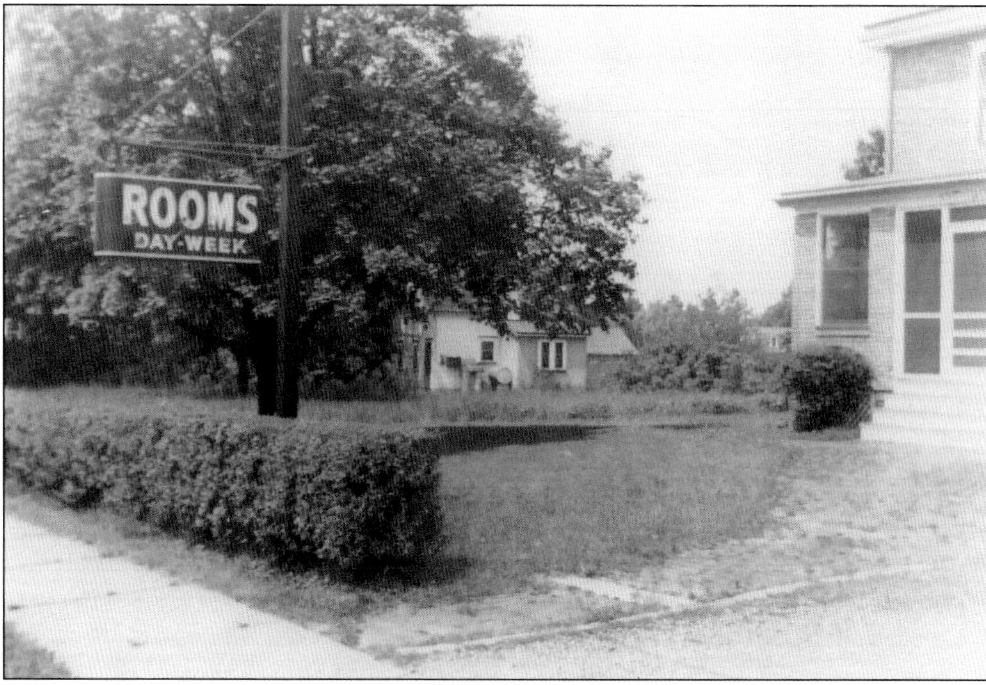

The Villa Anne Motel, pictured here around 1950, was advertised as a tourist home with rooms of a better type available by day or week. It provided a place to rest for weary travelers making their way along US Route 130 and was located on Crown Point Road or Route 44. Ann and Frank Coffiey ran the hotel. (Both, courtesy of Mary Ann Suiter.)

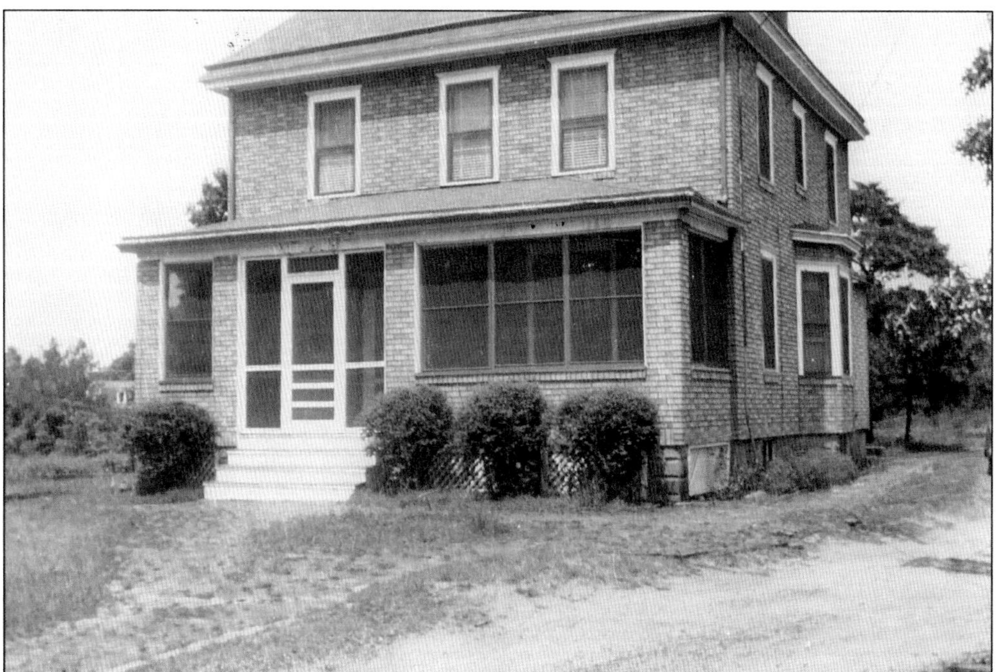

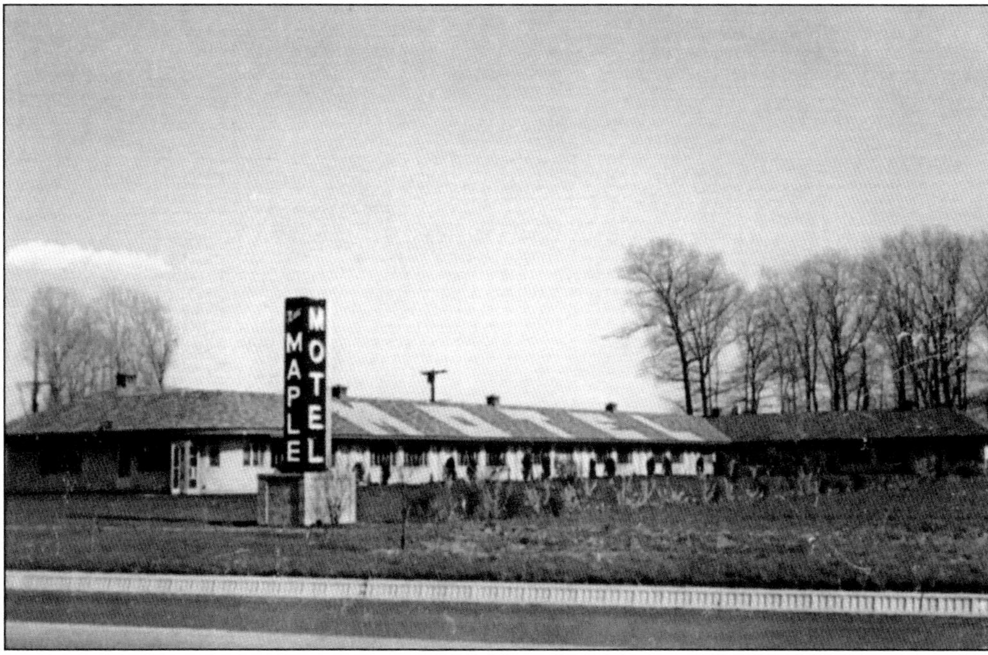

The Maple Motel was owned by Mr. and Mrs. John Gill and was located on Route US 130 Freeway in the Thorofare section of West Deptford. The phone number was TIlden 5-9757. It boasted deluxe, modern units and was open all year. (Courtesy of Larry Chester.)

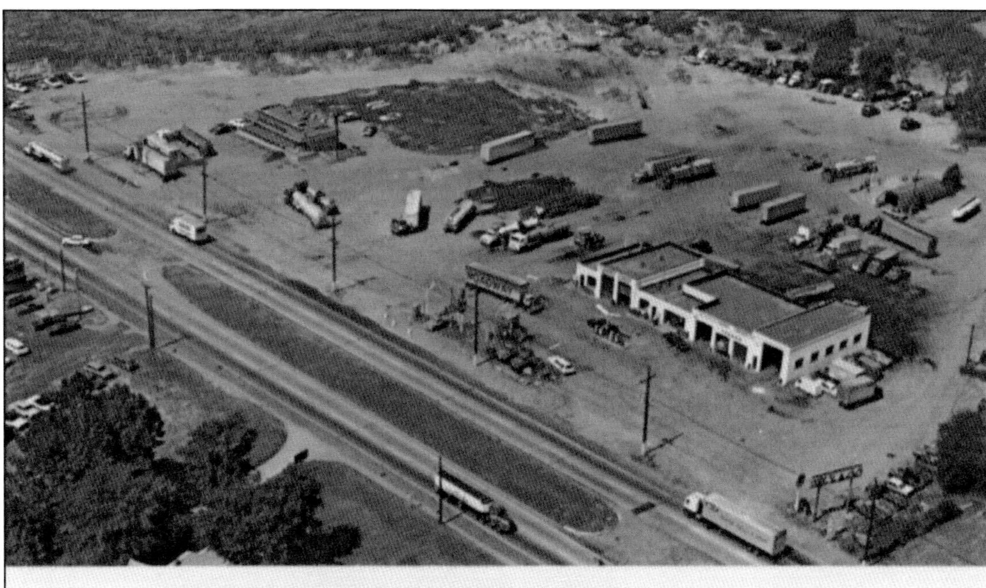

The Crown Point Truck Stop opened its doors in 1936. Known as the Crown Point Motor Park, it was located on Route US 130-295 in the Thorofare section of the township. Owned by Roy Weaver, the truck stop provided 24-hour service of Texaco fuel and gasoline, as well as truck rentals, truck repairs, road service, wrecker service, international truck sales, and parts. The truck stop also had a modern diner. (Courtesy of Larry Chester.)

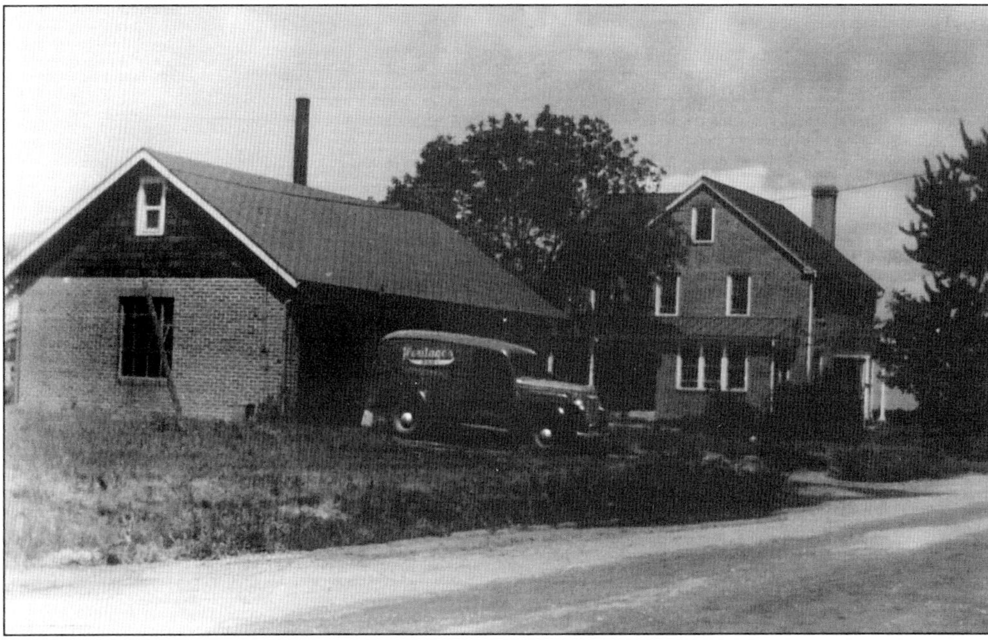

Heritage's Dairy Stores, Inc., began when brothers Harold H. "Grandpop Skeets" and Sam Heritage combined their 50-acre family farms as an innovative way to make money during the Great Depression. The family business began with just one cow and a Model A Ford, and with these two important components, milk was delivered to friends and neighbors living in the community. (Courtesy of Heritage's Dairy Stores.)

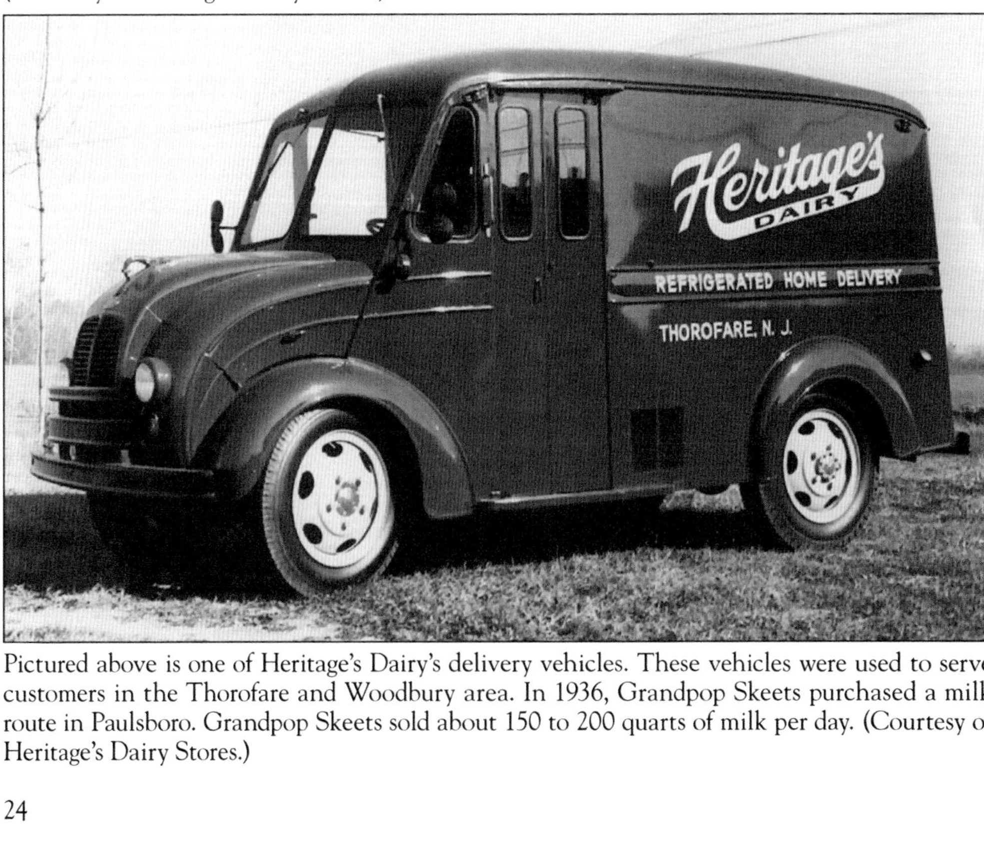

Pictured above is one of Heritage's Dairy's delivery vehicles. These vehicles were used to serve customers in the Thorofare and Woodbury area. In 1936, Grandpop Skeets purchased a milk route in Paulsboro. Grandpop Skeets sold about 150 to 200 quarts of milk per day. (Courtesy of Heritage's Dairy Stores.)

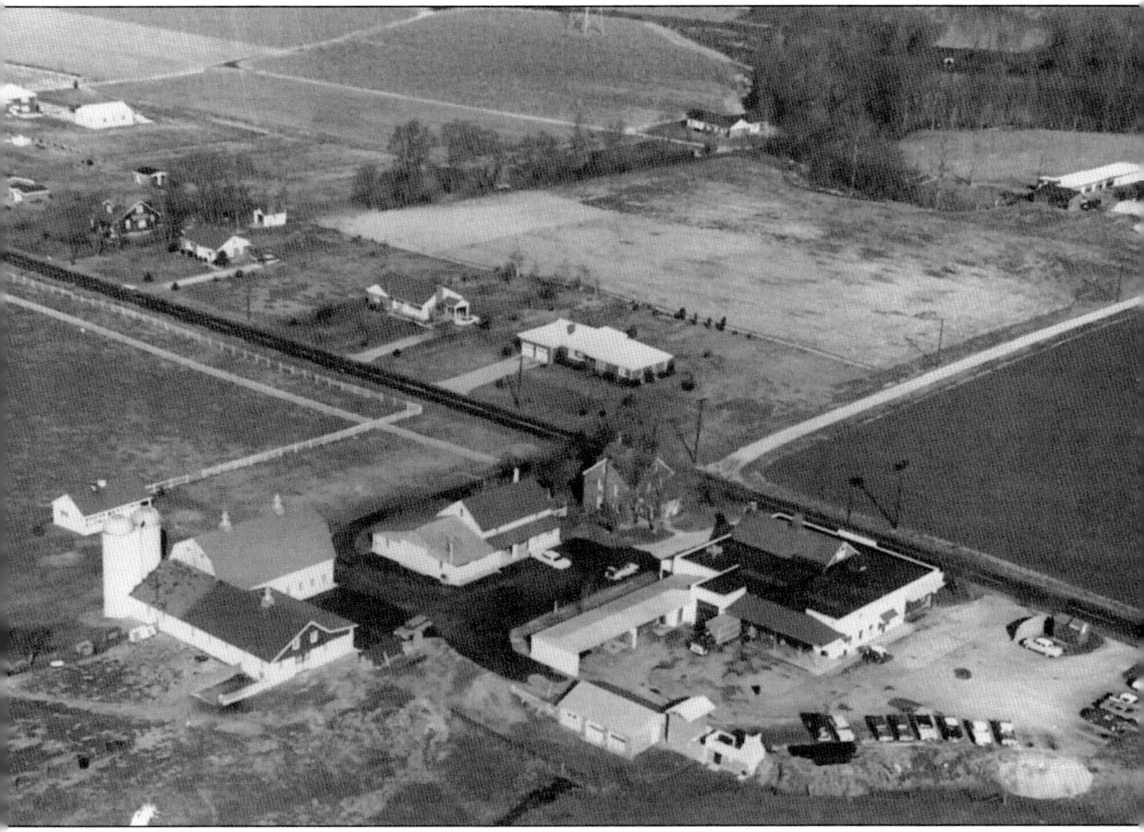

As seen in this aerial view, taken in the 1950s, the one-cow delivery service grew into a thriving dairy business. As the quart age of milk delivery gradually increased and the home delivery business decreased, Grandpop Skeets and son Harold H. Heritage Jr., known as "Skeets Jr.," investigated the possibility of opening a convenience store to serve the needs of the local families. (Courtesy of Heritage's Dairy Stores.)

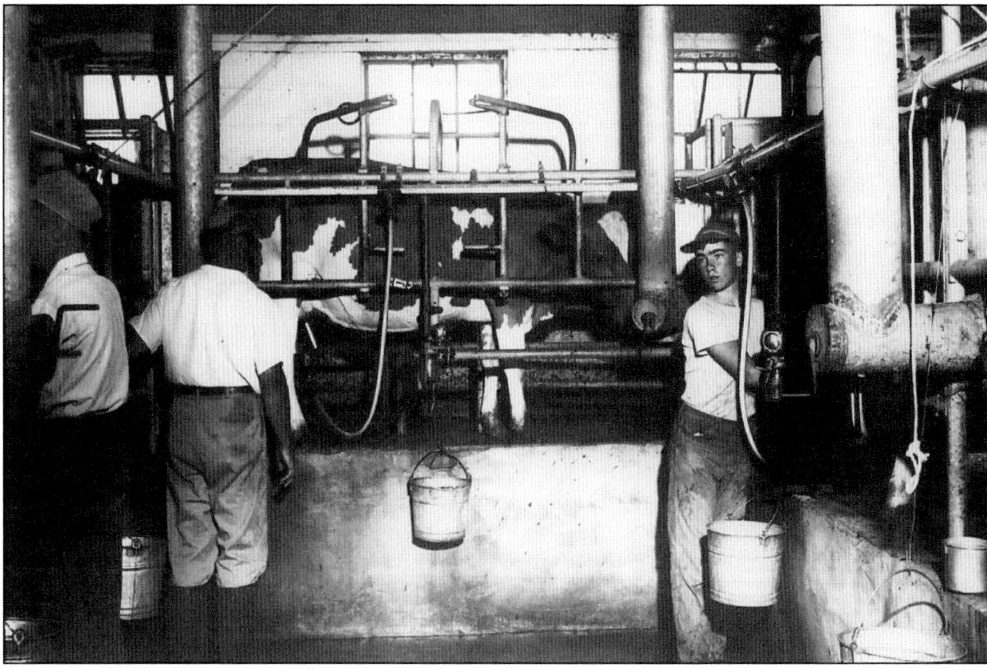

In the 1950s, modern technology took over, and cows were milked via milking machines, like the ones pictured. These machines replaced the need for hand milking. (Courtesy of Heritage's Dairy Stores.)

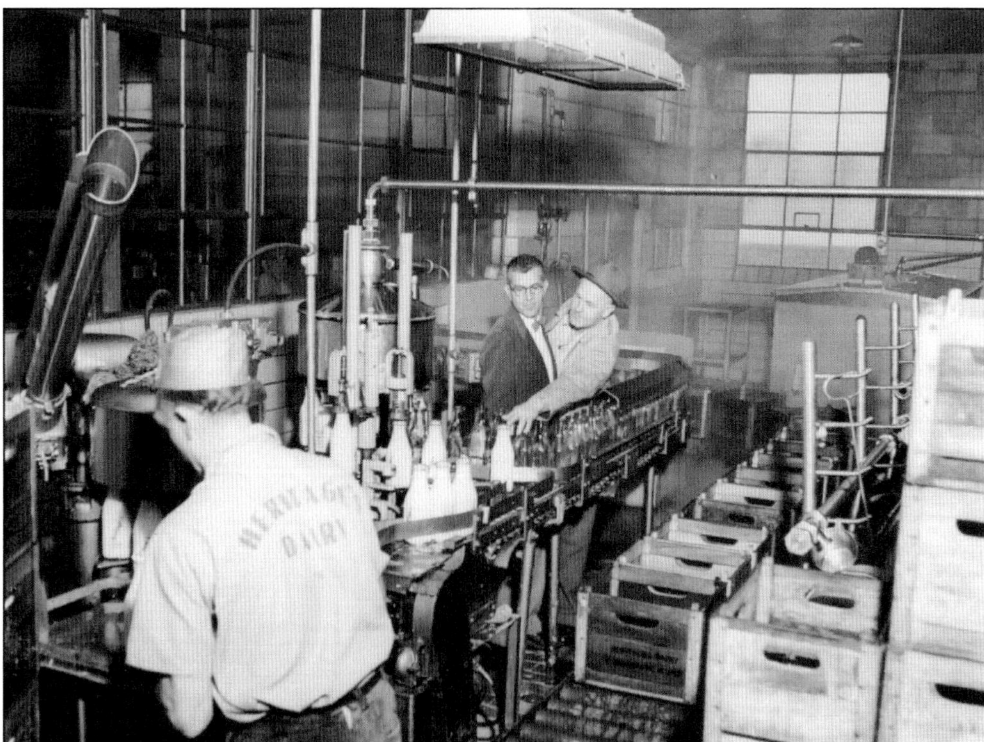

Pictured is the bottling plant at Heritage's Milk Plant. (Courtesy of Heritage's Dairy Stores.)

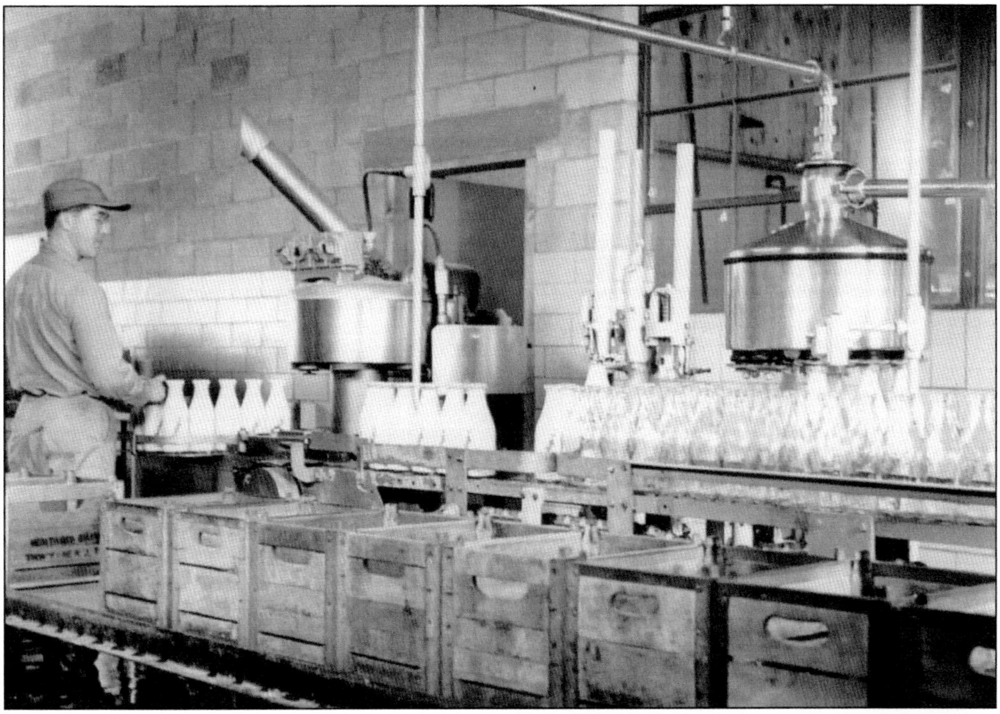

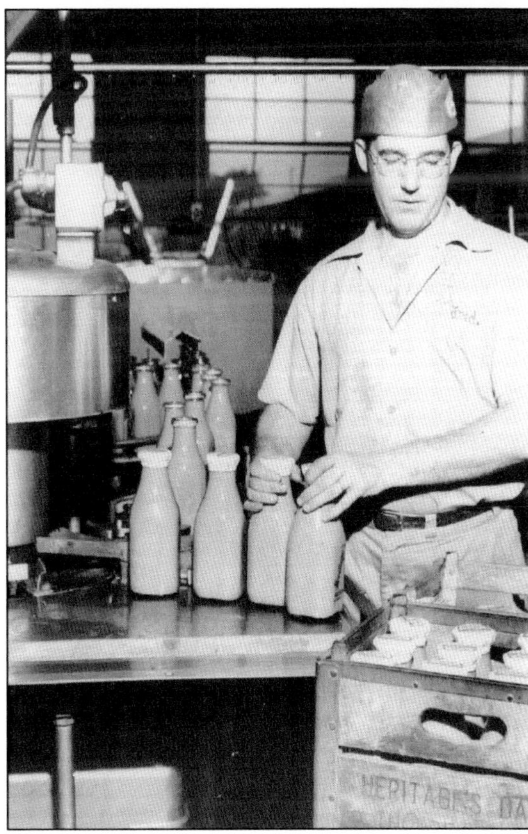

The bottling plant at Heritage's Dairy was housed on Jessup Road, next to the dairy. (Both, courtesy of Heritage's Dairy Stores.)

NEW PRICE SAVINGS

NOW AVAILABLE FOR HOME DELIVERY
STARTING JULY 1, 1960

HERITAGE'S

HOMOGENIZED VITAMIN "D" **MILK**

ON THE CONVENIENT ECONOMY

HALF GALLON

GLASS BOTTLE

NO DEPOSIT

ORDER TODAY FROM YOUR MILKMAN

Please deliver the following number of 1/2 gallons of Homogenized milk on my regular delivery days.

MON. TUE. WED. THUR. FRI. SAT.

(Please order in advance)

Signed ....

TEAR OFF HERE

HERITAGE'S

COMPLETE LINE OF DAIRY PRODUCTS

Homo. "A" Vit. "D" Milk	$ .31 qt.
Homo. "B" Vit. "D" Milk	.28 1/2 qt.
Homo. "B" Vit. "D" Milk	.54 1/2 gal.
Guernsey Milk	.30 qt.
Grade "B" Milk	.28 qt.
Chocolate Milk	.31 qt.
Skim (Fat-free) Milk	.25 qt.
Buttermilk	.28 qt.
Orange Drink	.38 1/2 gal.
Grape Drink	.38 1/2 gal.
Cottage Cheese	.28 12 oz.
Heavy Cream	1.69 qt.
Heavy Cream	.89 pt.
Heavy Cream	.47 1/2 pt.
Light Cream	.98 qt.
Light Cream	.51 pt.
Light Cream	.28 1/2 pt.
Half & Half Cream	.33 pt.

Pure Orange Juice
"Whipped" Butter
Large White Eggs
"Evergood" Margarine

} controlled by market

JESSUP ROAD THOROFARE, N. J.

TI 5-2855

Shown at left is a price list for the home delivery service of homogenized, vitamin D milk, and other dairy products around 1960. Pasteurization of Heritage's milk began in 1937. (Courtesy of Heritage's Dairy Stores.)

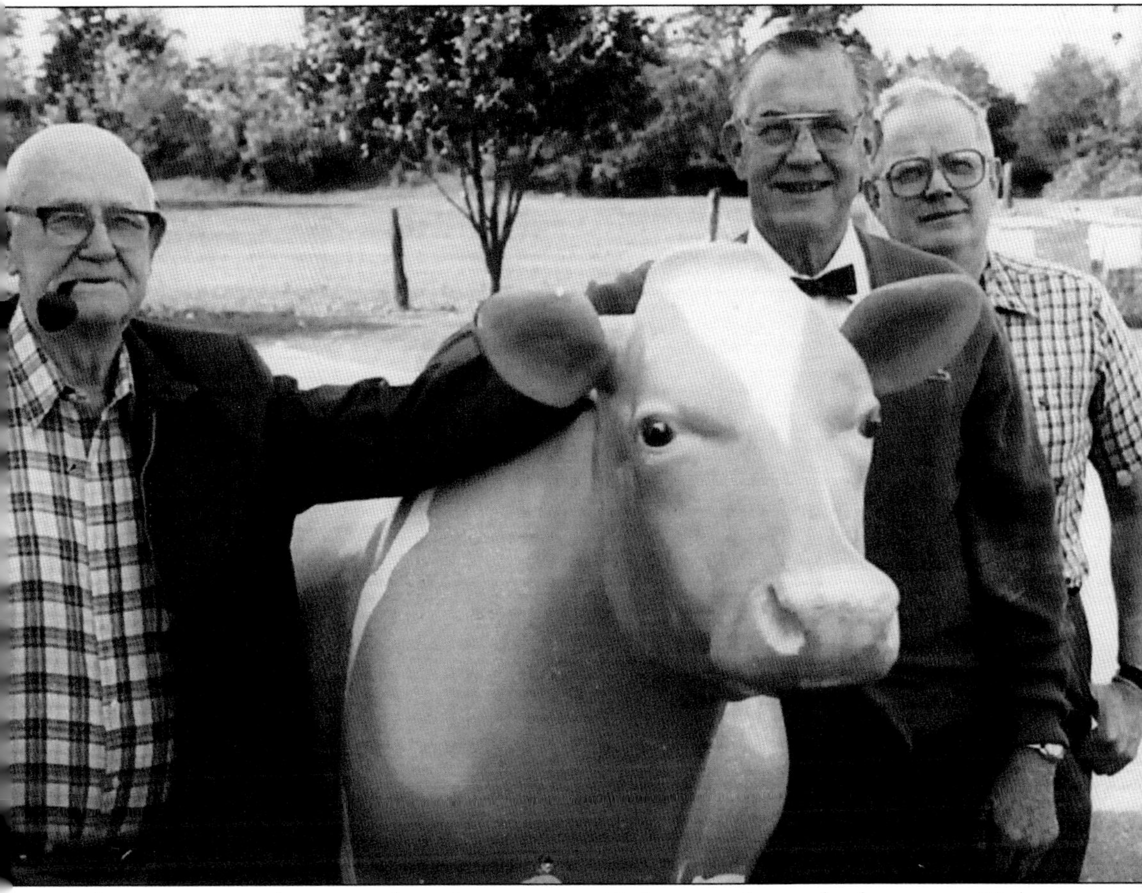

As business increased, more trucks and stores were added to meet the needs of customers. Today, Heritage's Dairy Stores, Inc., employs over 400 people and is currently operated by the founder's grandchildren Jack Heritage and Skeeter. Heritage's still uses its own unique milk recipe and continues the philosophy of M.A.G.I.C. (Making A Great Impression on our Customers), established by Grandpop Skeets (left), who is pictured with sons Skeets Jr. (center) and Windy (right) around 1986. (Courtesy of Heritage's Dairy Stores.)

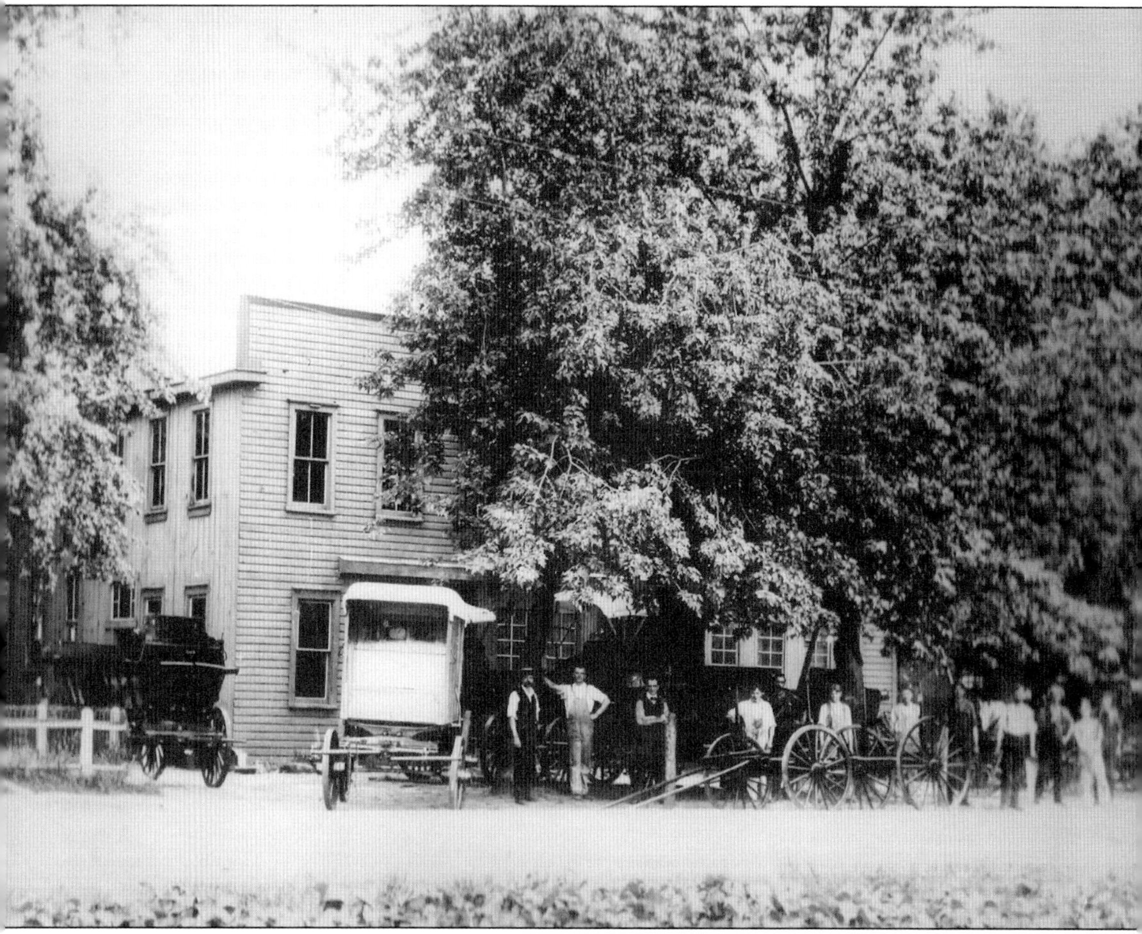

H.A. DeHart & Sons was founded in 1884 as a blacksmithing shop. The family business repaired wagons, which led to the manufacturing of new wagons. Pictured above is the original blacksmith shop in Thorofare. (Courtesy of H.A. DeHart & Son.)

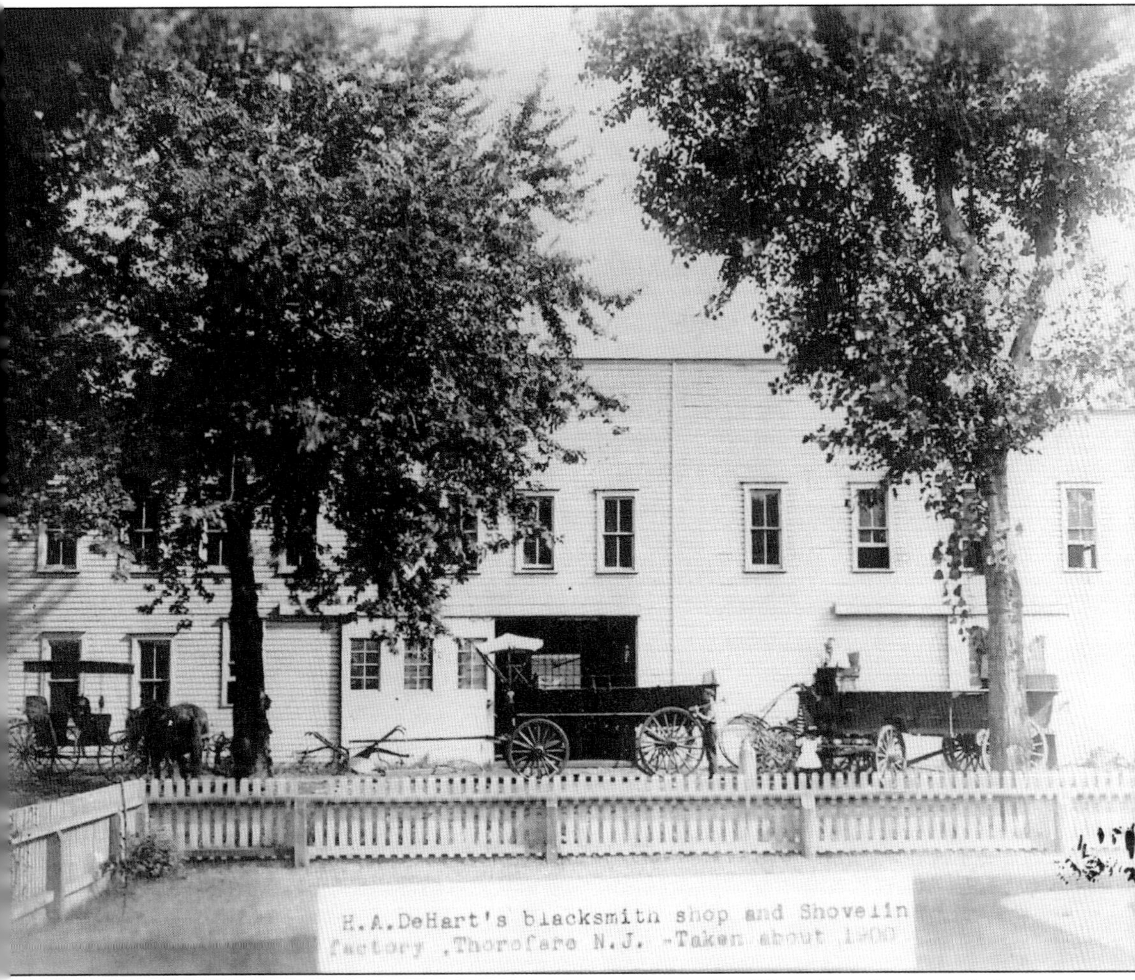

The H.A. DeHart blacksmith shop and shovelin factory, located in Thorofare, is pictured above. This picture was taken in the early 1900s. (Courtesy of H.A. DeHart & Son.)

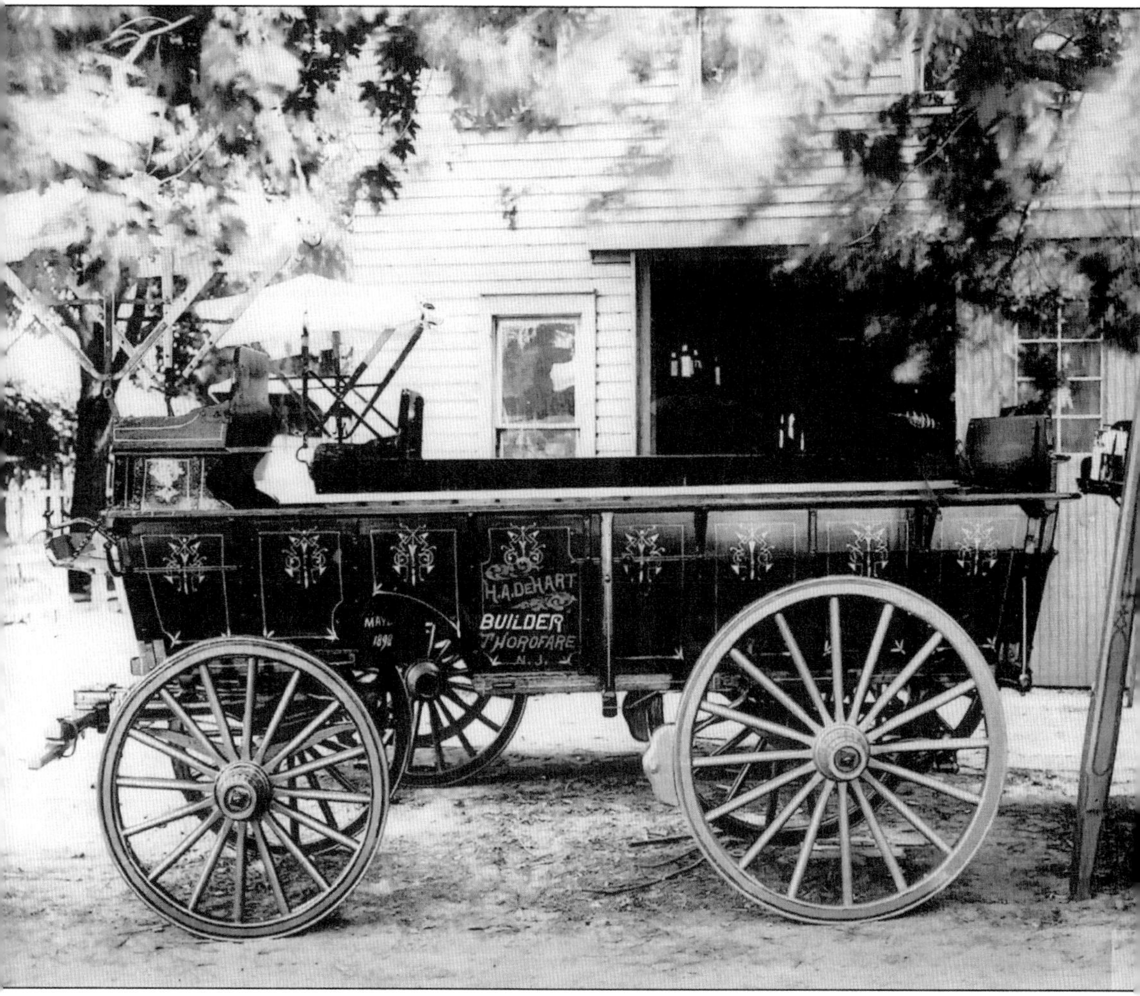

Dated May 1898, this photograph shows that the H.A. DeHart & Son Wagon Company built this Shelving wagon. (Courtesy of H.A. DeHart & Son.)

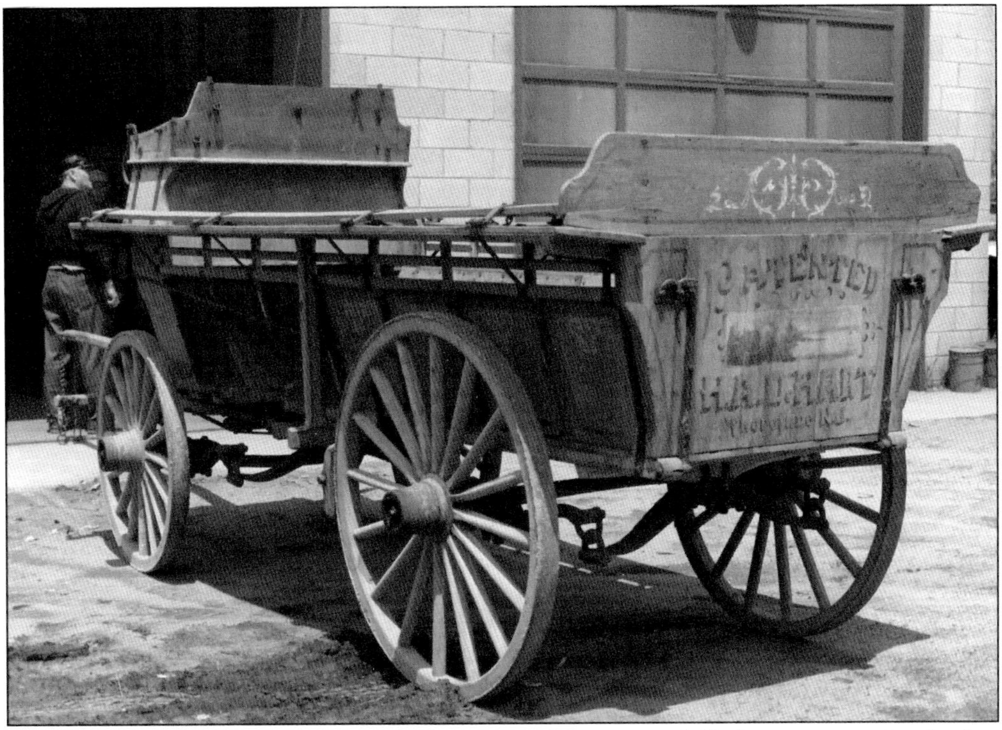

In the 1970s, DeHart's took to refurbishing one of the original Shelving wagons for display. (Courtesy of H.A. DeHart & Son.)

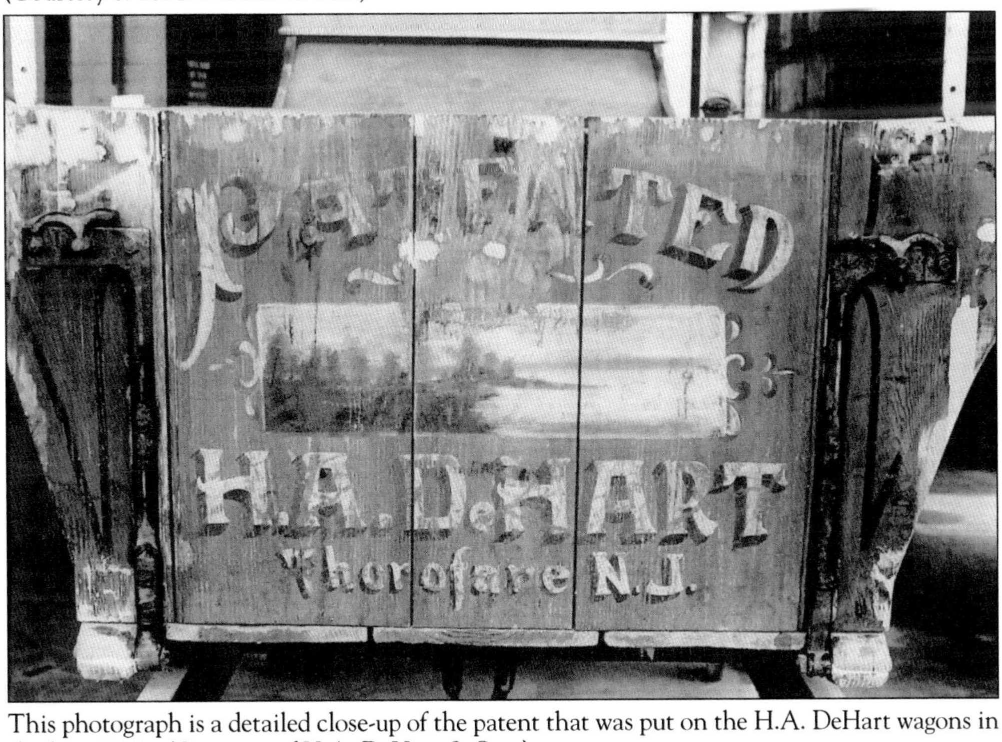

This photograph is a detailed close-up of the patent that was put on the H.A. DeHart wagons in the late 1800s. (Courtesy of H.A. DeHart & Son.)

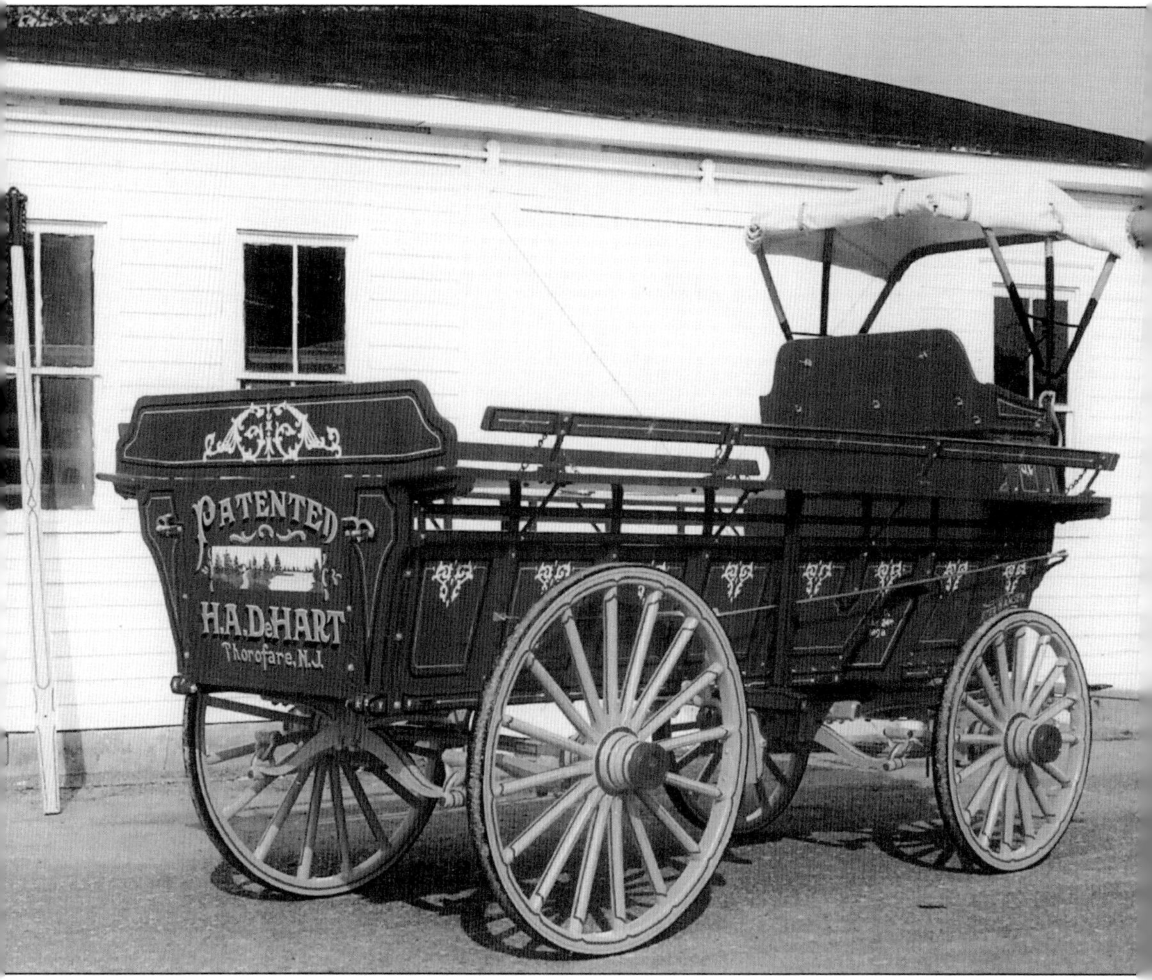

Pictured above is the 1898 DeHart Cut-Under Shelving wagon, which was refurbished in the 1970s. The DeHart Cut-Under Shelving wagon was used in the late 19th century to carry farm products from southern New Jersey to markets in Philadelphia. The patent allowed for navigation of congested city streets. Note the huge rear wheels, which allowed easy passage over deeply rutted country roads. Wagons of this type were loaded in a unique pyramid arrangement to allow for greater capacity. (Courtesy of H.A. DeHart & Son.)

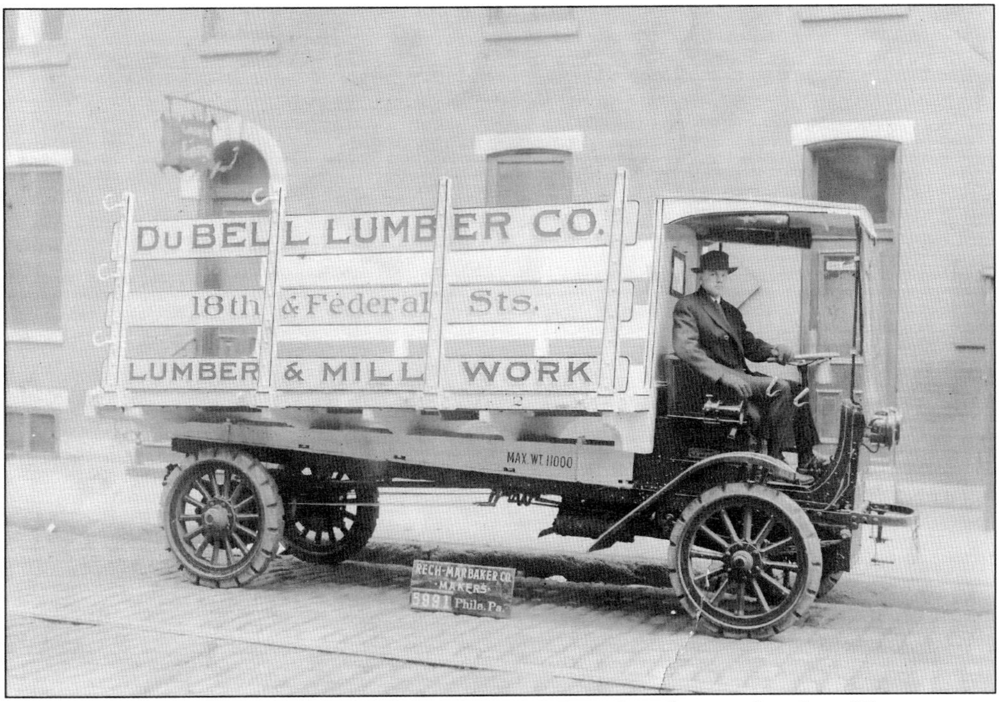

With the advent of the automobile, H.A. DeHart & Son altered its product line. The company began to build truck chassis with bodies to fit. Here is the DuBell Lumber Company truck that was manufactured by H.A. DeHart & Son on May 4, 1922. (Courtesy of H.A. DeHart & Son.)

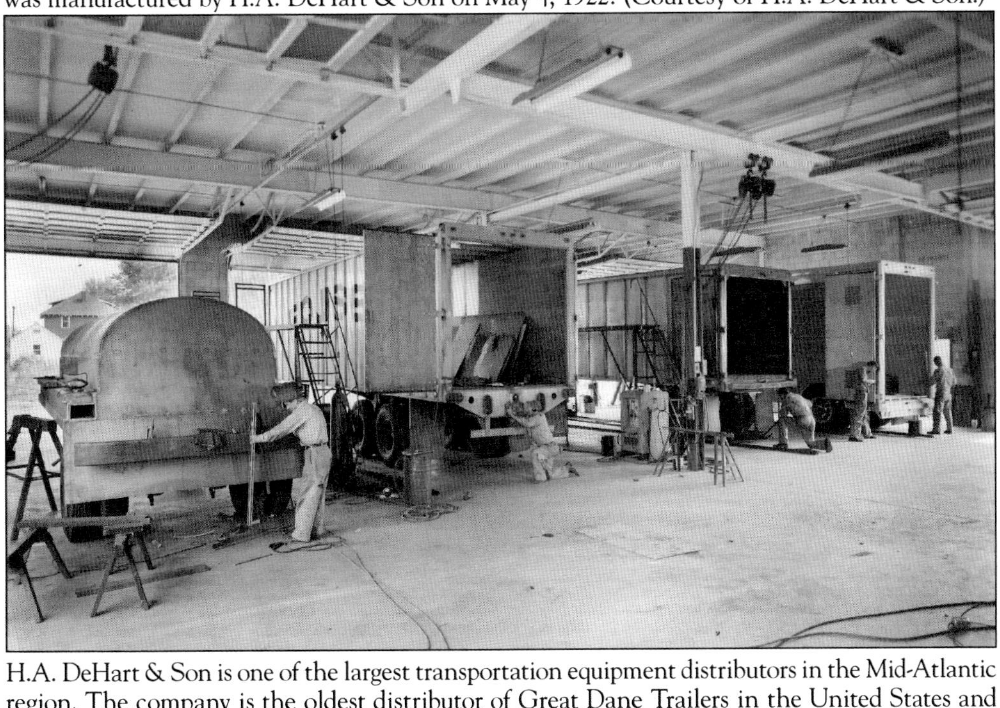

H.A. DeHart & Son is one of the largest transportation equipment distributors in the Mid-Atlantic region. The company is the oldest distributor of Great Dane Trailers in the United States and holds the exclusive license to market the Great Dane product line in the tristate area. Working on trailers are shop mechanics. (Courtesy of H.A. DeHart & Son.)

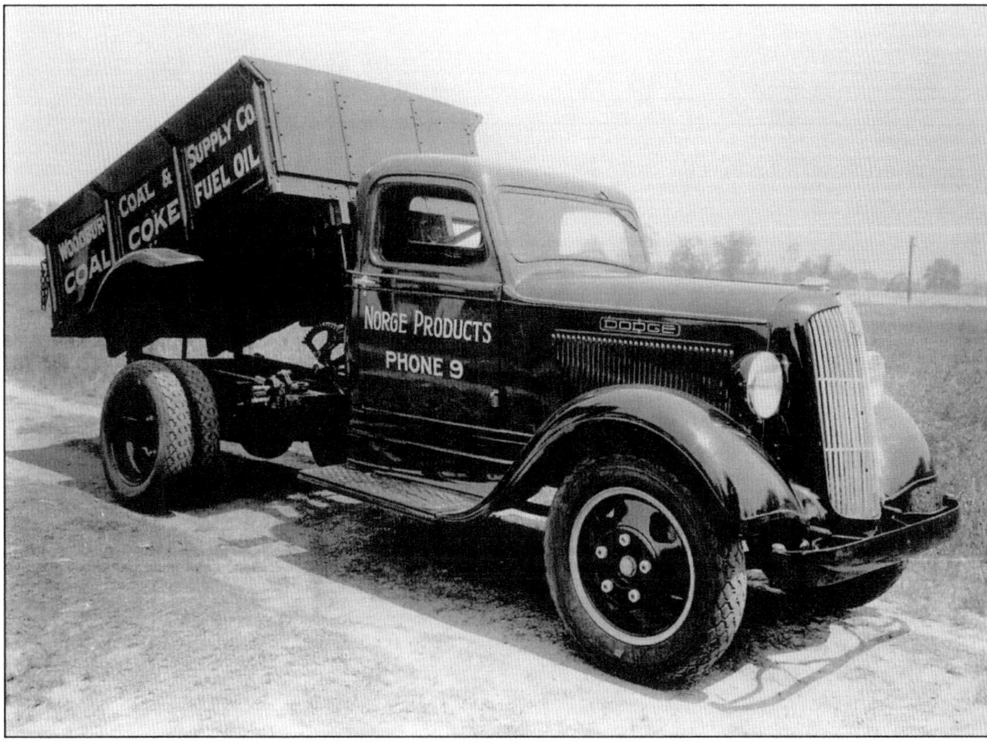

The Woodbury Coal and Supply Company purchased this truck from the H.A. DeHart truck company. (Courtesy of H.A. DeHart & Son.)

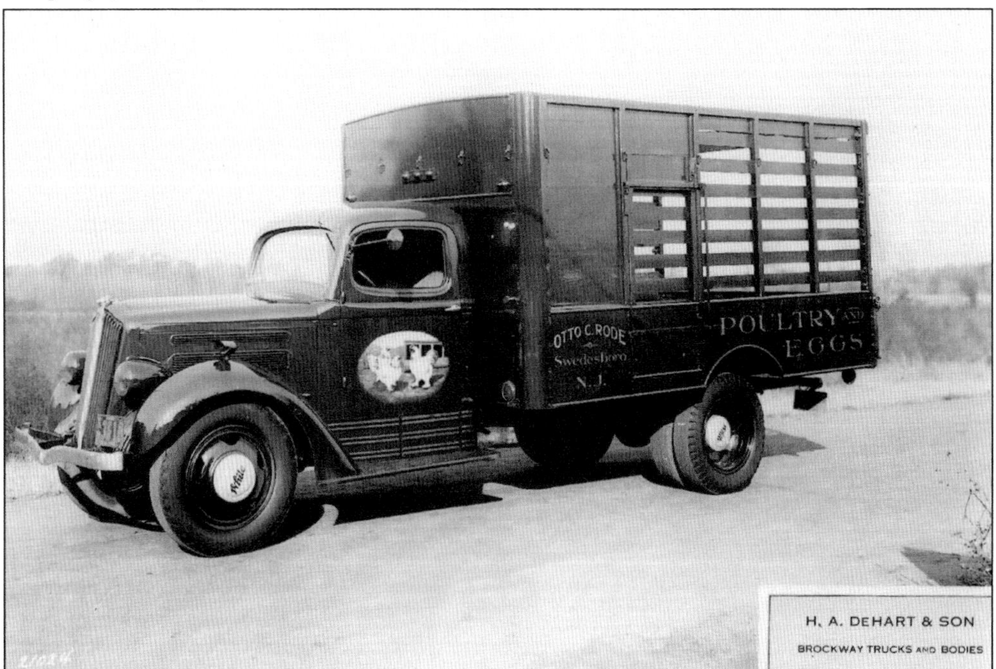

Pictured is another variation of the truck that was purchased by Otto C. Rode from the H.A. DeHart truck company. (Courtesy of H.A. DeHart & Son.)

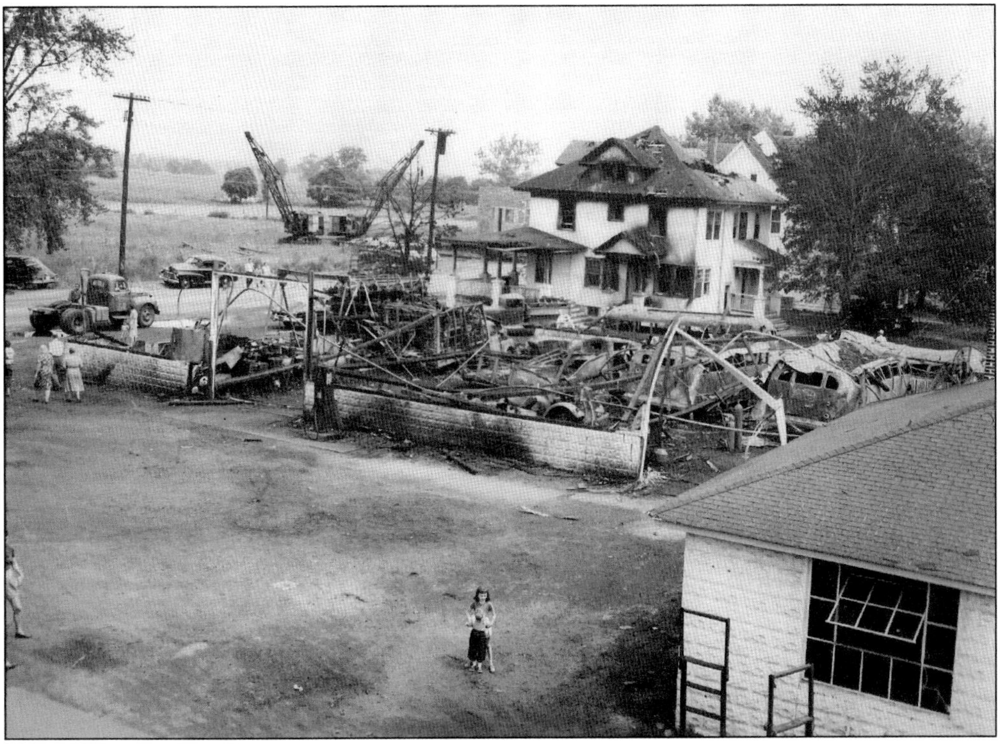

A major fire in August 1950 temporarily halted production, but the company rebuilt and continued to thrive as a major truck and trailer company. (Both, courtesy of H.A. DeHart & Son.)

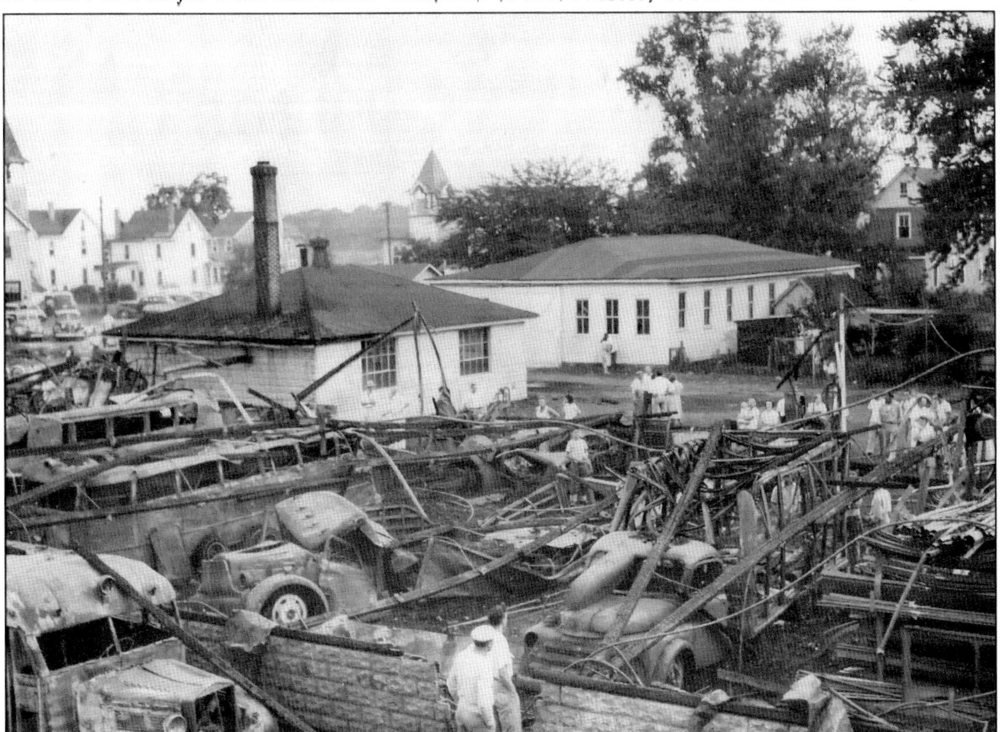

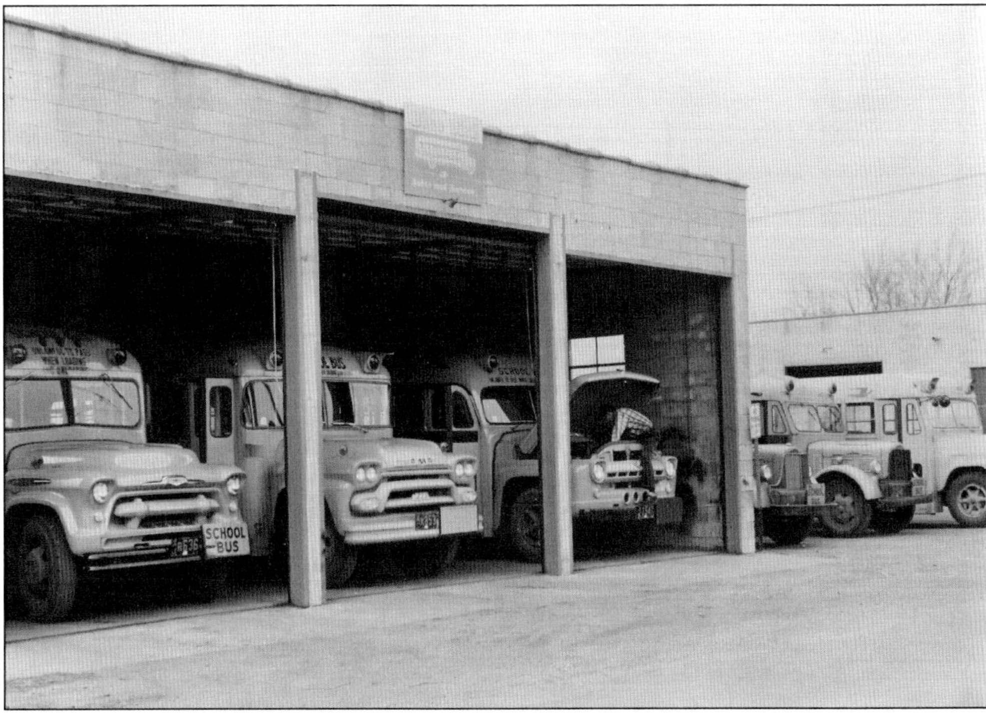

DeHart's machine shop has always been a busy place. Here, a shop mechanic is shown working on one of the many buses owned and operated by the DeHart company. H.A. DeHart was a family-owned business until 1987. At this time, employees of the company purchased a majority of the issued stock under an employees stock ownership plan. (Courtesy of H.A. DeHart & Son.)

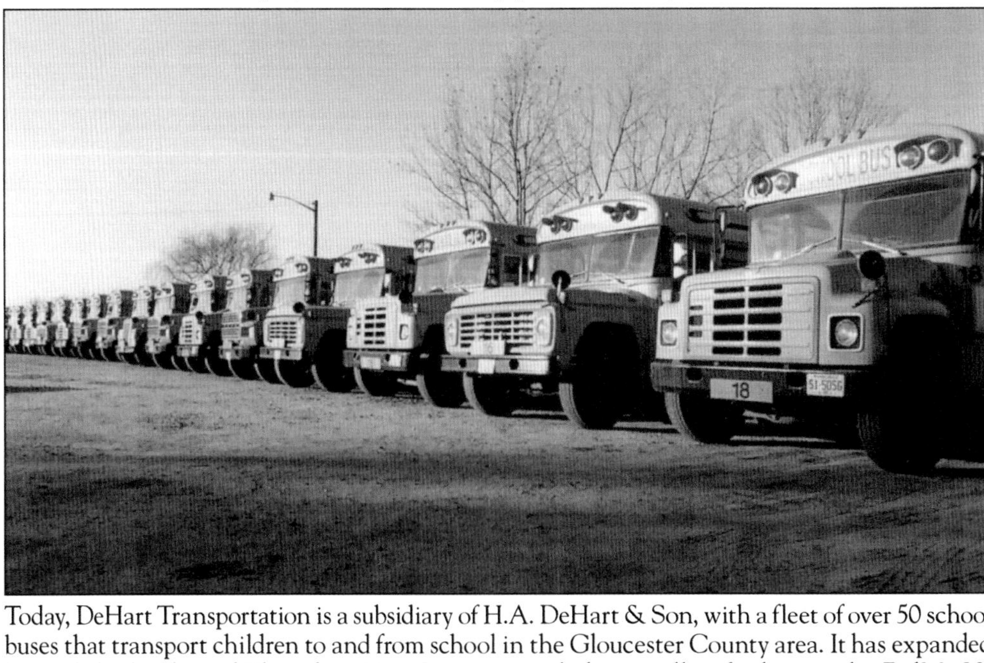

Today, DeHart Transportation is a subsidiary of H.A. DeHart & Son, with a fleet of over 50 school buses that transport children to and from school in the Gloucester County area. It has expanded beyond the borders of Thorofare, New Jersey, to include a satellite facility on the DelMarVa Peninsula. (Courtesy of H.A. DeHart & Son.)

Three
People and Families

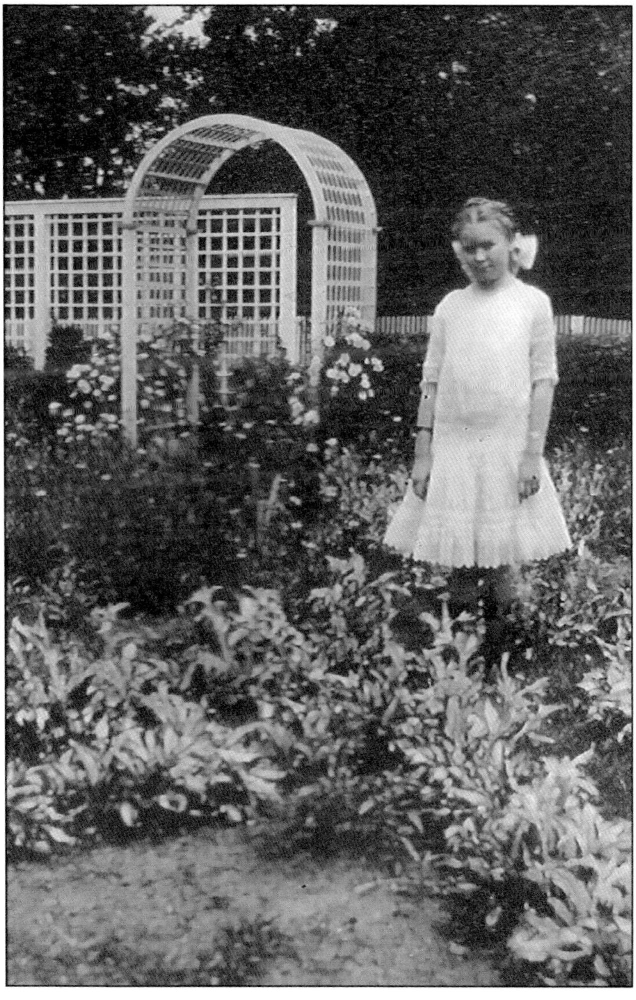

While the men were in Europe fighting the battles of World War I, their families stayed home and worked to help support the war effort. Pictured is Mae Pearl Quickmire Turner, who lived with her family on the grounds of the Woodbury Bag Loading Munitions Plant during the war. (Courtesy of Sondra Turner Dankel.)

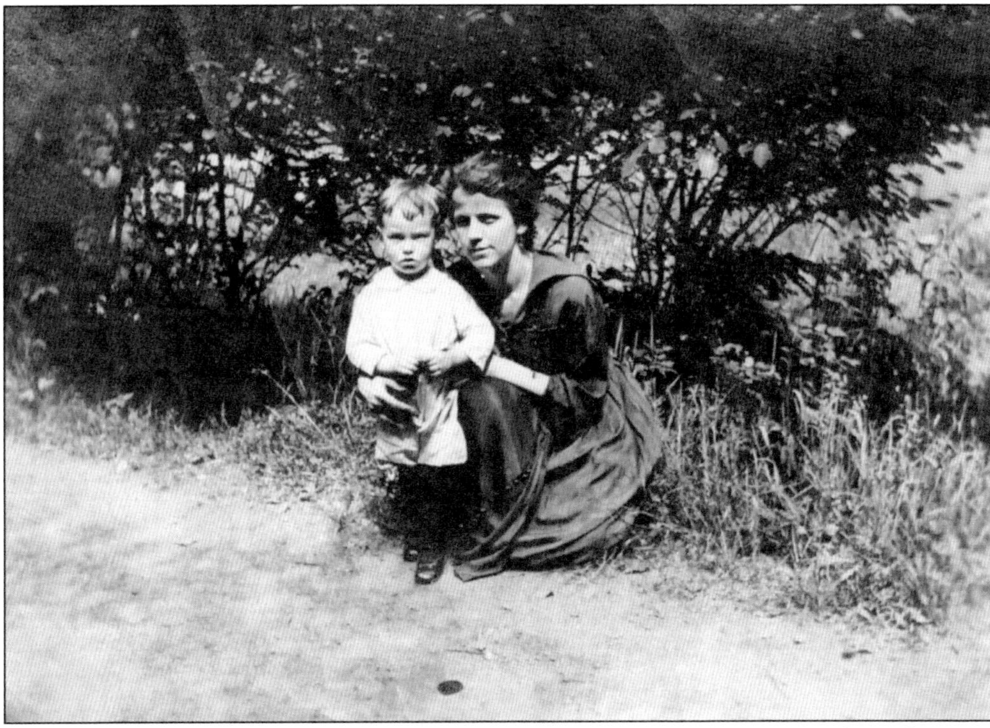

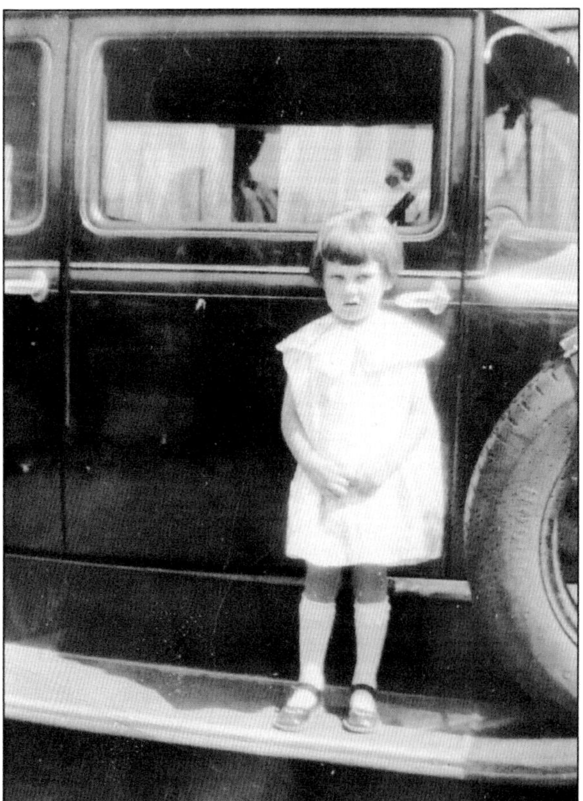

Above, Florence Nicolai and son Rodger are pictured around 1920, and at left, daughter Florence Nicolai is shown around 1930. The Nicolai family settled and worked in the Verga section of the township. (Both, courtesy of Florence Kappeler.)

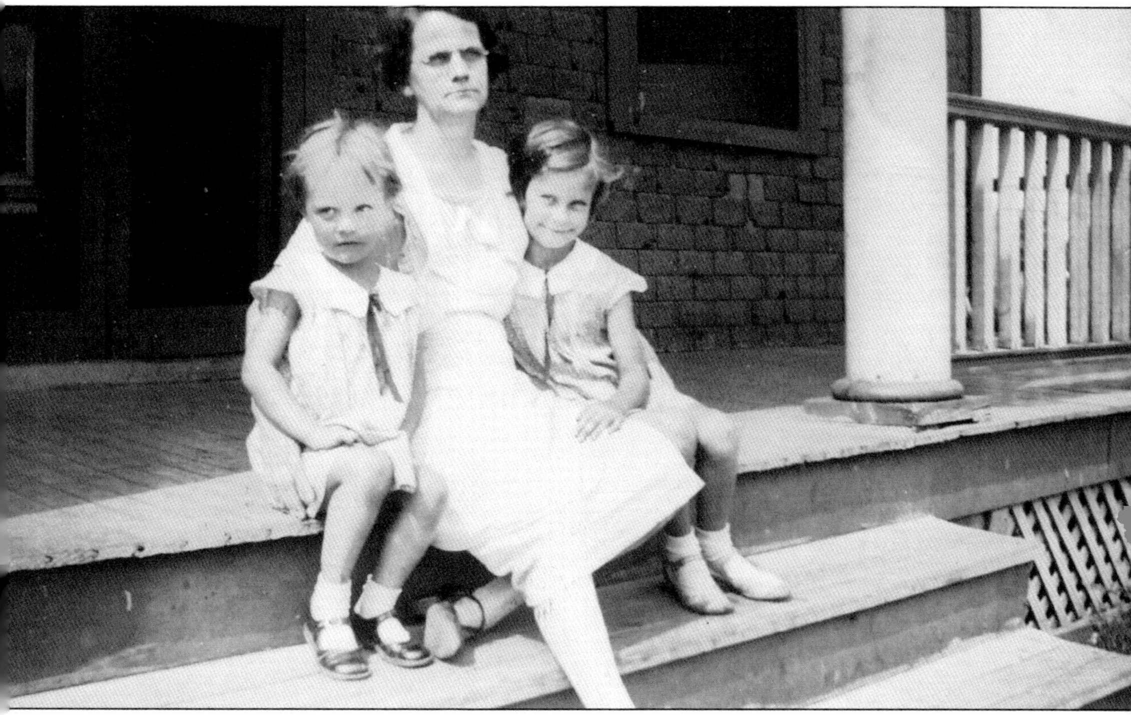

Florence Nicolai is pictured with her daughters Jane and Florence in 1934. (Courtesy of Florence Kappeler.)

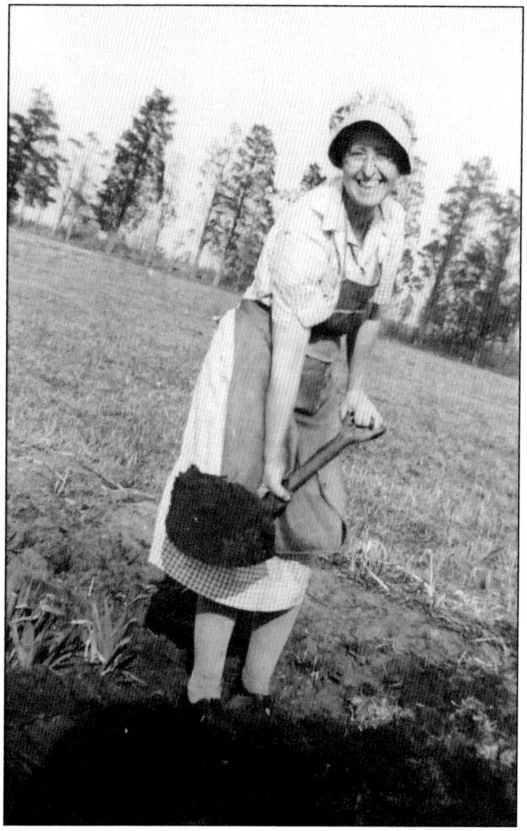

Marian Budd is digging in her iris garden on March 31, 1943. (Courtesy of Pearl Dehner.)

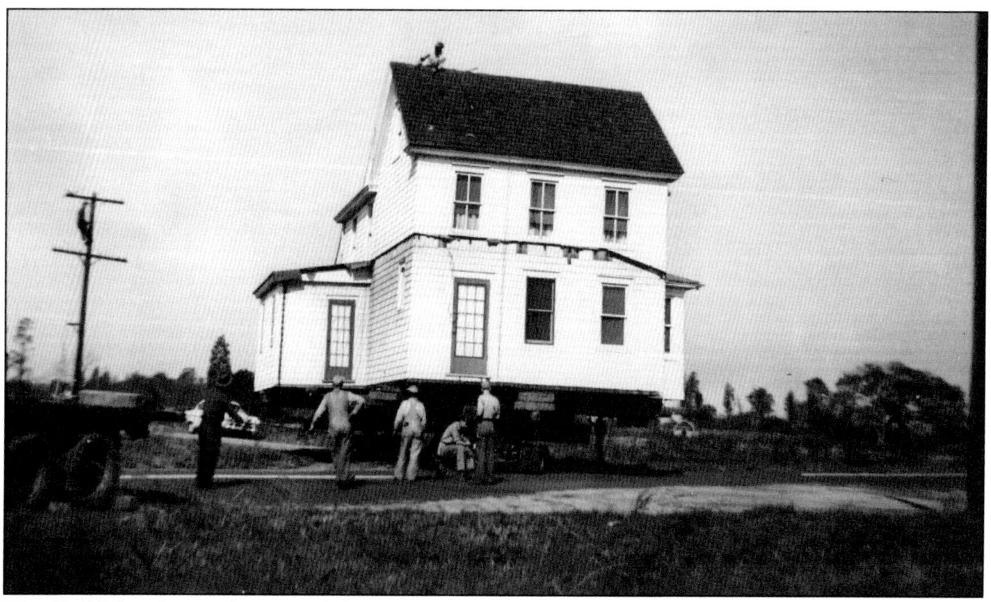

The Budd family members resided for many years on Delaware Street until the expansion of the highways and roadways forced them to move their home from Delaware Street to Crown Point Road. The Budd family home was hoisted onto a trailer and moved slowly to its new location. Note that the telephone wires had to be removed for this move. (Courtesy of Pearl Dehner.)

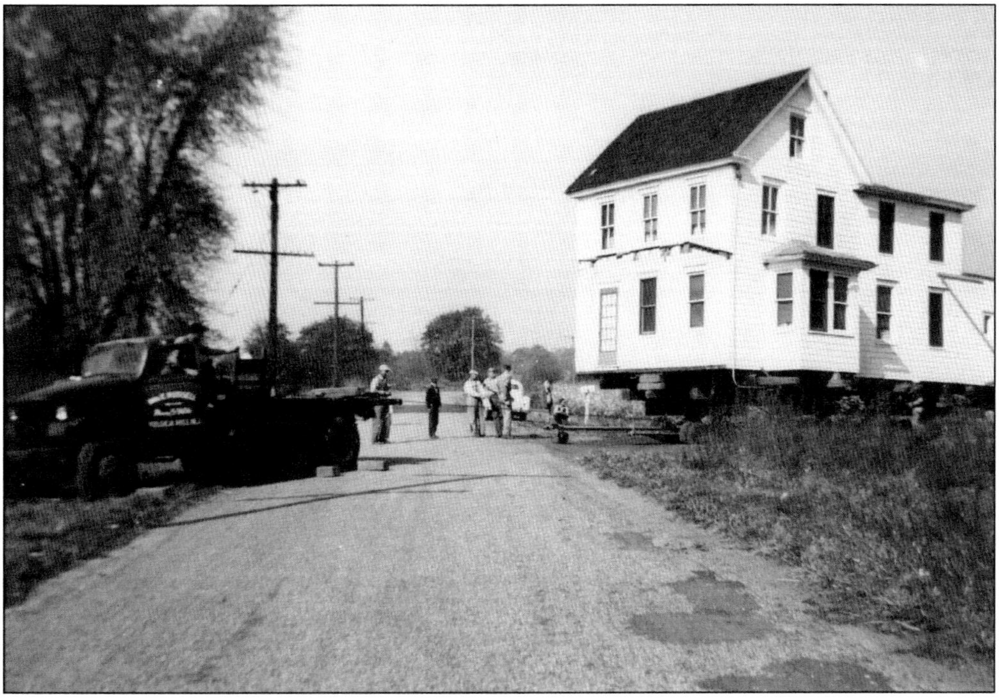

The Budd house is slowly moved down Delaware Street toward its new home on Crown Point Road. Workers from William E. Russell House Movers, out of Mullica Hill, New Jersey, were hired to move the home in the 1940s. (Both, courtesy of Pearl Dehmer.)

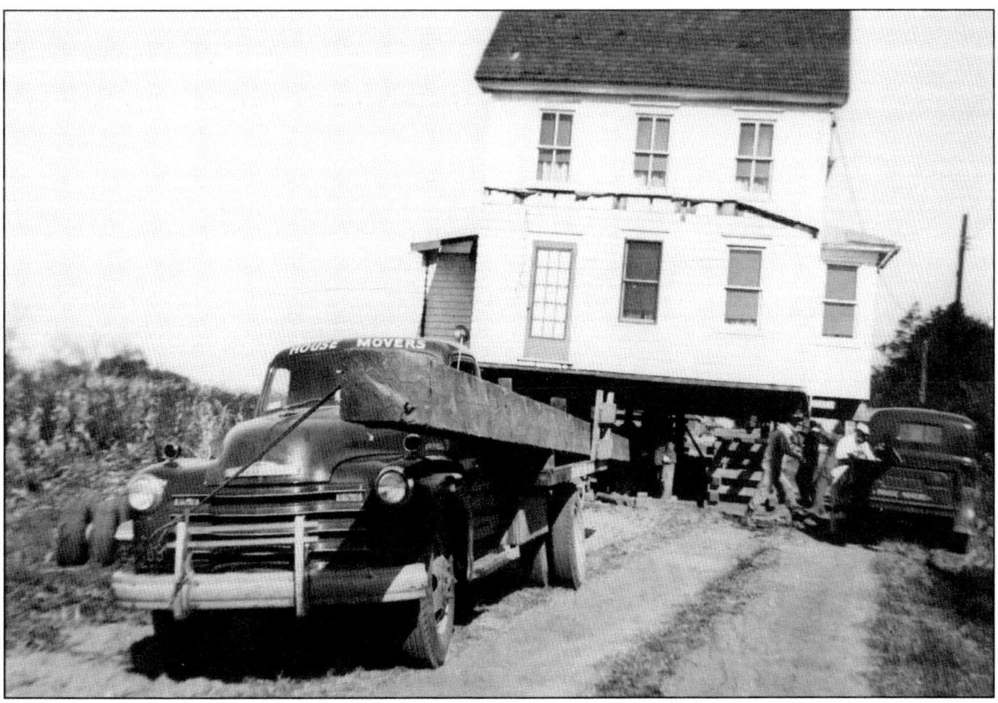

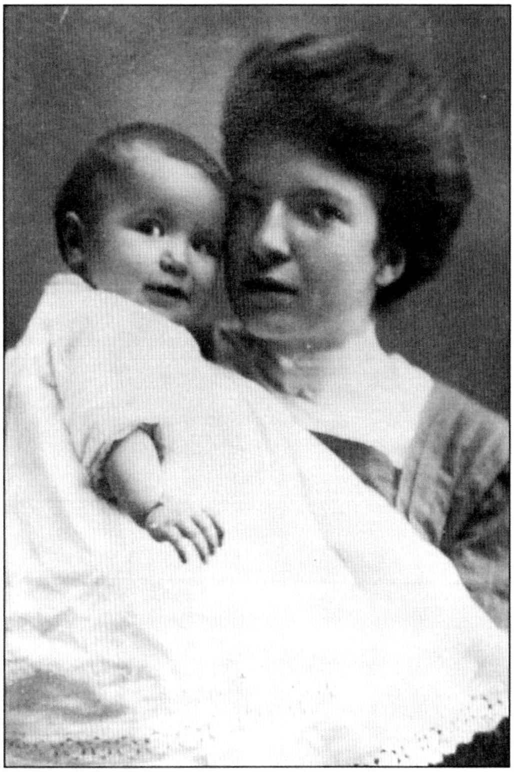

Charles Bowers is pictured with his mother, Hazel Bowers. Charles Bowers was born in 1910 and grew up in the Thorofare section of West Deptford. (Courtesy of Pearl Dehner.)

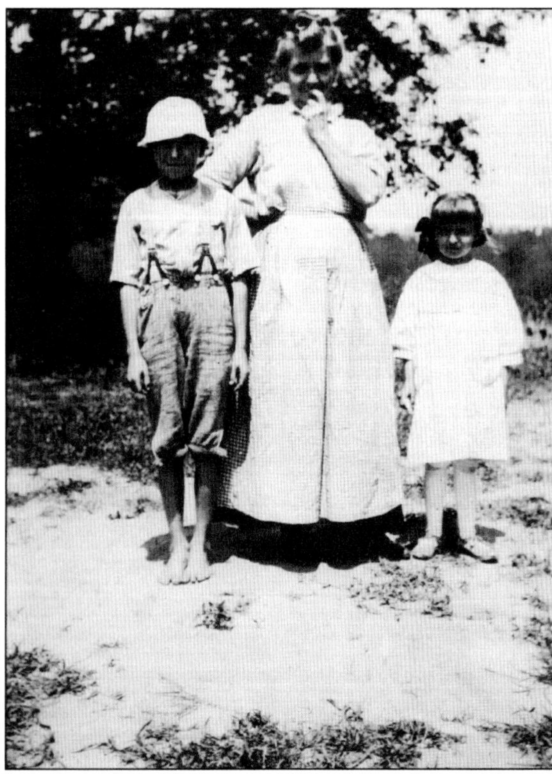

Ten-year-old Charles Bowers poses with six-year-old sister Tutsie Bowers and grandmother Mary Louise Day. The picture was taken on Delaware Street. (Courtesy of Pearl Dehner.)

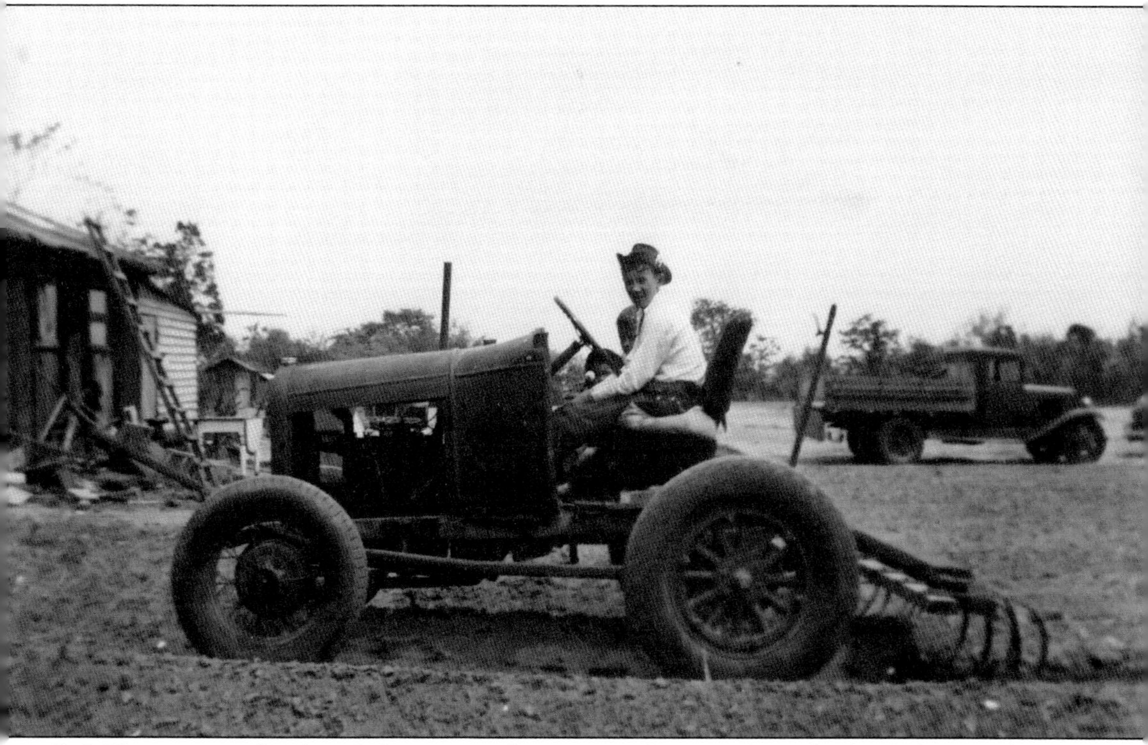

Bob Thompson and Wilson Dehner spent the summer of 1943 working the family farm. Wilson is driving, Bob sits next to him, and at Bob's knee is Wilson's niece Barbara Ann McDowell (Tameo). The picture was taken on the Dehner Farm. (Courtesy of Pearl Dehner.)

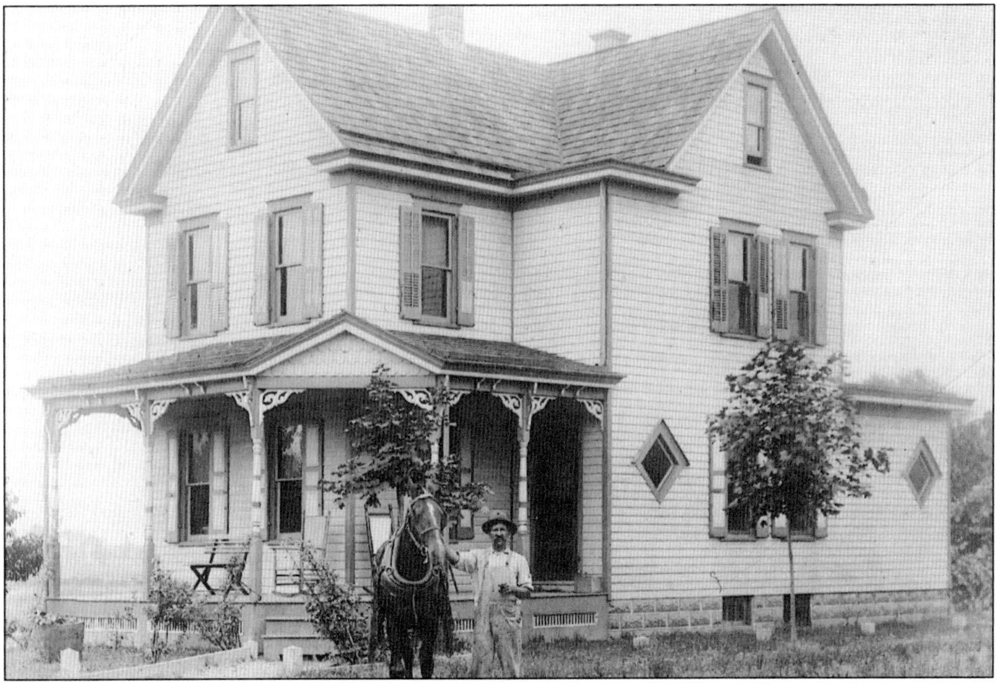

This Victorian farmhouse was located in Thorofare and belonged to William and Mary Emma (Davis) Bowers. The house was located at the end of the row of homes on the same side of the street as the Thorofare School. Out front are William Bowers and his horse. The house was torn down in 1962. (Courtesy of Charles Leonard.)

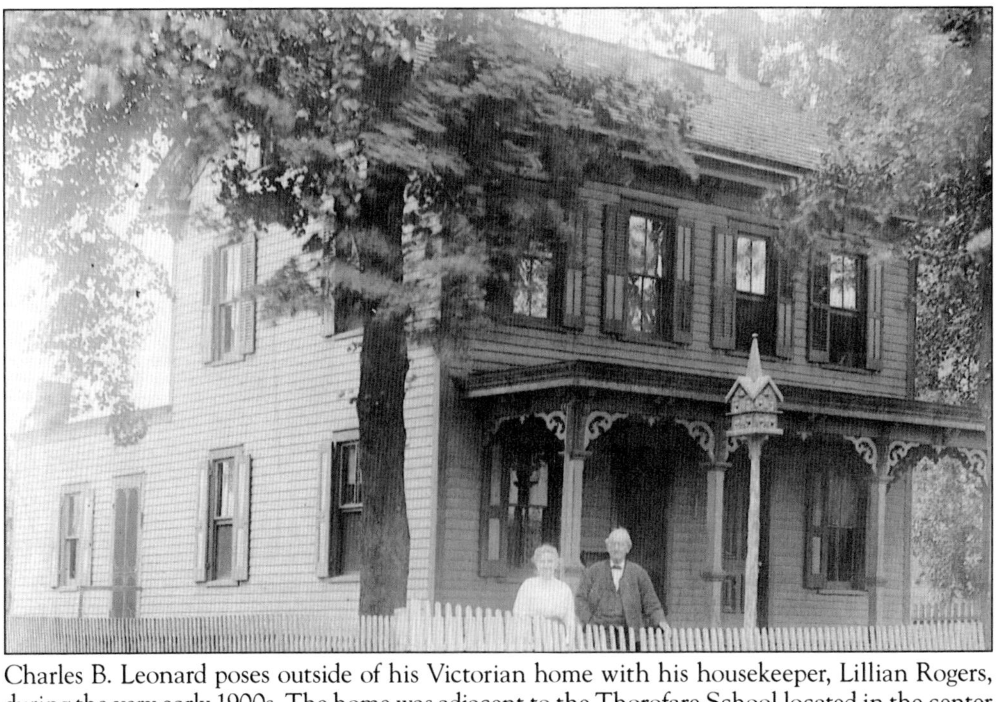

Charles B. Leonard poses outside of his Victorian home with his housekeeper, Lillian Rogers, during the very early 1900s. The home was adjacent to the Thorofare School located in the center of town. (Courtesy of Charles Leonard.)

Pictured on her horse Flora is Mae Quickmire, who did her part during World War I by living and working at the Woodbury Bag Loading Munitions Plant with her family. The plant was run by the MacArthur Brothers Engineering Company. (Courtesy of Sondra Turner Dankel.)

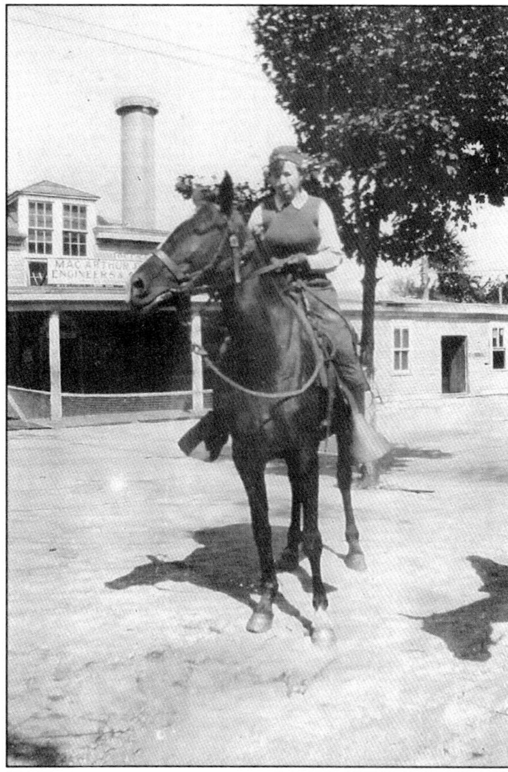

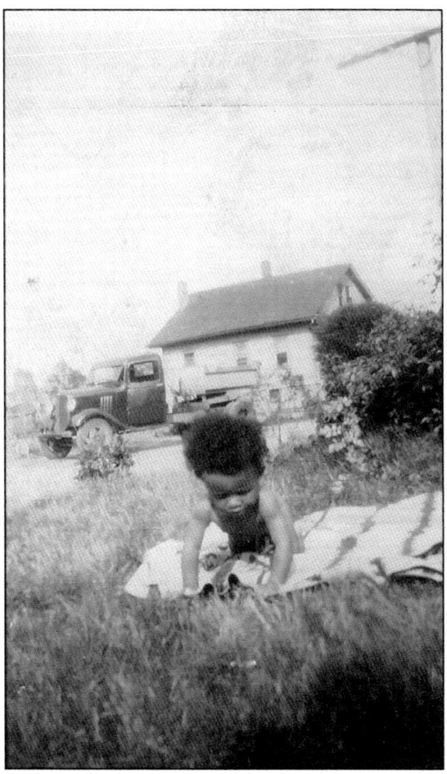

Pictured is Frederick "Fred" Purnell, exploring the yard of his West Deptford home. Fred Purnell has lived his entire life in West Deptford Township. He attended the Thorofare Colored School, the township's only segregated school. The home pictured in the background belonged to the Reverend George Alfred Johnson. Having studied ministry at Temple University, Reverend Johnson was a local preacher at Campbell African Methodist Episcopal (AME) Church and was asked to take on the mission that had been started by Fred Purnell's father, William P. Purnell; his mother, Della. E. Purnell; and neighbor Frances Johnson. (Courtesy of the Purnell family.)

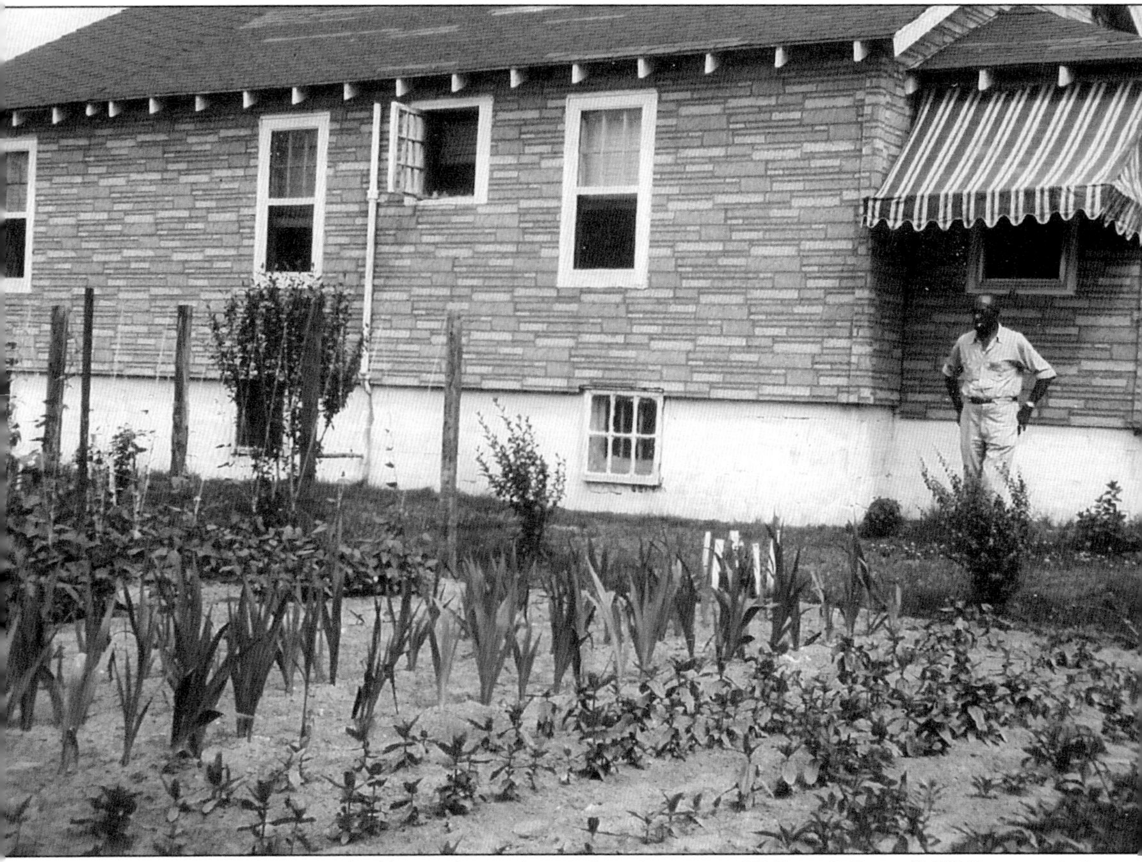

Outside of his West Deptford home, located on Salem Avenue, is William P. Purnell. William settled with his family in West Deptford during the early 1900s. (Courtesy of the Purnell family.)

Four

Public Services

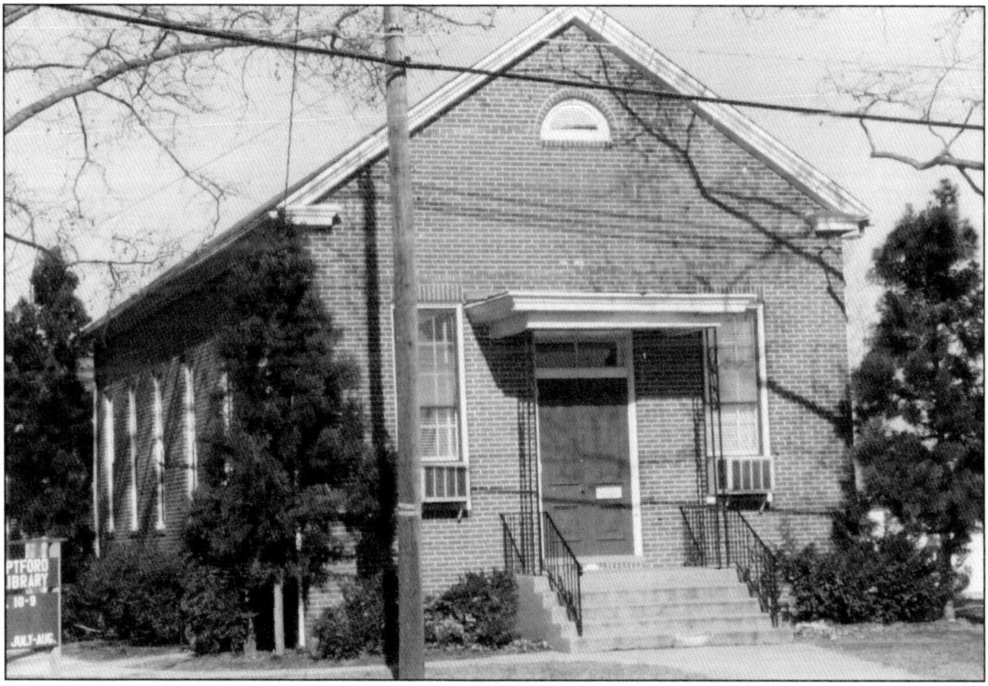

This building, located on Crown Point Road, was first used as the West Deptford Township Municipal Building. When the new municipal building was opened, the old structure became a new home for the West Deptford Free Public Library. The West Deptford Free Public Library was first located in a family home and then moved to the Thorofare No. 3 School before making this building its new home. The library moved to its present location in 1987. (Courtesy of the West Deptford Free Public Library.)

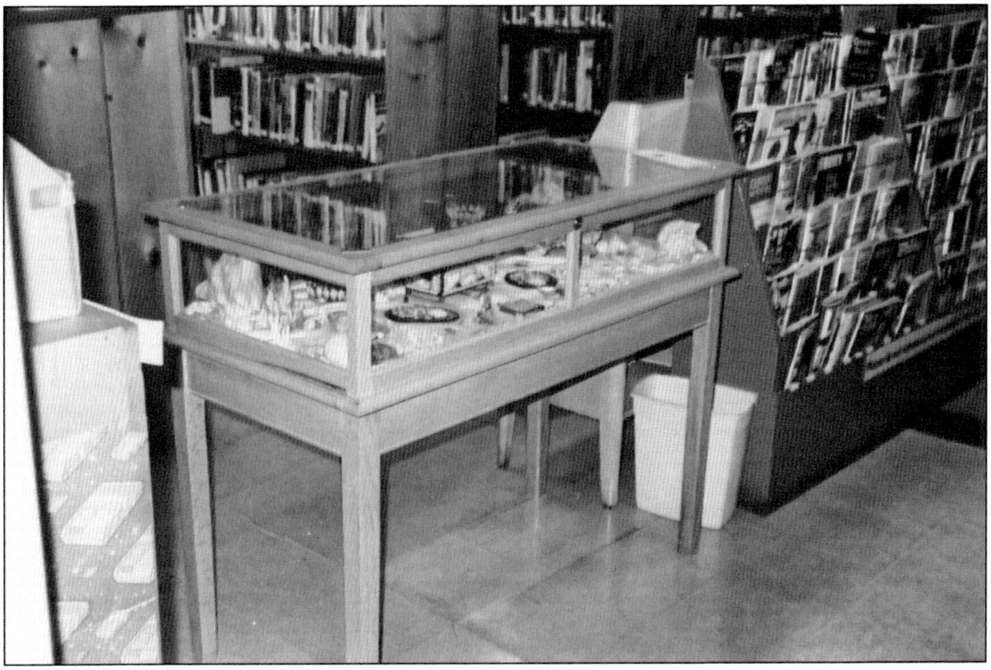

Pictured above is an inside glimpse of the library when it was located in a building on Crown Point Road. In the display case is a collection belonging to a library patron. In the background are stacks and shelves available for use by those at the library. Below, library staff members Robin Turner (left) and Gerrie Schwebel work in the information area of the library. (Both, courtesy of the West Deptford Free Public Library.)

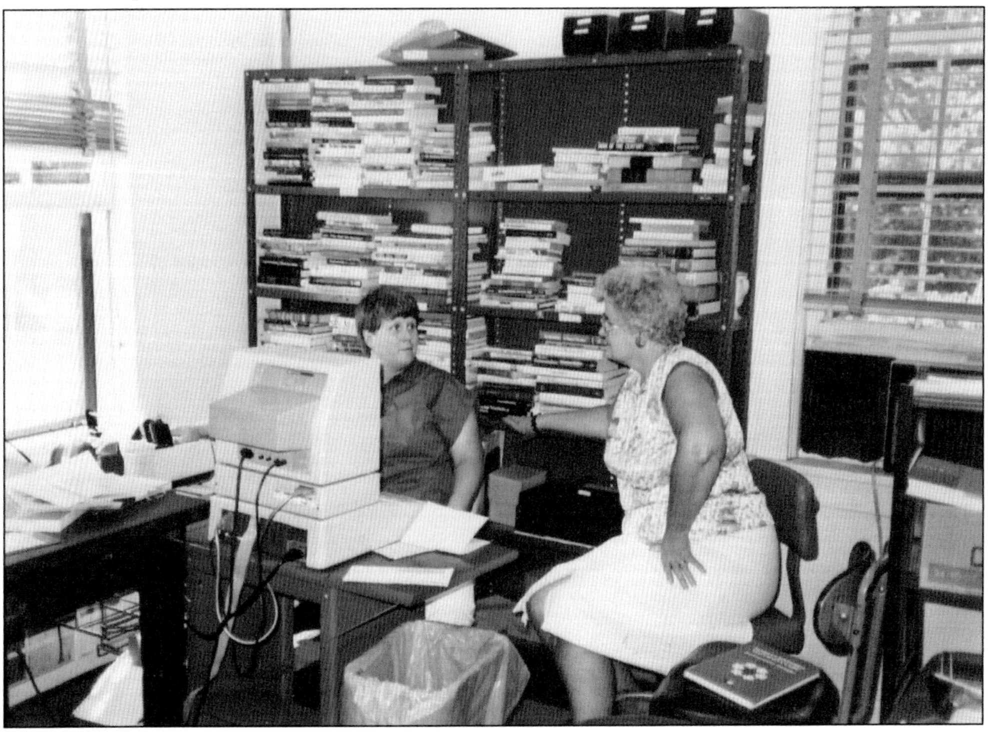

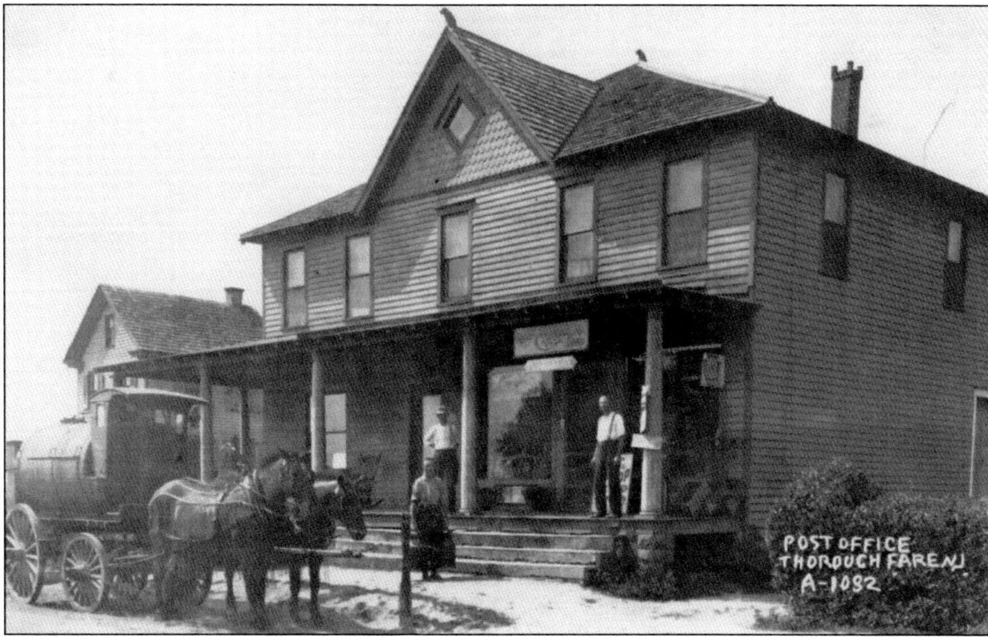

The Thoroughfare Post Office is the only post office located within the borders of West Deptford Township. It has been a part of the community since the 1800s. The spelling of Thoroughfare was due to the fact that the town was a true thoroughfare for people traveling between Woodbury and Paulsboro. (Above, courtesy of Sam Fuss; below, courtesy of Charles Leonard.)

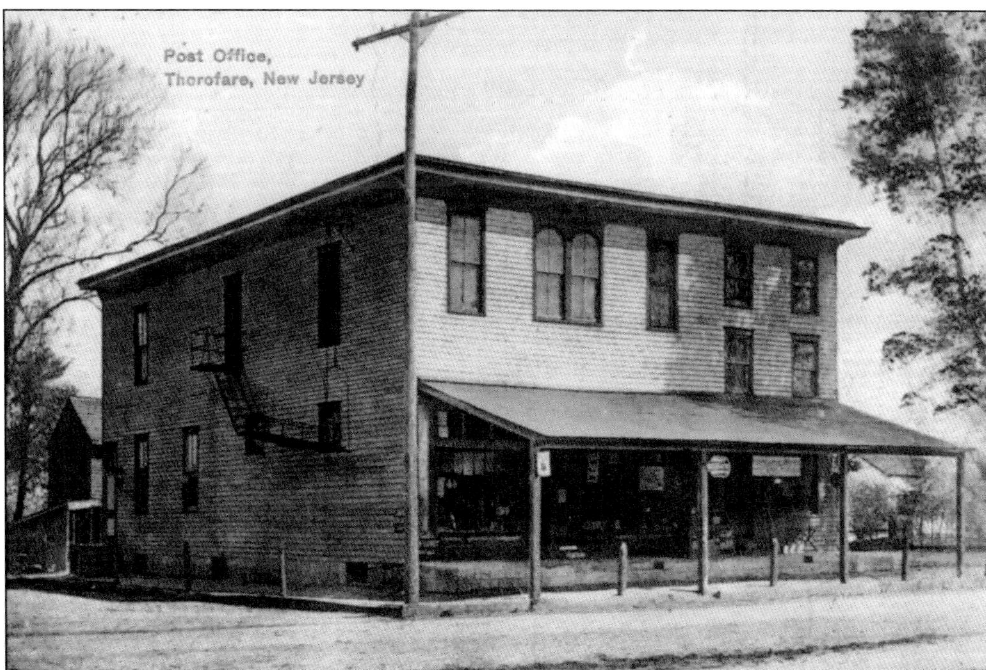

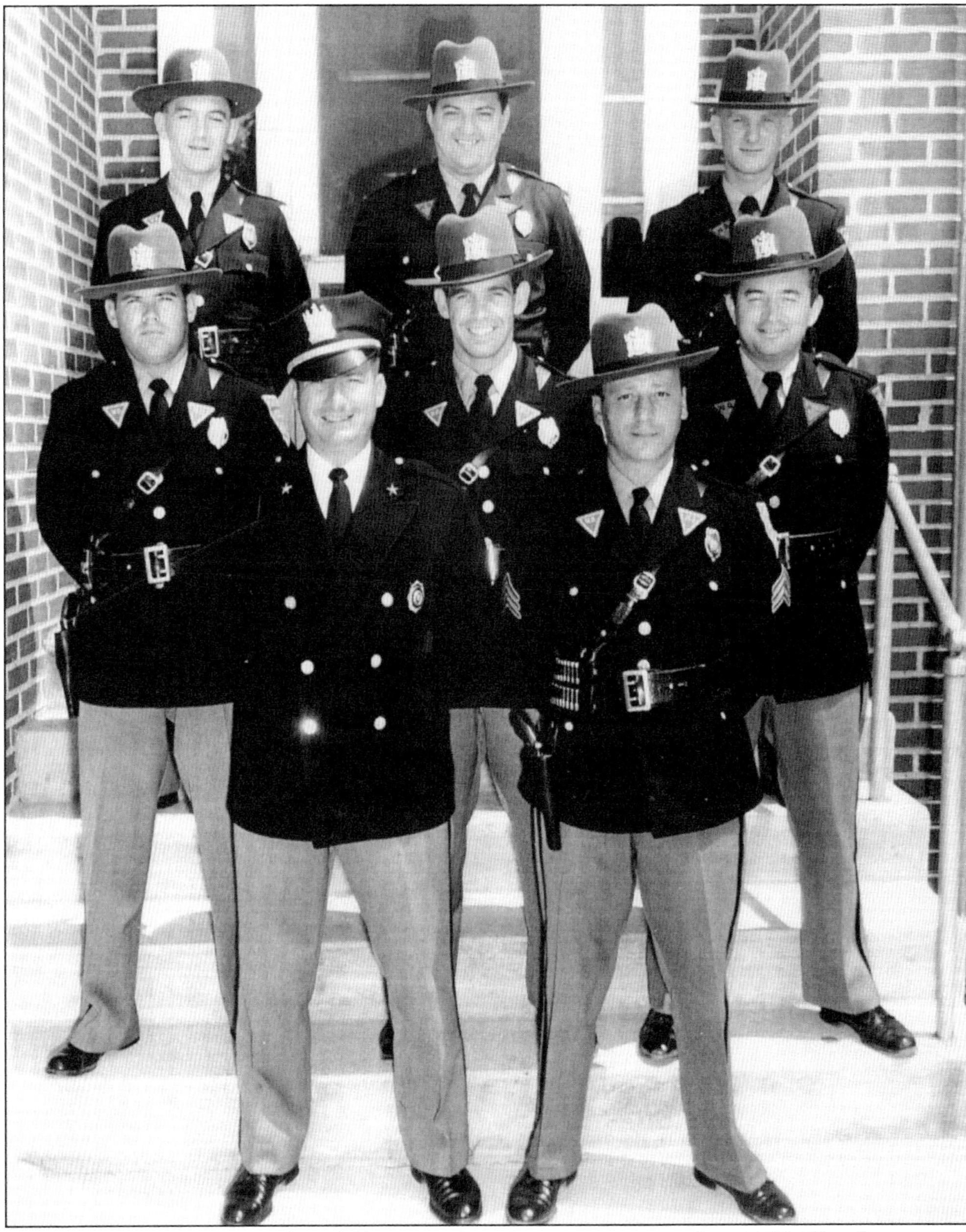

West Deptford Township's first full-time police department started in 1957. The department began with eight full-time officers. Today, the police department boasts 41 police officers and two canine members. Members of the 1957 department are, from left to right, (first row) Chief Walter Miller and Sgt. Frank Polio; (second row) John Neveling, Joe Ellis, and Sam Fuss; (third row) Lou Brammel, Frank Purvenis, and Henry Press. (Courtesy of Pat Perry.)

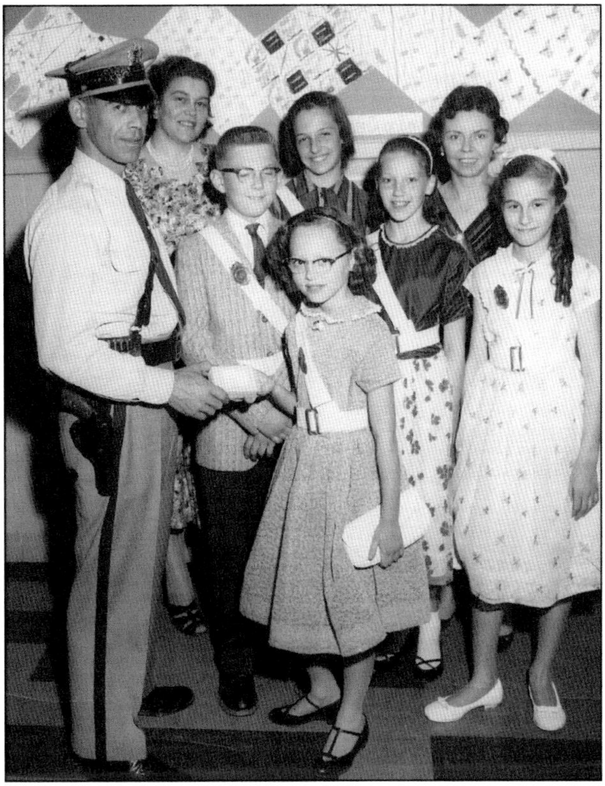

West Deptford police officer Joe Ellis recognizes local school safety patrol members. Public outreach has always been an important goal of the West Deptford Police Department.

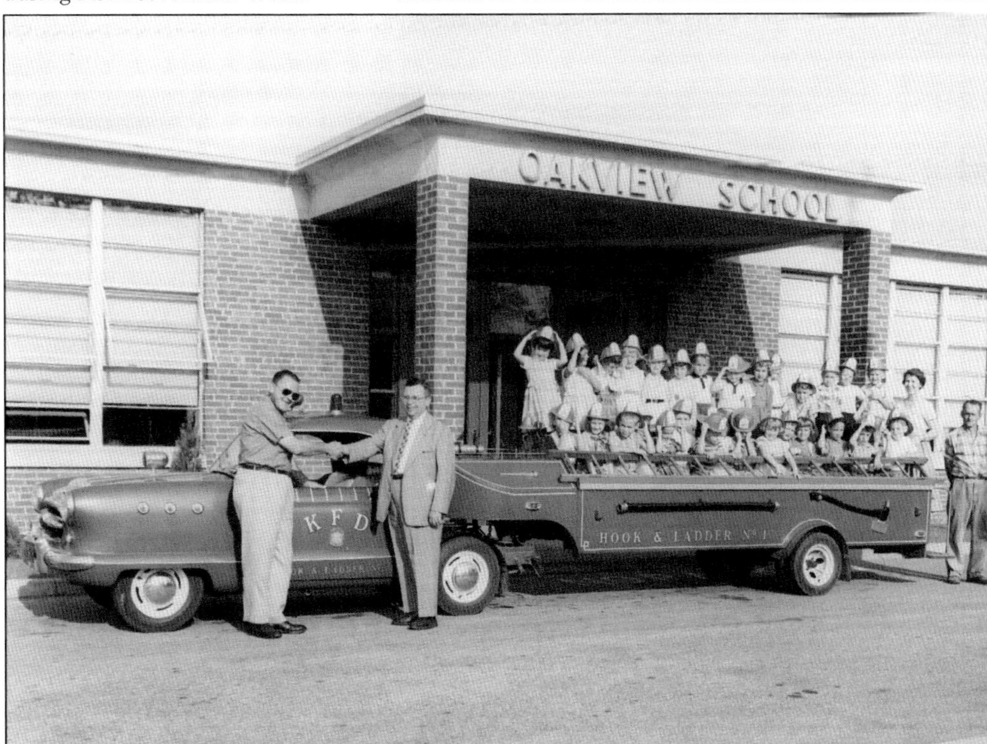

Like the police department, the West Deptford volunteer fire companies pride themselves on reaching out into the community. Keeping township residents safe is the number one priority for both departments. Here, students from the Oakview Elementary School received a ride during Fire Prevention Week.

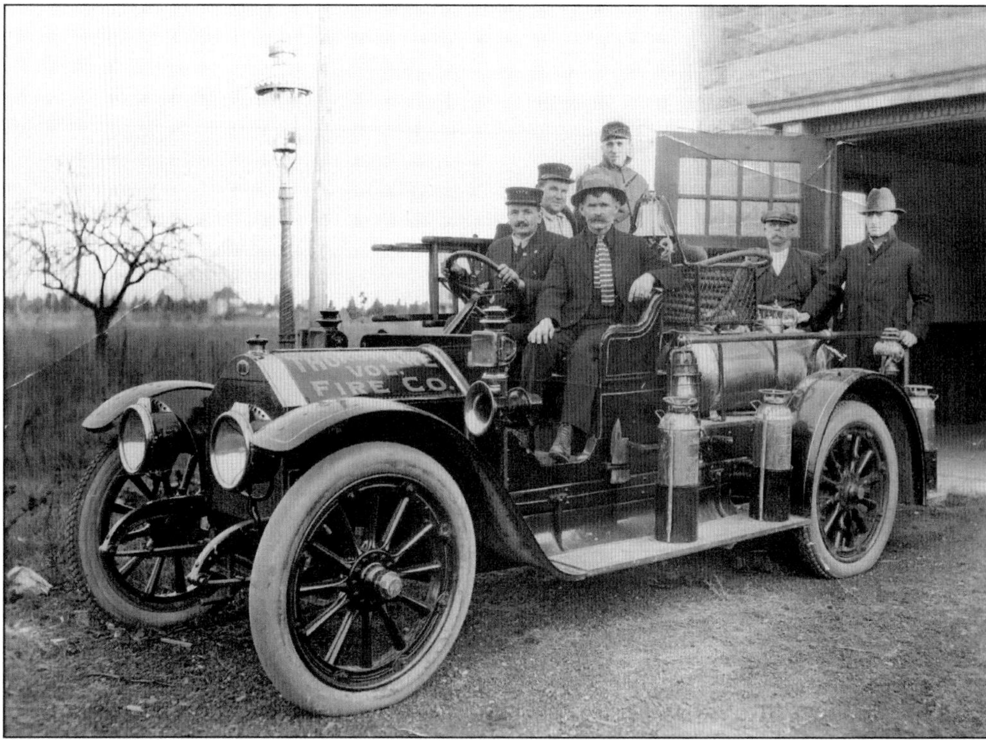

The Thorofare Volunteer Fire Company began in 1910, which makes it the oldest in West Deptford. In 1915, members show off their first motorized fire truck. Driving is Blane Hughes, while Barney Rambo sits in the passenger's seat. Bill Clement and Issac Bowers are seated behind the driver, while Bill Rambo rides on the left rear and Ed Shirk rides on the right. (Courtesy of Charles Bowers.)

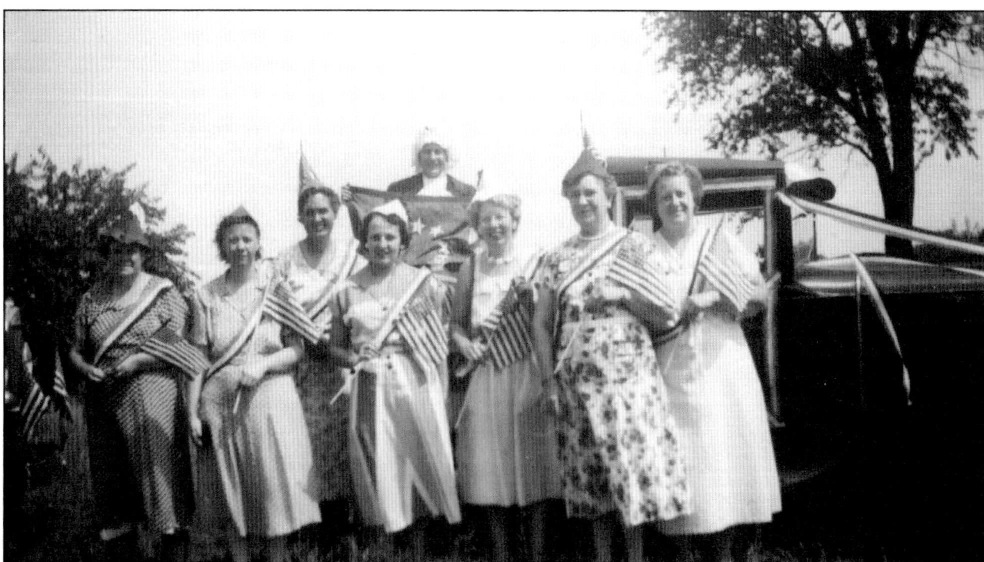

The Thorofare Ladies Auxiliary poses for a patriotic picture on July 4, 1952. (Courtesy of Pearl Dehner.)

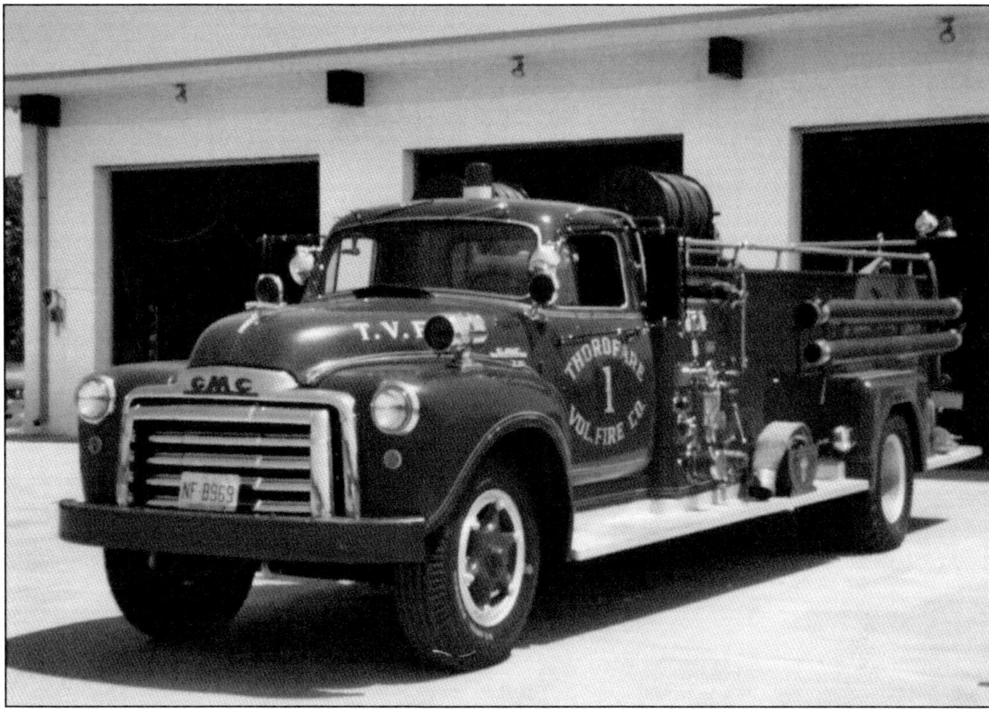

For over 100 years, Thorofare Volunteer Fire Company has provided fire protection to the community. The company has changed with the times and currently provides marine rescue, industrial fire fighting, and extrication services. Pictured are just two of the fire trucks that have been used to fight fires within the township. (Both, courtesy of Thorofare Volunteer Fire Company.)

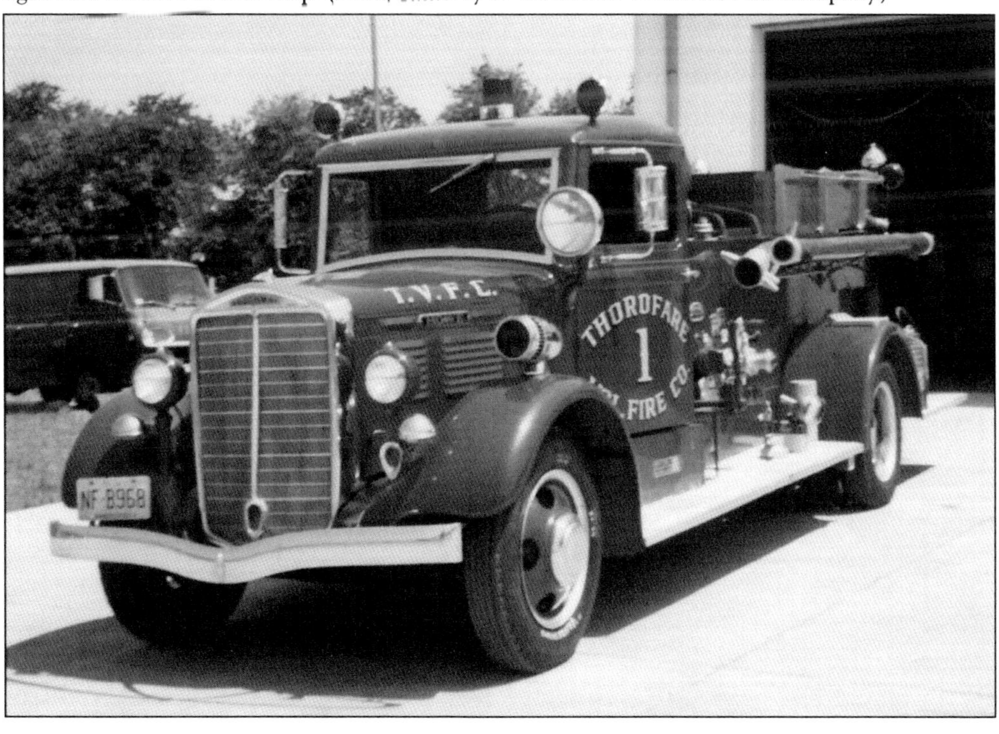

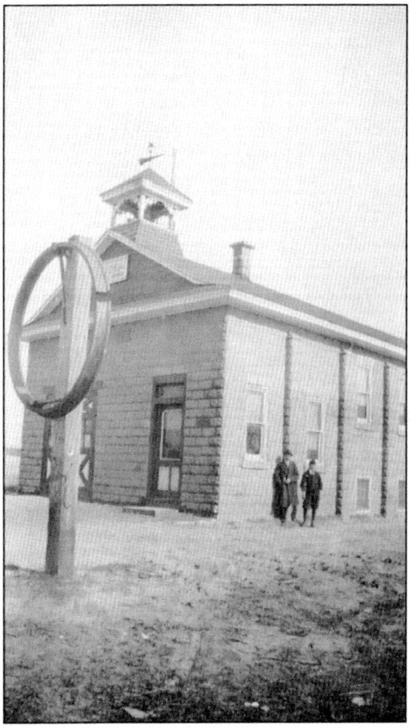

In 1916, a group of five men met in a home to discuss ways to provide fire protection to the rapidly expanding Verga neighborhood. The first selection of officers was held on July 7, 1916, and the West Deptford Fire Company was formed. Within two weeks, the name was changed to the Verga Volunteer Fire Company No. 1. In January 1917, a lot was purchased from a Mrs. Sharp, and a tent was erected on the site where meetings could be held. By the fall of that year, ground was broken for the first building. Pictured at left is the original Verga firehouse. Pictured below is the Verga firehouse addition, which was needed to house equipment. (Both, courtesy of Verga Volunteer Fire Company No. 1.)

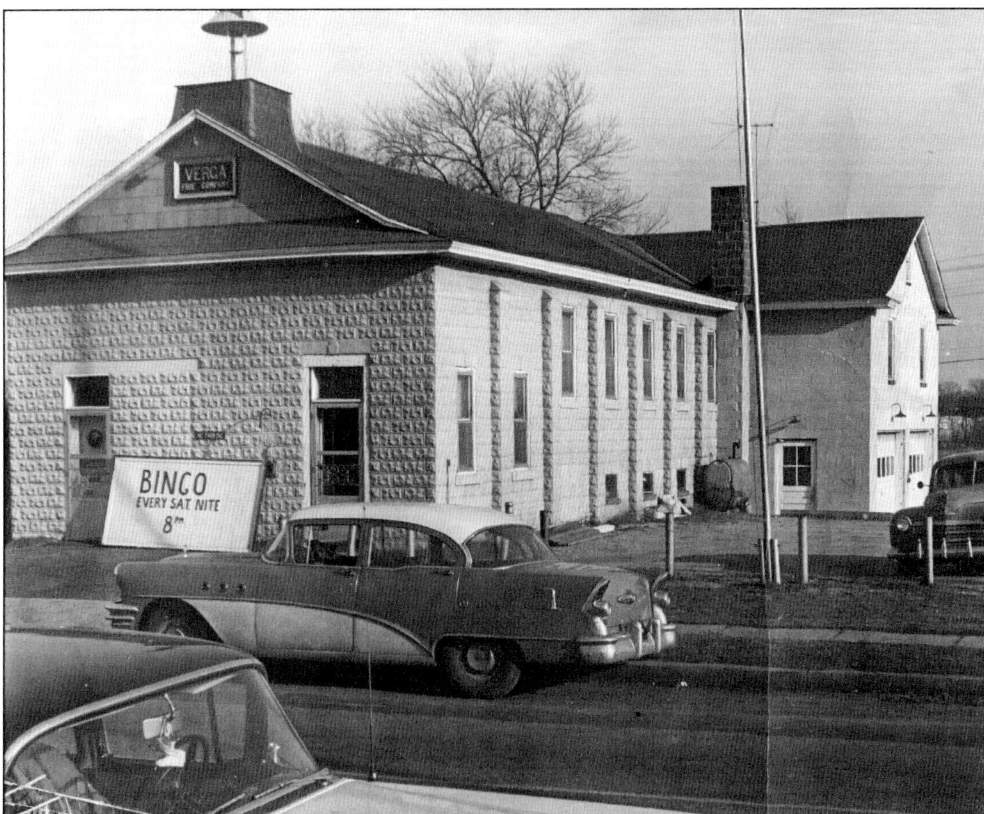

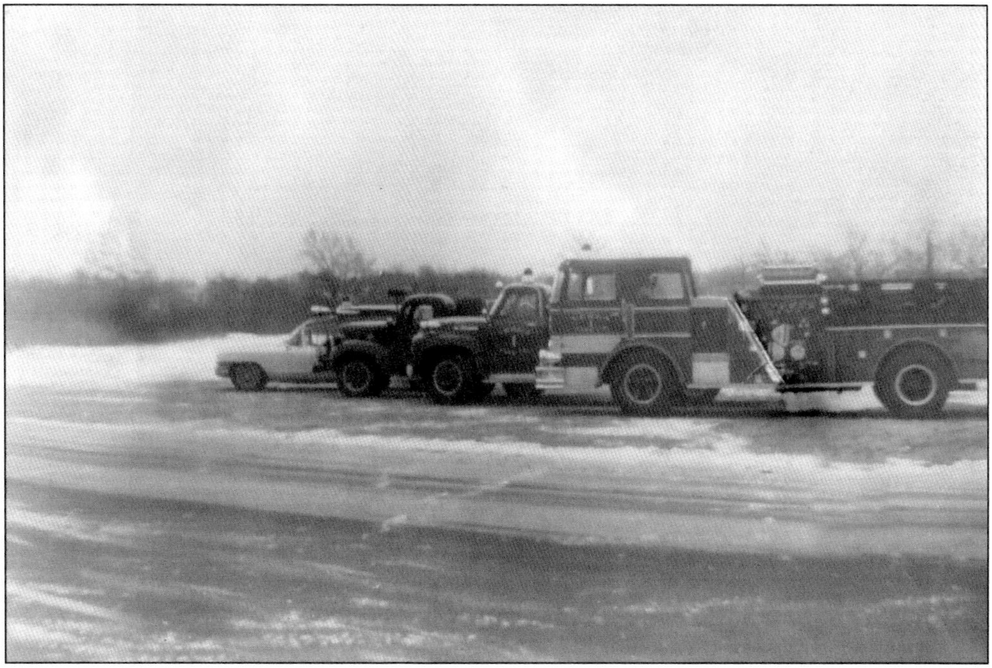

Pictured are an ambulance and three fire trucks belonging to the Verga Volunteer Fire Company No. 1. The fire company housed the ambulance that was used for the northern end of the township. (Courtesy of Verga Volunteer Fire Company No. 1.)

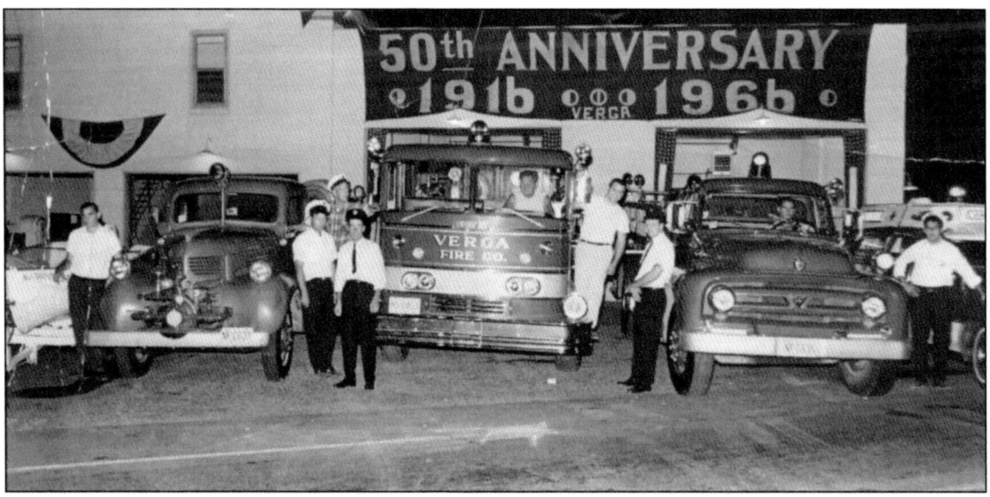

Verga Volunteer Fire Company No. 1 celebrates 50 years of service to the community. (Courtesy of Verga Volunteer Fire Company No. 1.)

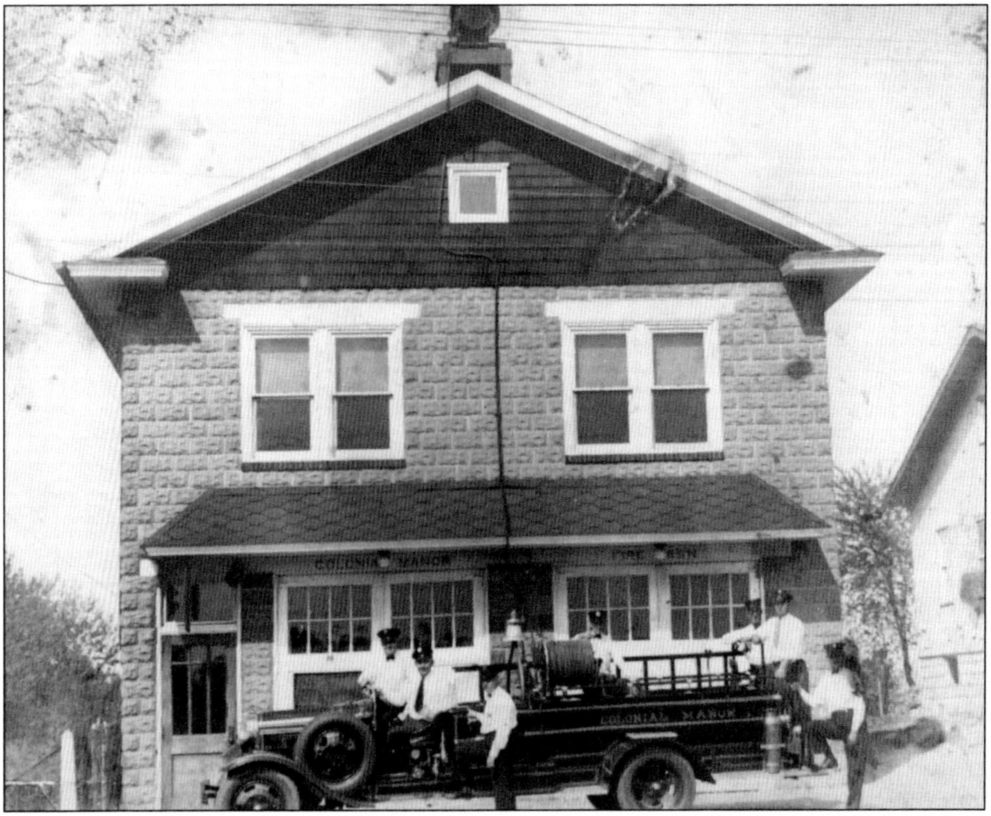

The Colonial Manor Fire Association was organized on February 23, 1922. In 1923, the fire association acquired its first building from a Mr. Love of the Colonial Land Company for $725 at the corner of Colonial and Lincoln Avenues. Shown above is Colonial Manor Fire Association's first official home. Also shown is the company's first fire truck. The truck was originally a chemical horse-drawn truck purchased in 1923 from the Philadelphia Fire Company. The Colonial Manor Fire Association members placed this body on an old Buick car chassis, donated by a Mr. Friel. Two weeks later, the association adopted crimson and gold as the official colors. (Both, courtesy of the Colonial Manor Fire Association.)

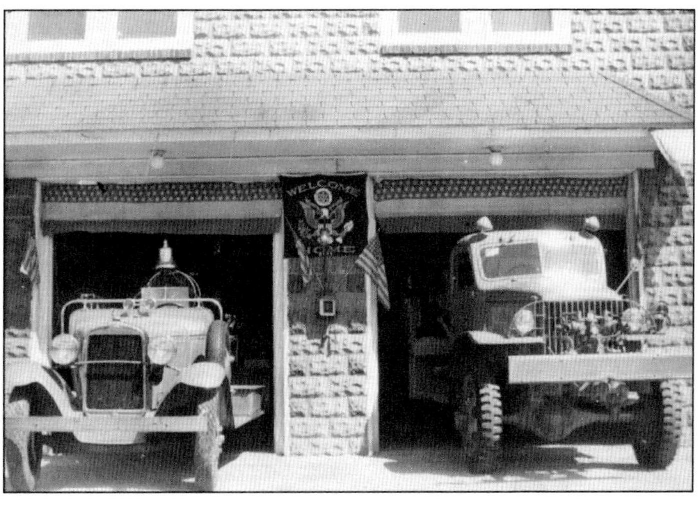

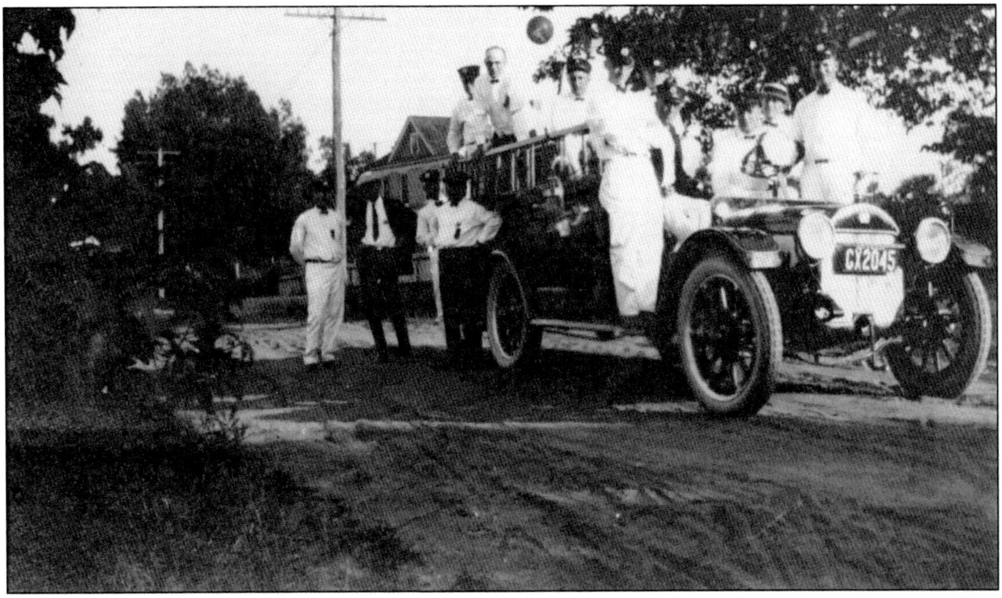

Pictured around 1925 on one of Colonial Manor's dirt roads is the Colonial Manor Fire Association. Standing in the back of the fire truck, second from the rear, is Leo Janson. (Courtesy of Grace Janson.)

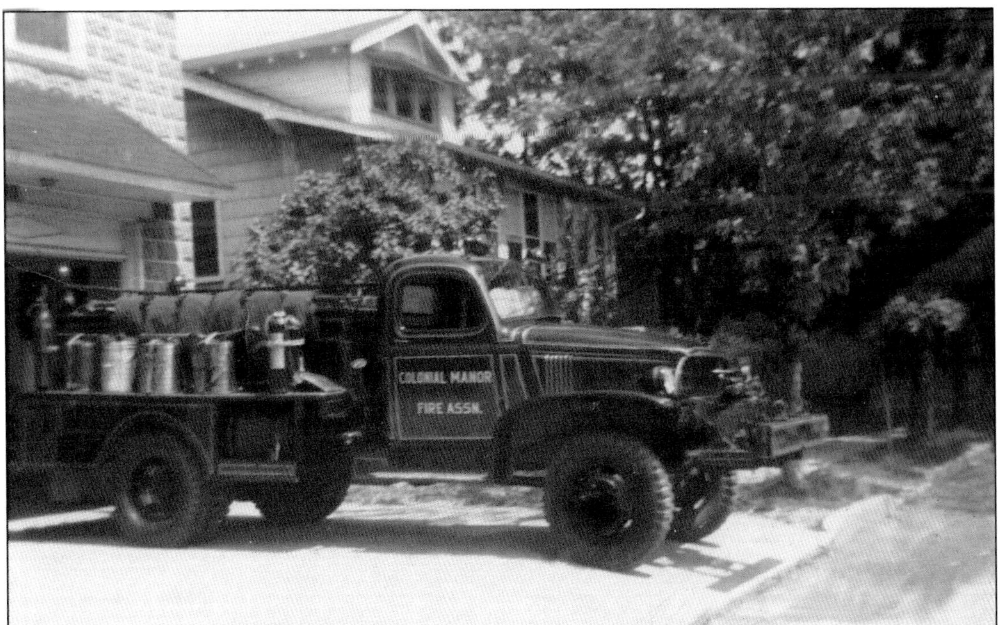

A lone fire truck awaits its next call outside the Colonial Manor Fire Association. (Courtesy of Ethel Coates.)

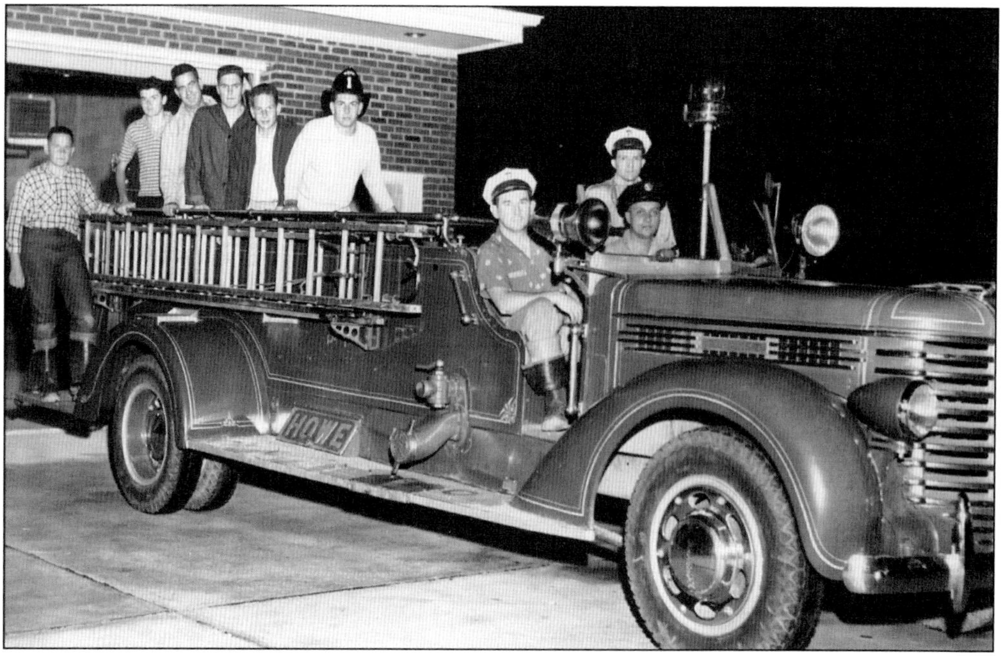

The Greenfields Fire Association started in June 1956. The firehouse stands on Budd Boulevard in the Greenfields neighborhood. Pictured in 1959 are George Bradley Jr., David Brennan, Doug Brown, Paul Higgins, David Vaughan, Charles Vaughan, George Bradley, Charles Cole, and Vern Evans. The firefighters are seated on a 1941 Diamond-T Howe Pumper. (Courtesy of Greenfields Fire Association.)

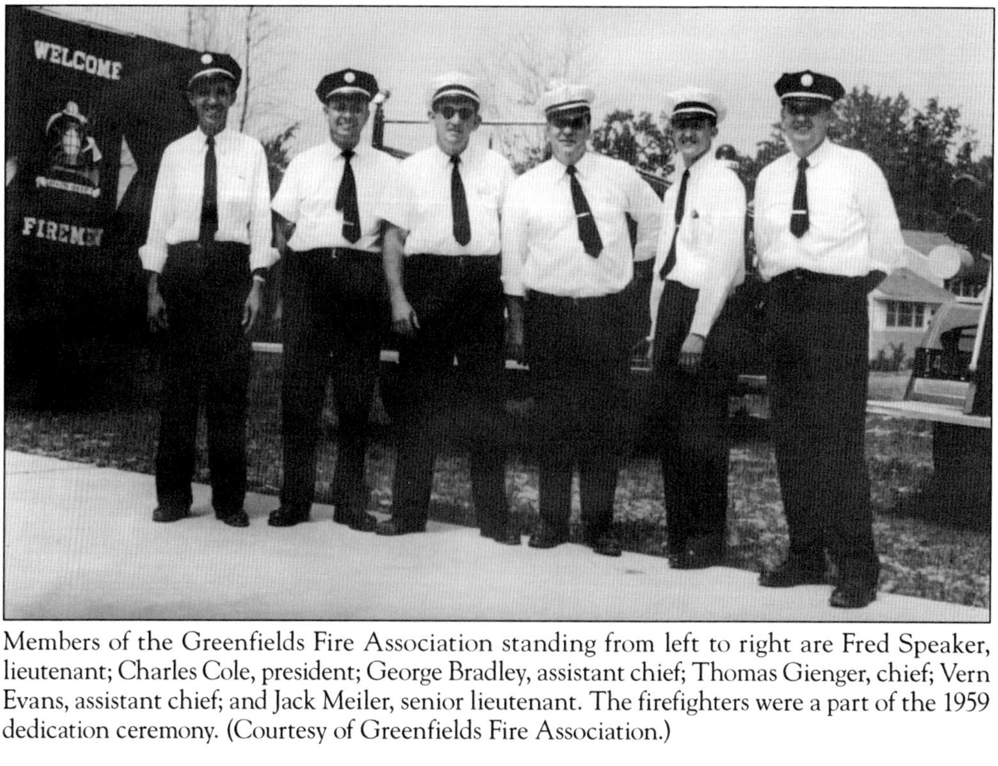

Members of the Greenfields Fire Association standing from left to right are Fred Speaker, lieutenant; Charles Cole, president; George Bradley, assistant chief; Thomas Gienger, chief; Vern Evans, assistant chief; and Jack Meiler, senior lieutenant. The firefighters were a part of the 1959 dedication ceremony. (Courtesy of Greenfields Fire Association.)

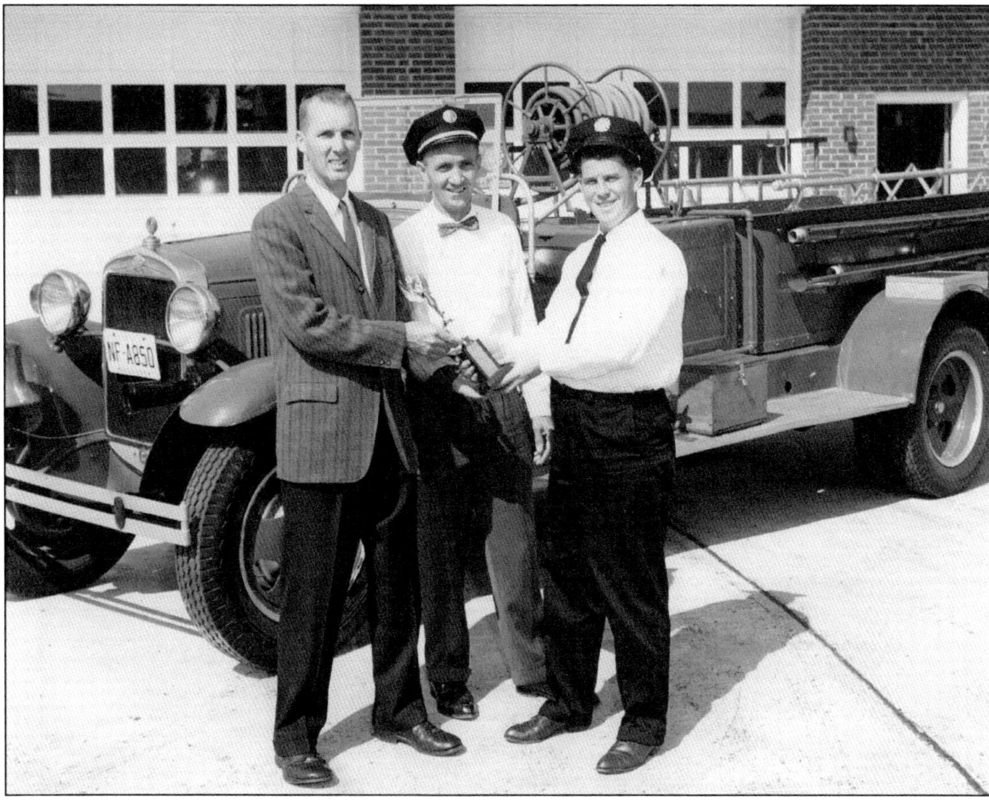

Receiving an award outside of the Greenfields Fire Association is Wade K. Monroe, while Fred Speaker looks on. In the background is the Greenfields Model A Ford fire truck. (Courtesy of Greenfields Fire Association.)

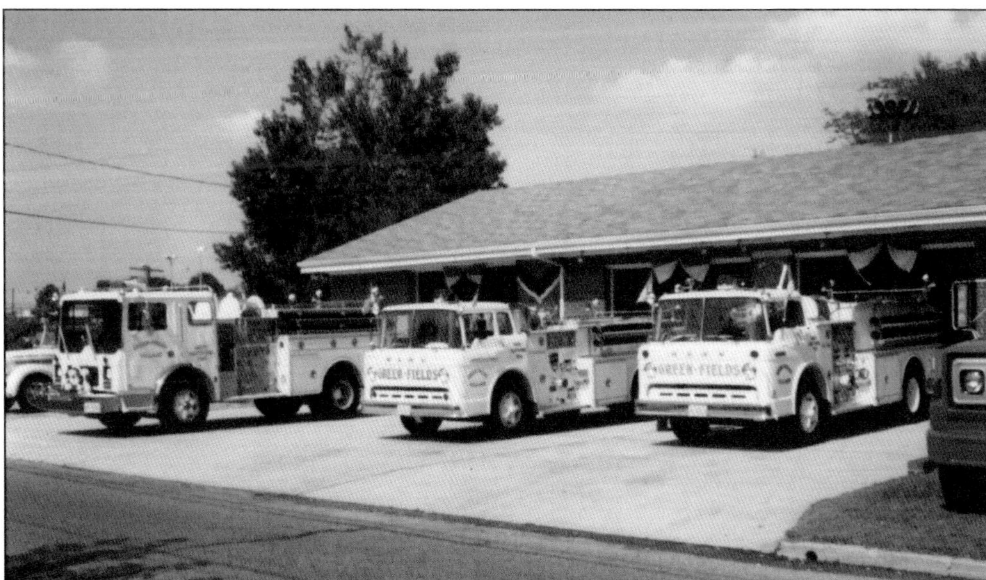

The Greenfields firehouse is pictured with company fire trucks on display. (Courtesy of Greenfields Fire Association.)

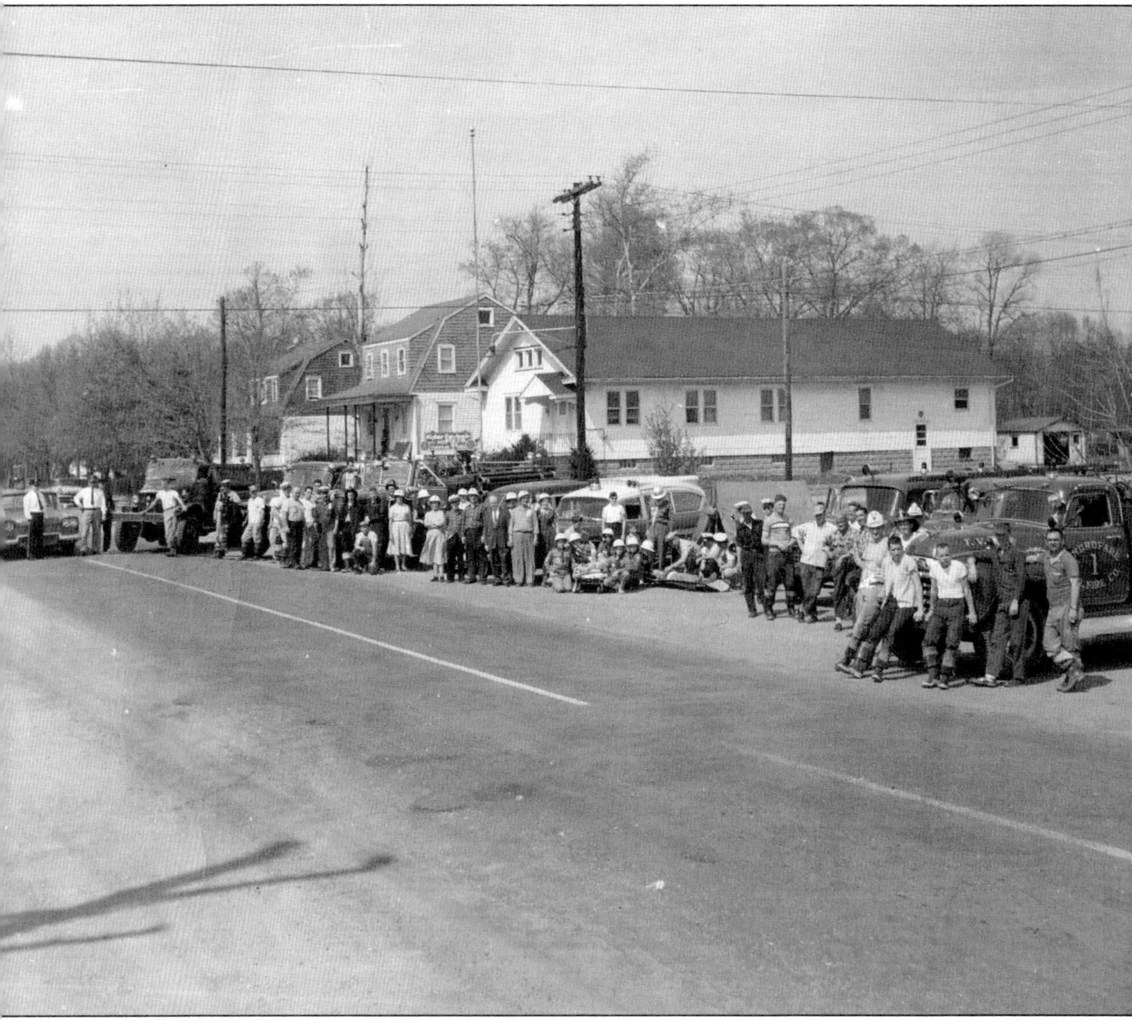

Although members belong to individual fire companies that protect each section of the township, members of the four fire companies come together as one to celebrate and protect the residents of West Deptford Township. (Courtesy of Verga Volunteer Fire Company No. 1.)

Five

EDUCATION

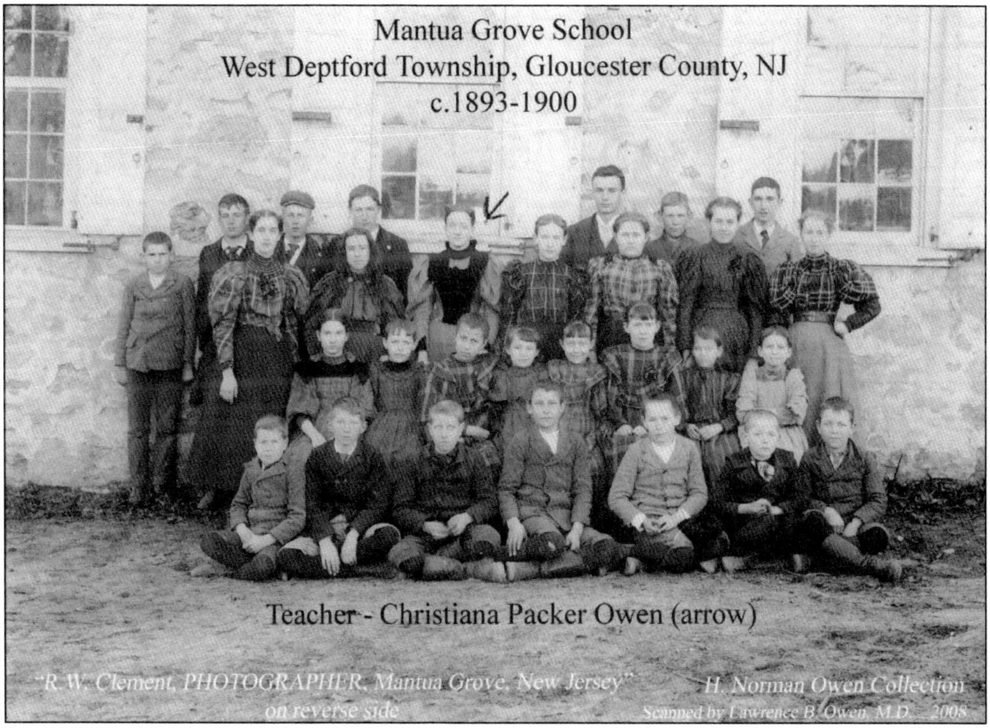

Mantua Grove School opened in 1822. The school was a small wooden structure. It was not until 1842 that the small stone school was built at its current location on Kings Highway. The ground for the school was donated by Joseph Tatum of the Society of Friends. Mantua Grove School was the longest running elementary school in Gloucester County. Pictured is Christiana Packer Owen's class of students around the late 1800s. (Courtesy of Lawrence B. Owen, MD.)

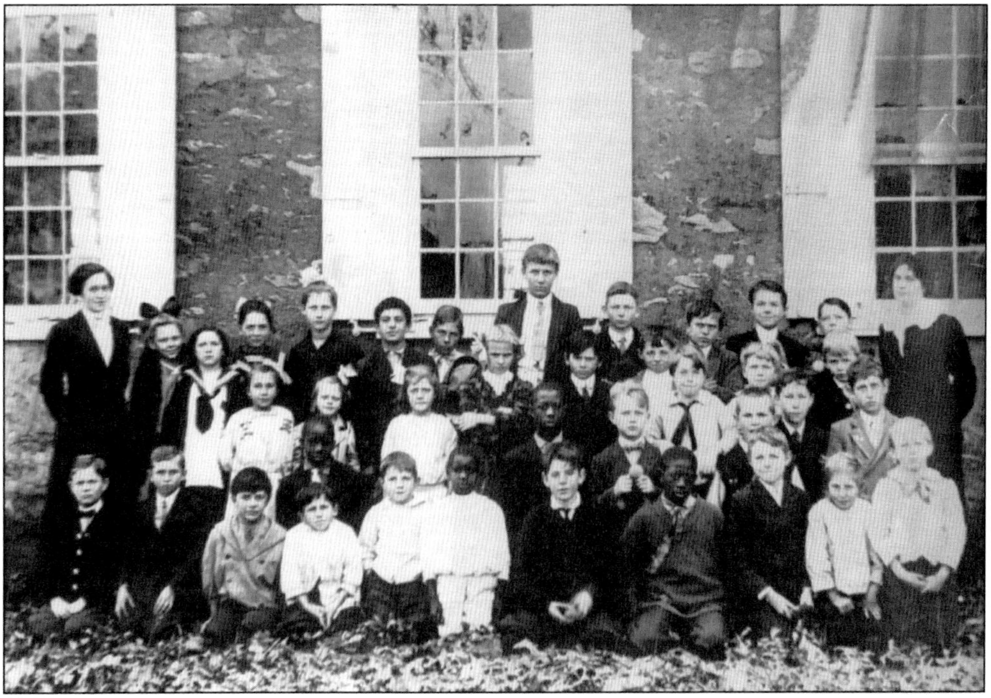

Mantua Grove Schoolhouse, known as the little gray stone schoolhouse, was the oldest running elementary school in Gloucester County, New Jersey. It was built in 1842 and operated as a school for over 125 years. Pictured is the class of 1902. Below is a class picture from the old Thorofare School around 1896. (Both, courtesy of Ernest and Bert Parks.)

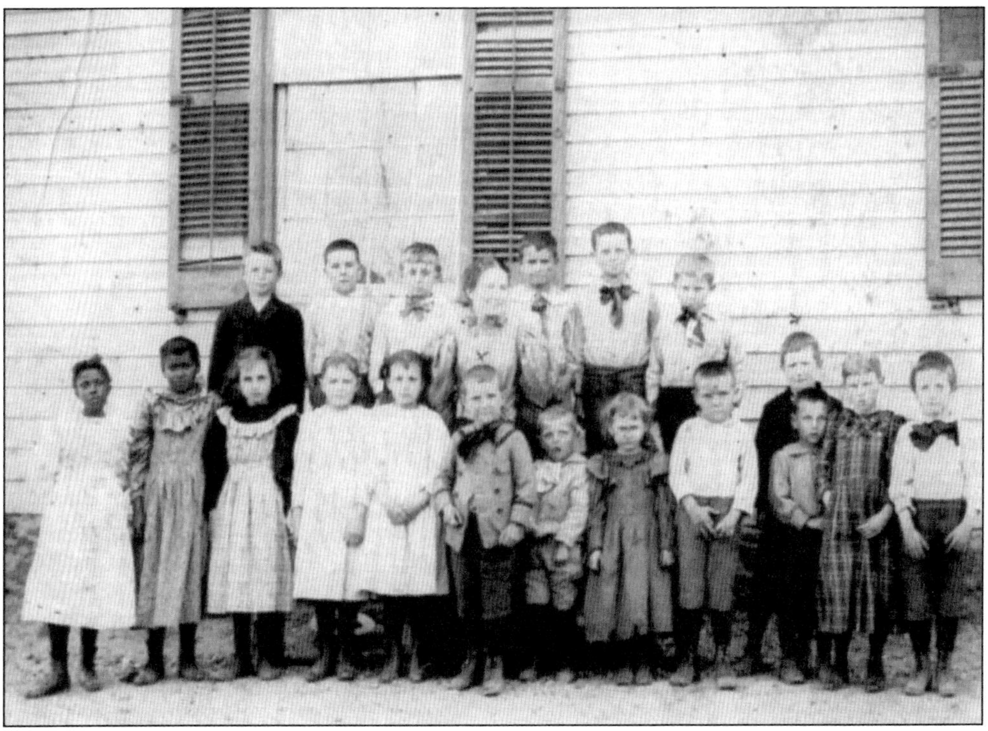

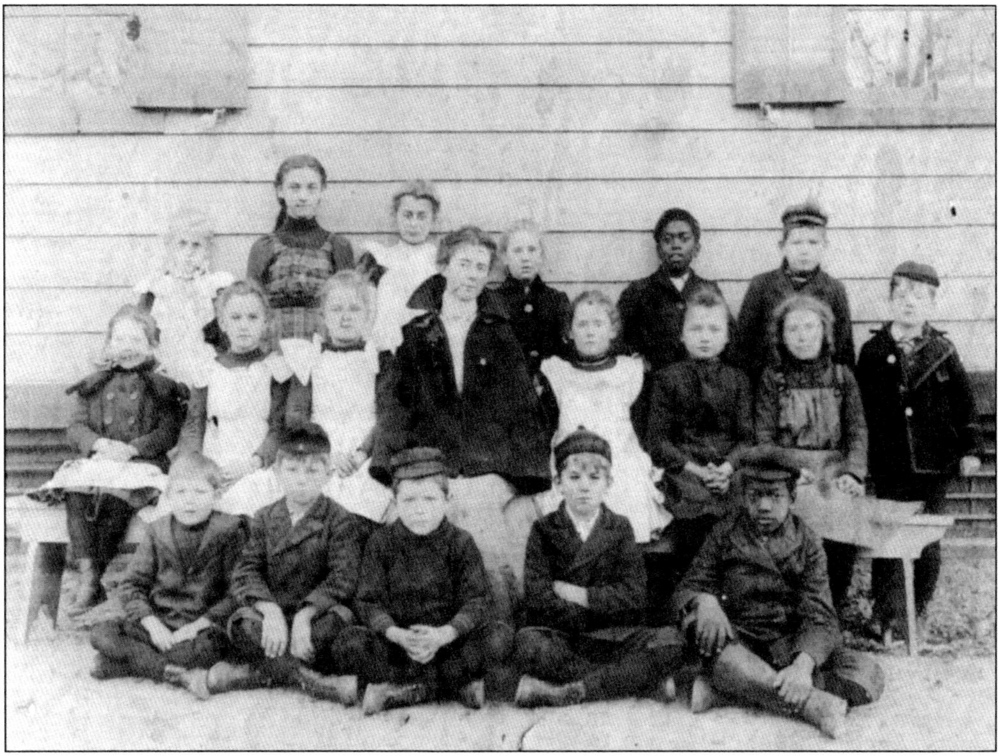

Children pose outside the old Thorofare School for their class pictures in the early 1900s. (Both, courtesy of Charles Leonard Jr.)

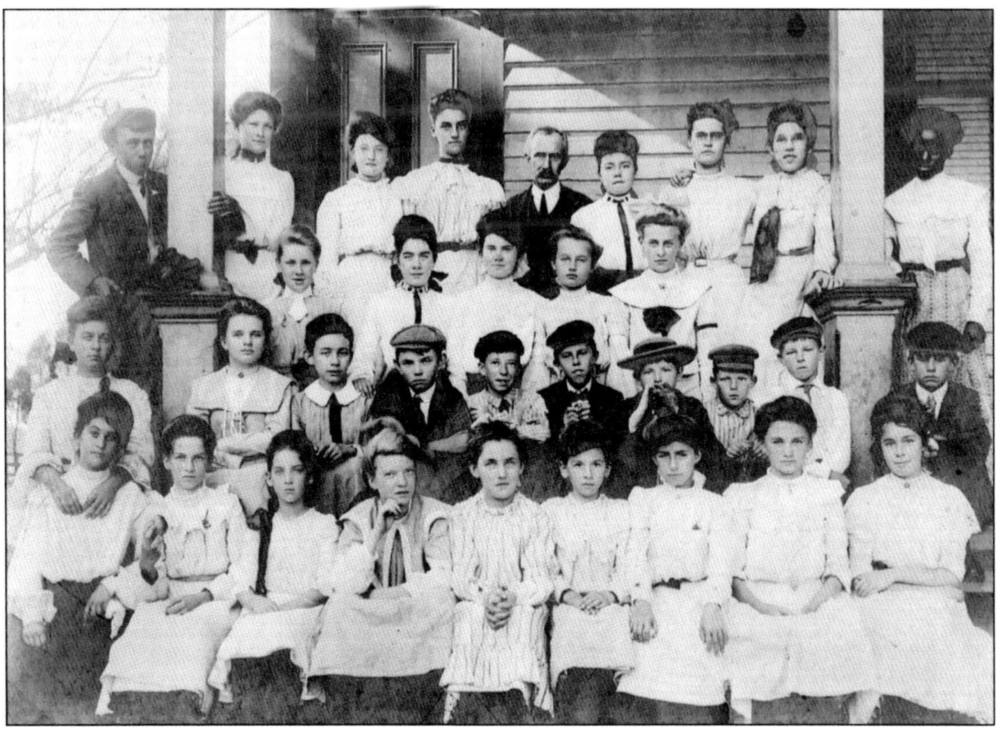

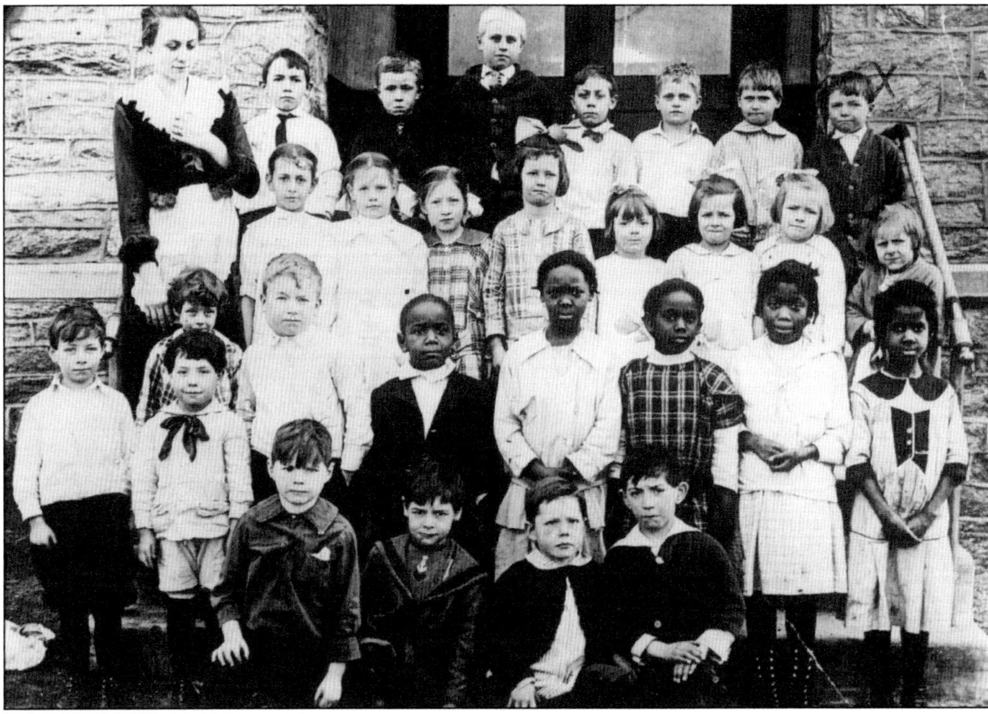

As the 1800s came to an end, the need for another school was evident. In 1896, the Red Bank No. 1 School was built on the corners of Red Bank and Hessian Avenues. In 1965, the Red Bank No. 2 School was built on Philadelphia Avenue. In 1976, the Red Bank No. 1 School was closed and remained unoccupied until 1998, when the Scouting groups within the township refurbished it for use. Pictured is a class from the old Thorofare School, one of the first schools in West Deptford Township. Pictured in the last row at far right is Charles Bowers. (Courtesy of Pearl Dehner.)

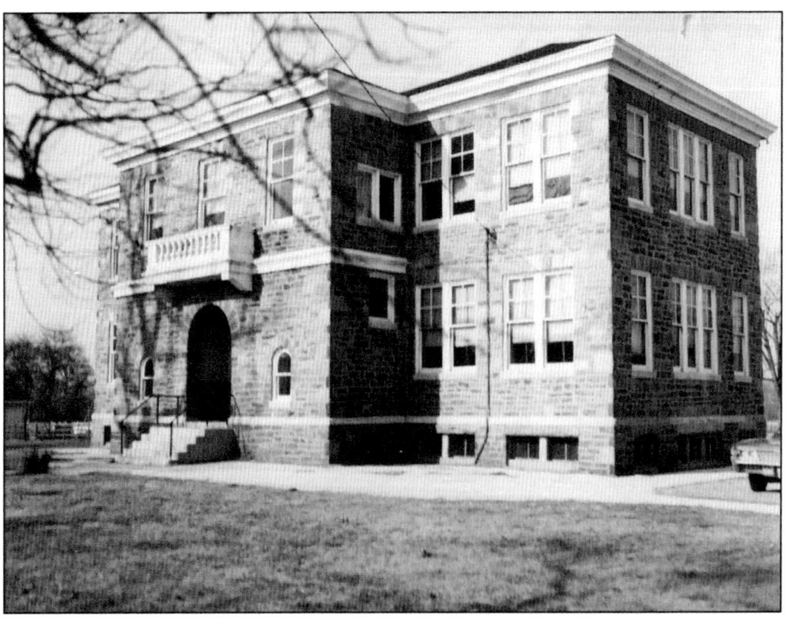

The Thorofare No. 3 School opened in 1905. Located on Old Crown Point Road, this property is currently home to the West Deptford Little Theater.

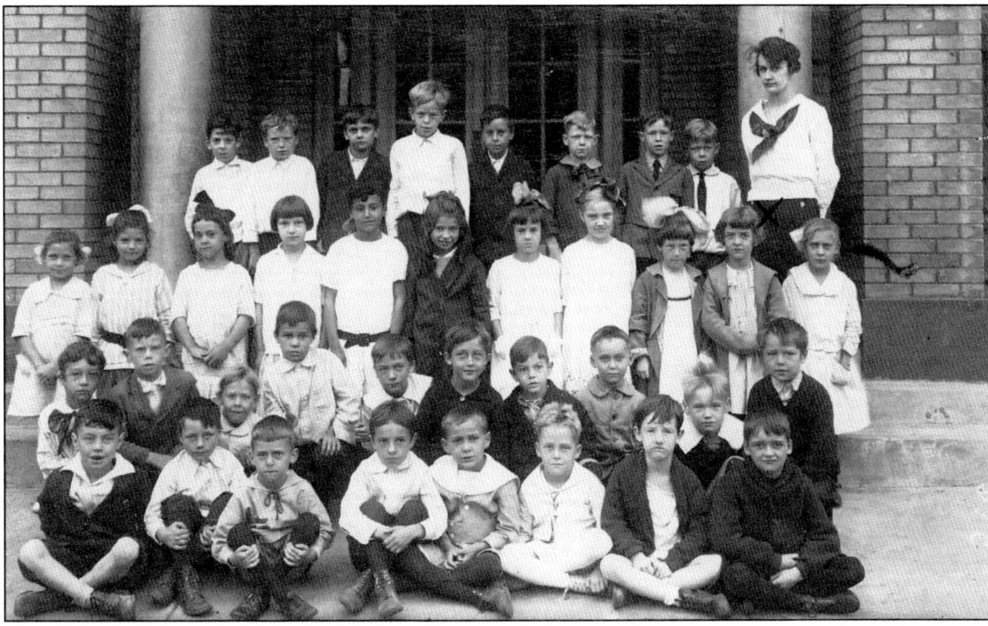

The Verga School was located on Verga Avenue in the northern end of the township. The school opened in 1922. Standing in the third row, second from the right, is Thelma Addason. (Courtesy of Pearl Dehner.)

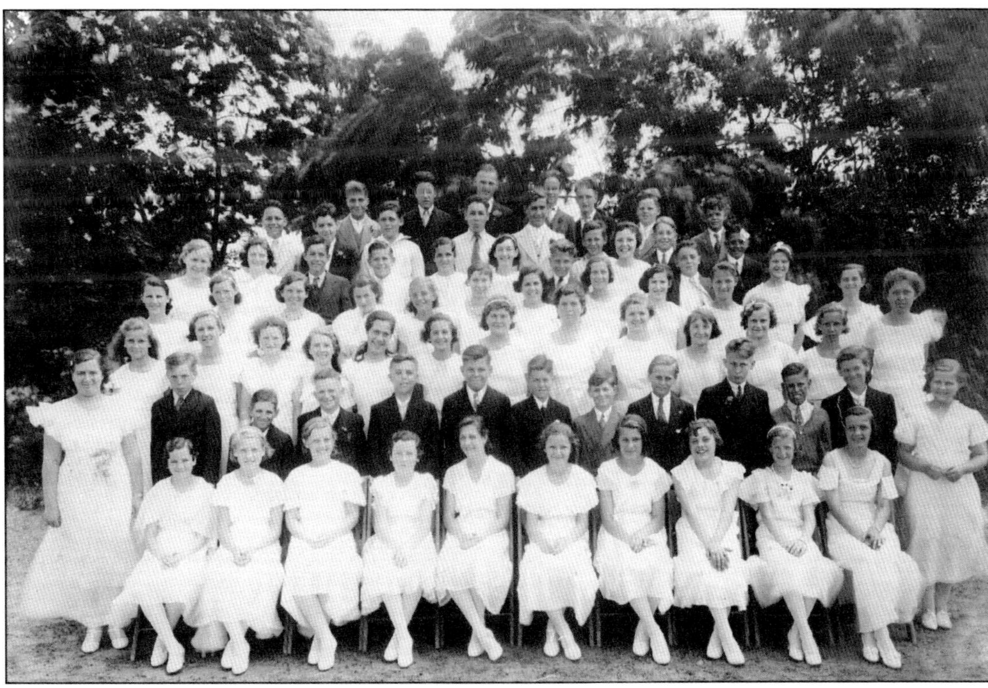

The 1934 eighth-grade class from the Verga School poses for a graduation photograph. It was not until 1972 that the township built a middle school, which continues to educate children attending the fifth through the eighth grades.

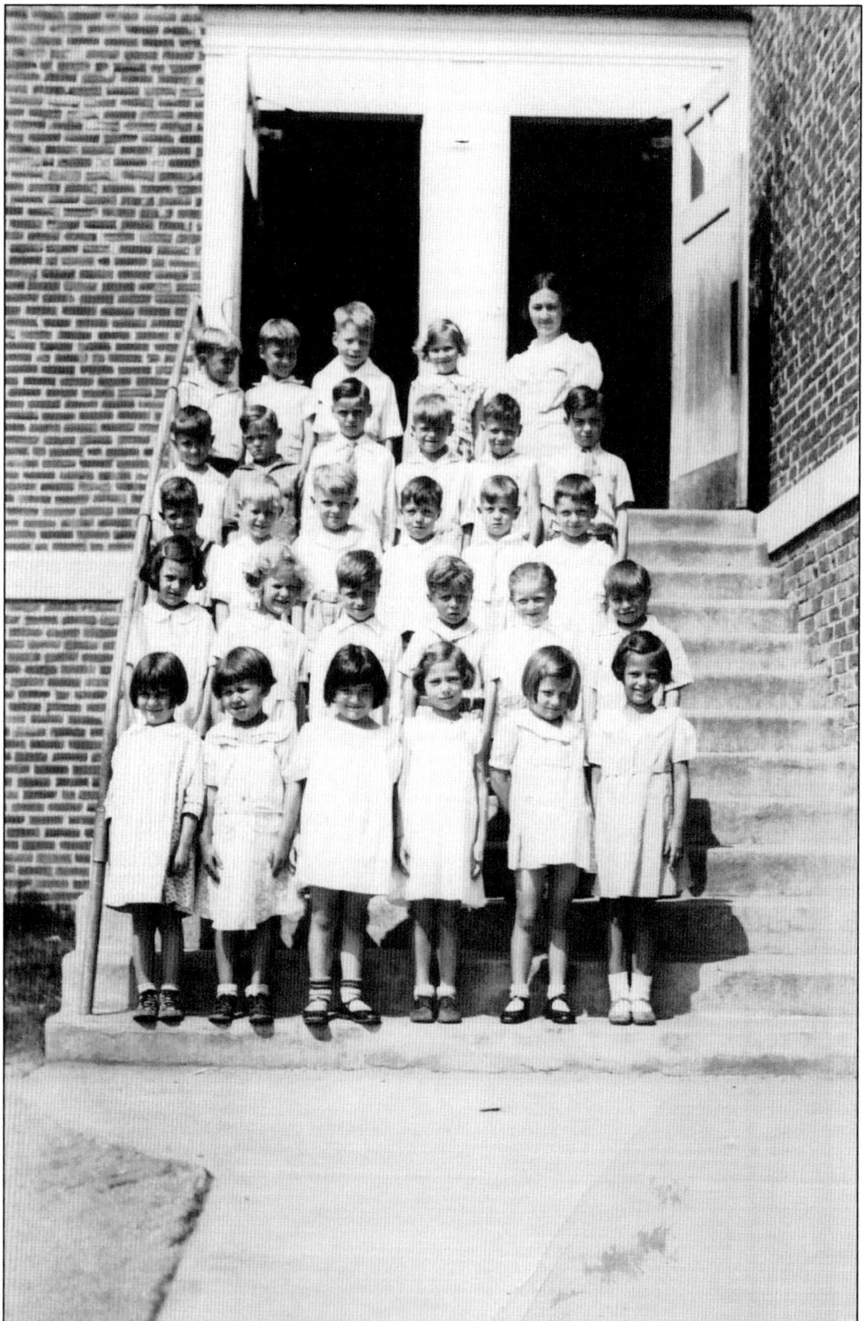

Colonial Manor School opened in 1929 at a cost of $66,000 and stood on Hessian Avenue. It opened the same year as the Mantua Terrace School, which opened at a cost of $45,000. At the request of the African American population that lived in West Deptford at that time, the Thorofare Colored School was built at a cost of $23,200. It was later known as the Thorofare No. 4 School and was used as a nonsegregated educational center. Located at the corner of Salem Avenue and Crown Point Road, it was closed and torn down in 1986. Pictured are Colonial Manor teacher Dorothy Detwiler (McGrail) and her class around 1930. (Courtesy of Grace Janson.)

The children attending Colonial Manor School affectionately knew Walter Shin as "Grandpop Shin." He was the first custodian of the school. Pictured is Grandpop Shin, raising the American flag at the start of another school day. (Courtesy of Herbert Lancaster.)

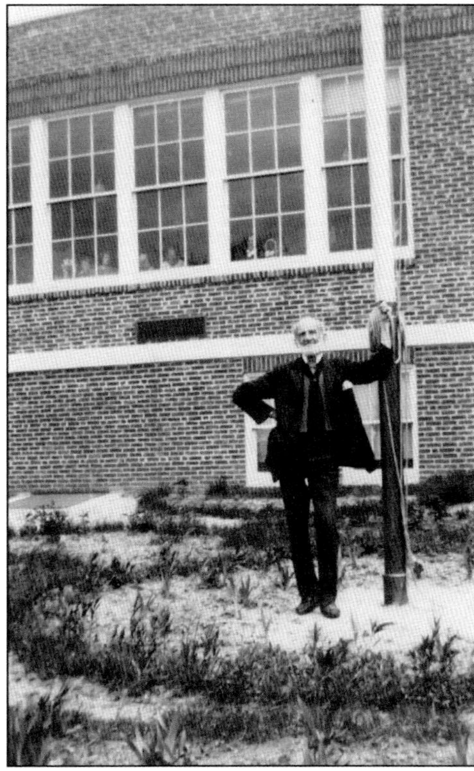

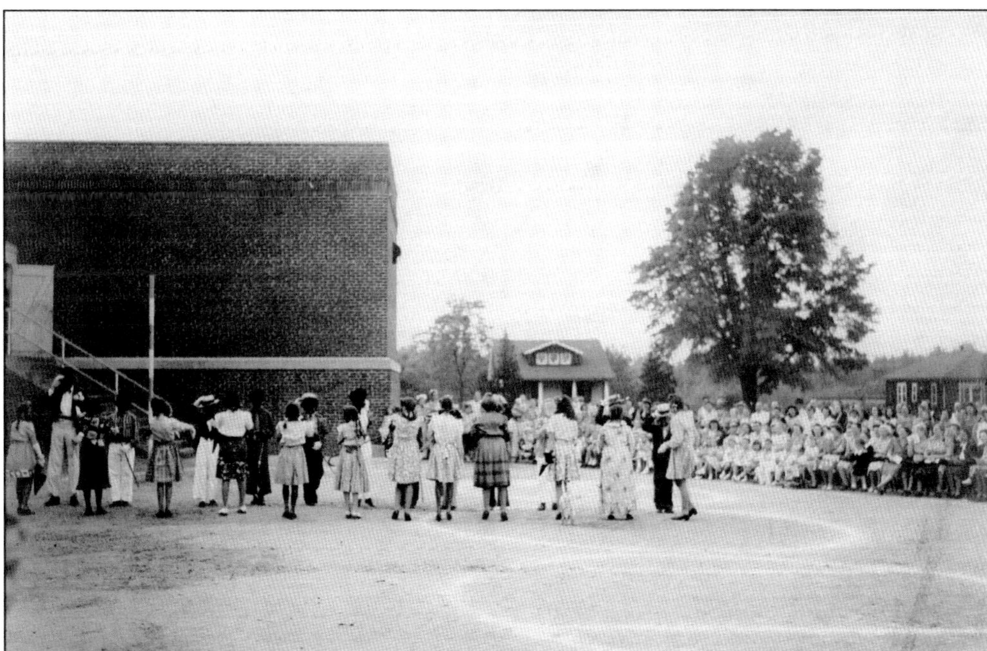

Children at the Colonial Manor School are seen putting on one of many outdoor performances for their excited parents. This May Day celebration was an annual tradition at the school. The dance they are performing is called the "Cakewalk." (Courtesy of Grace Janson.)

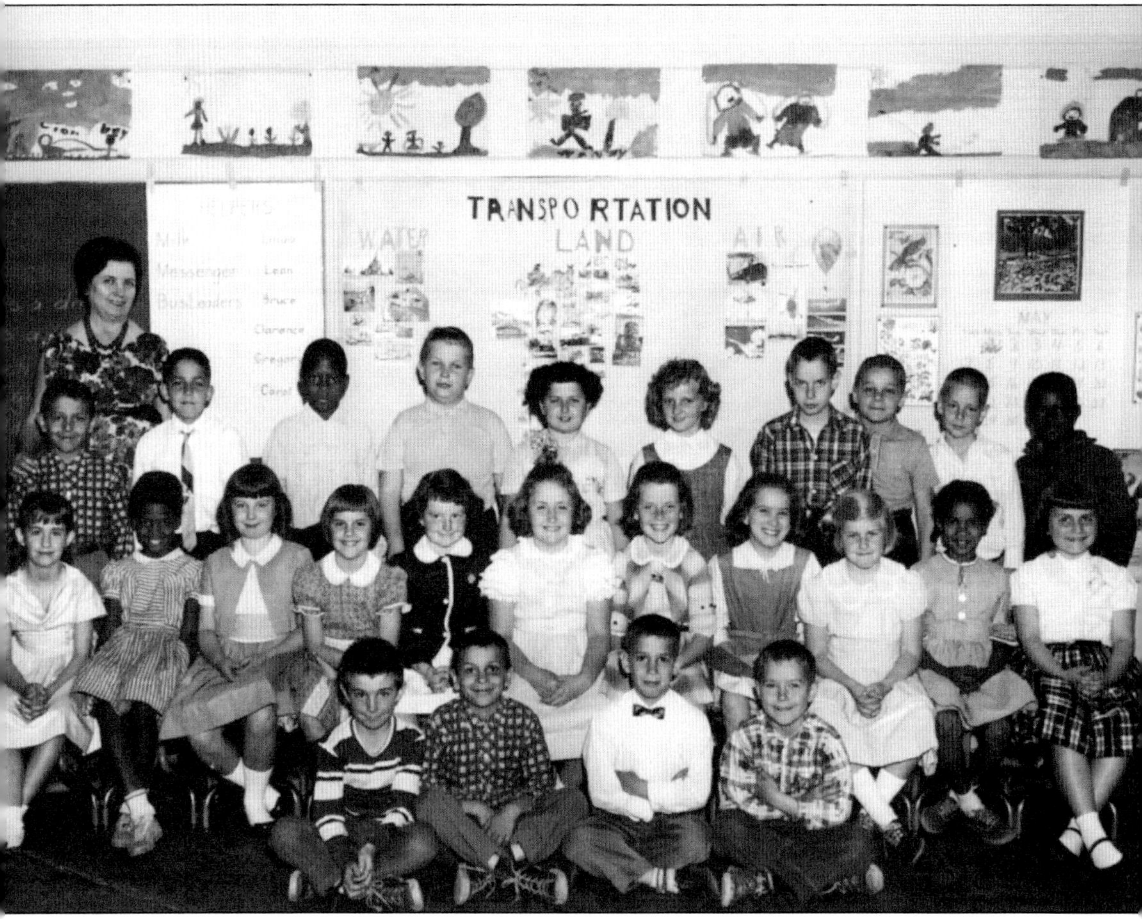

Pictured is Mrs. DeVinny's third-grade class at the Thorofare No. 4 School, located close to the township municipal building. This photograph was taken after the school was desegregated. (Courtesy of Deborah A. Richman.)

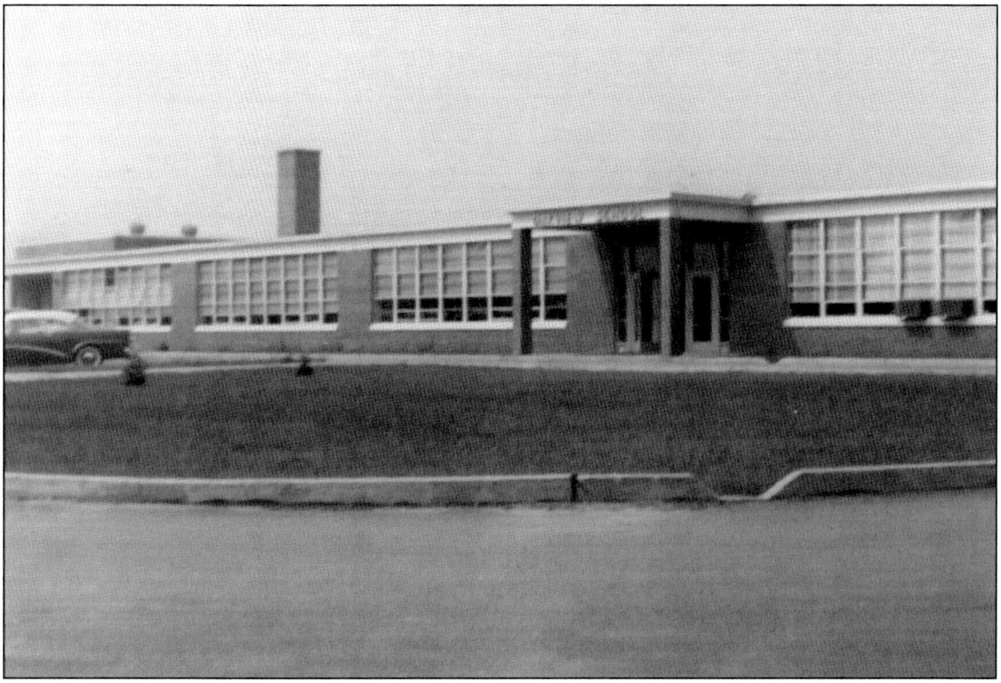

Oakview Elementary School was built in 1954 at the end of DuBois Avenue at the cost of $360,000. Children began class in April 1955. Two additions have been added, the latest of which was built in 1997. (Courtesy of Donna Tull.)

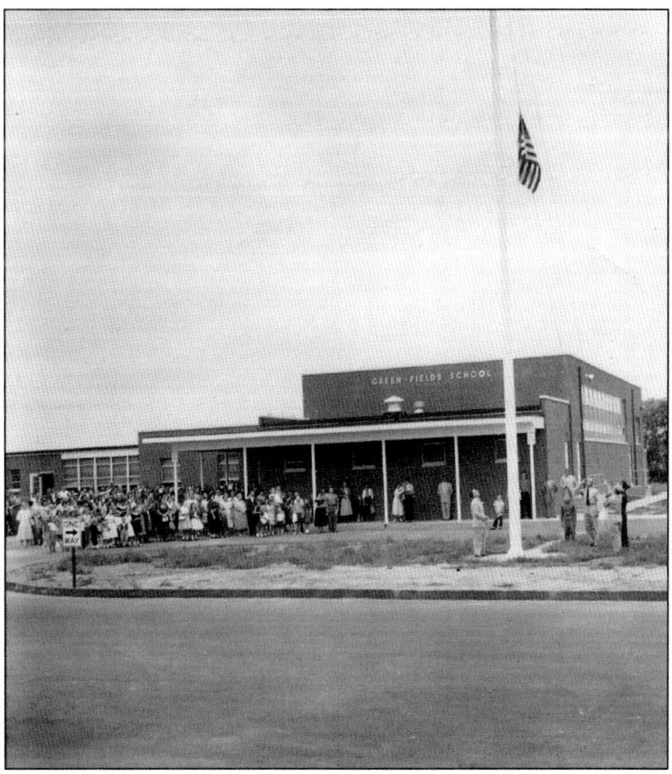

Green-Fields Elementary School was built on Hill Avenue in 1956 at a cost of $300,000. Children began to attend classes in September 1957. Additions were made to the building in 1965 and 1990 to keep up with the increases in the population.

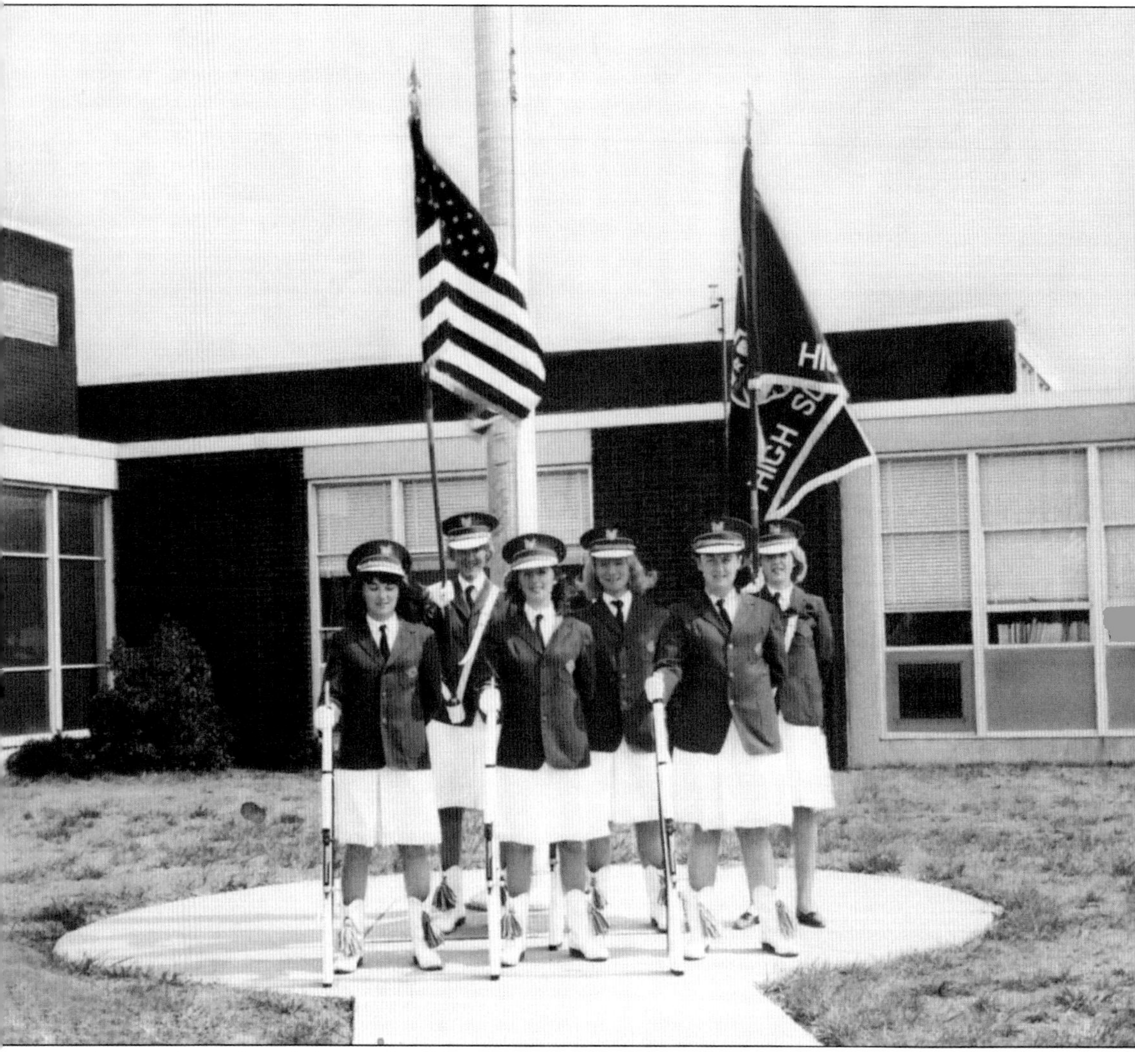

Pictured are, from left to right, (first row) Linda Sharrod, Diane Wallace, and Janice Stevens; (second row) Pat Frantz, Janie Toppin, and Ann Flannery. They were the first color guard team of the new West Deptford High School. The high school opened in 1960 with an incoming freshman class. A new incoming class was added each year. In 1964, the first senior class graduated from West Deptford High School.

Six
Soupy Island

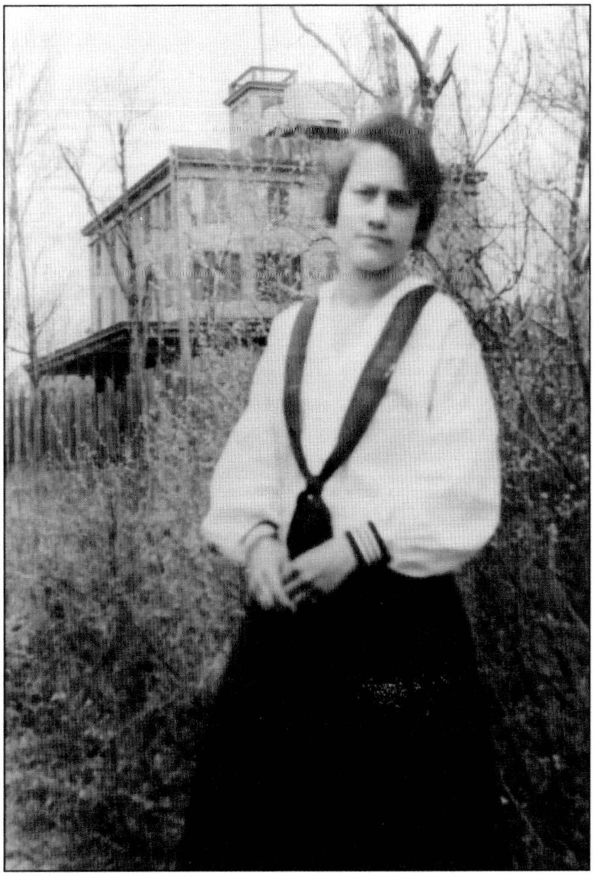

Over 135 years ago, conditions in Philadelphia during the cholera epidemic became so deplorable that a group of concerned citizens decided that sick children needed to be taken out of the city and given the opportunity to spend time outdoors in the fresh country air. So began the Sanitarium Association of Philadelphia, currently known as Sanitarium Playground of New Jersey, Inc. Mary Combs, an heiress to a snuff fortune, was known as Soupy Island's number one benefactor. Pictured is Eva Nickerson, whose family was employees of the sanitarium. In the background is the hospital. (Courtesy of the Bornmann family.)

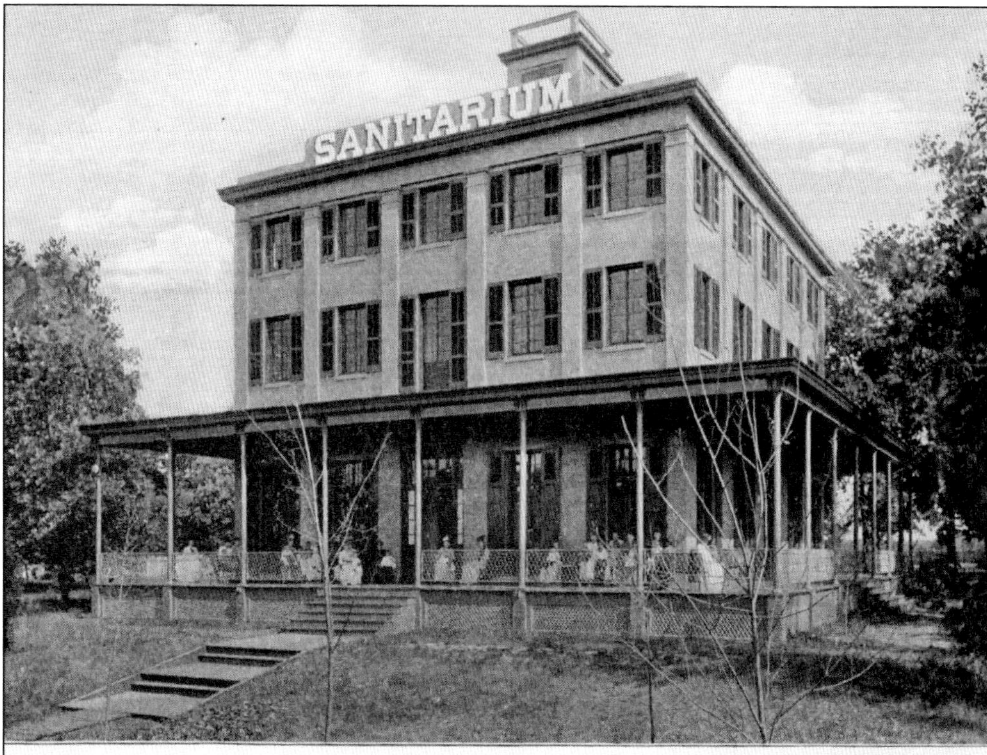

THE HOSPITAL

As the use of the facility grew, the Sanitarium Playground of New Jersey, Inc., recognized the need to relocate. A total of 104 acres was purchased in West Deptford Township, slightly north of National Park. The organization sold most of the acres, keeping just the 13 acres where Soupy Island continues to operate today. An old hotel was converted into a hospital where sick children could stay for free for up to two weeks. It operated until 1936, when it was torn down. The current Soupy Island swimming pool is located where the basement of the old hotel once existed. Shown below is a typical hospital ward. Since the sanitarium cared for children of all ages, rooms were filled with cribs and cots. (Both, courtesy of Bornmann family.)

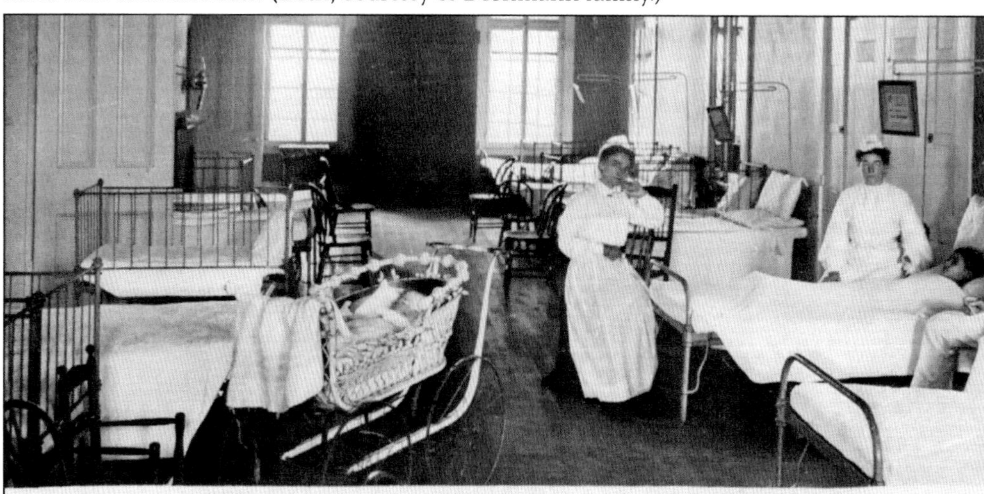

A WARD IN THE HOSPITAL

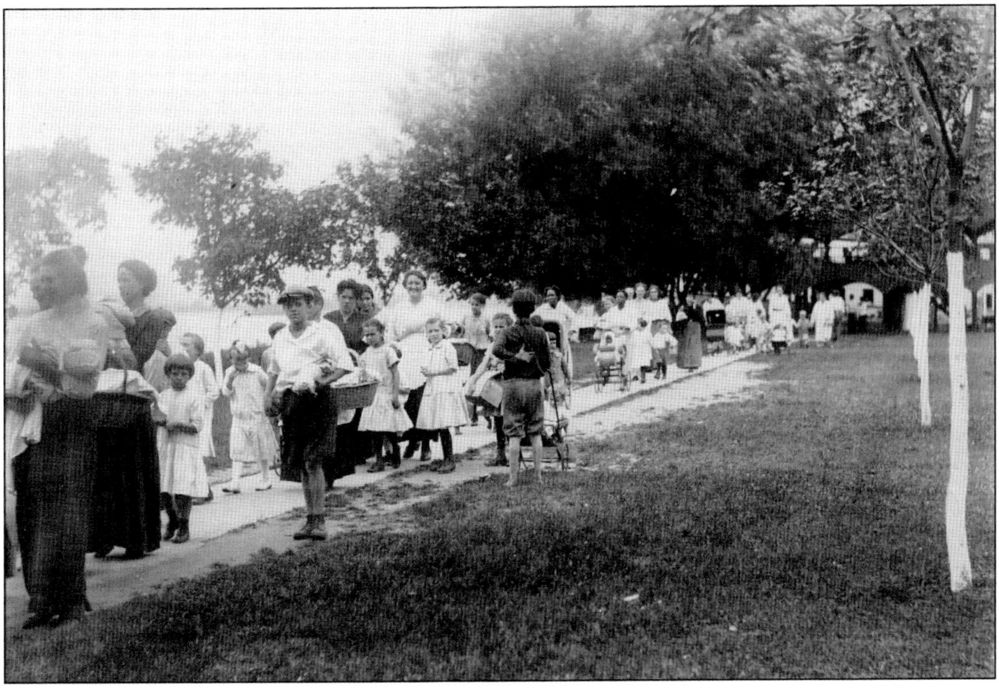

Children travel to and from Soupy Island in many different ways. In the early years, children traveled to the island by ferry or trolley. Later, children came by car or bus. Upon arrival, accurate counts were made for bookkeeping purposes. (Both, courtesy of the Bornmann family.)

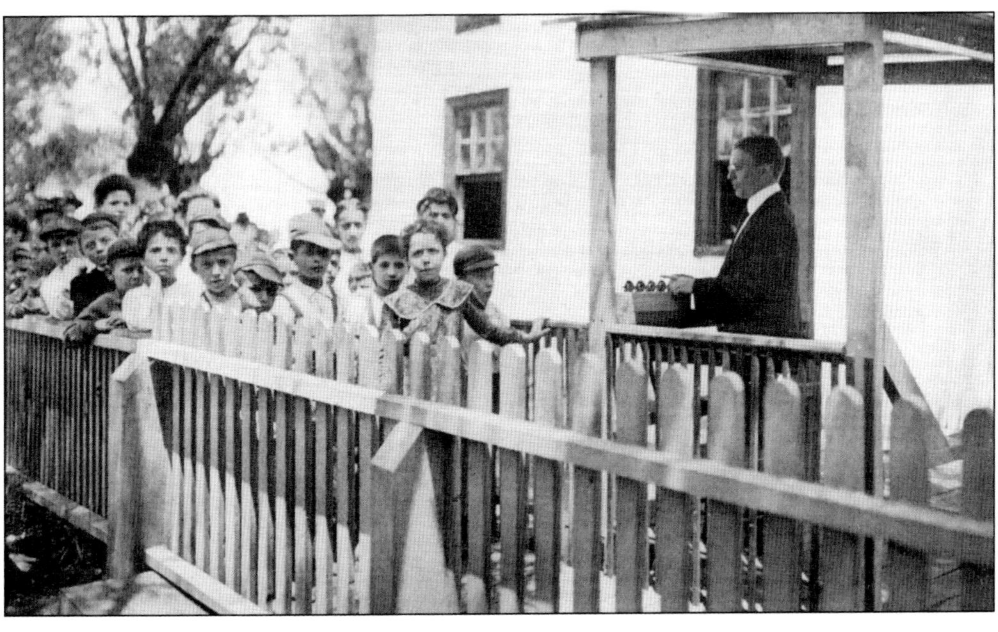

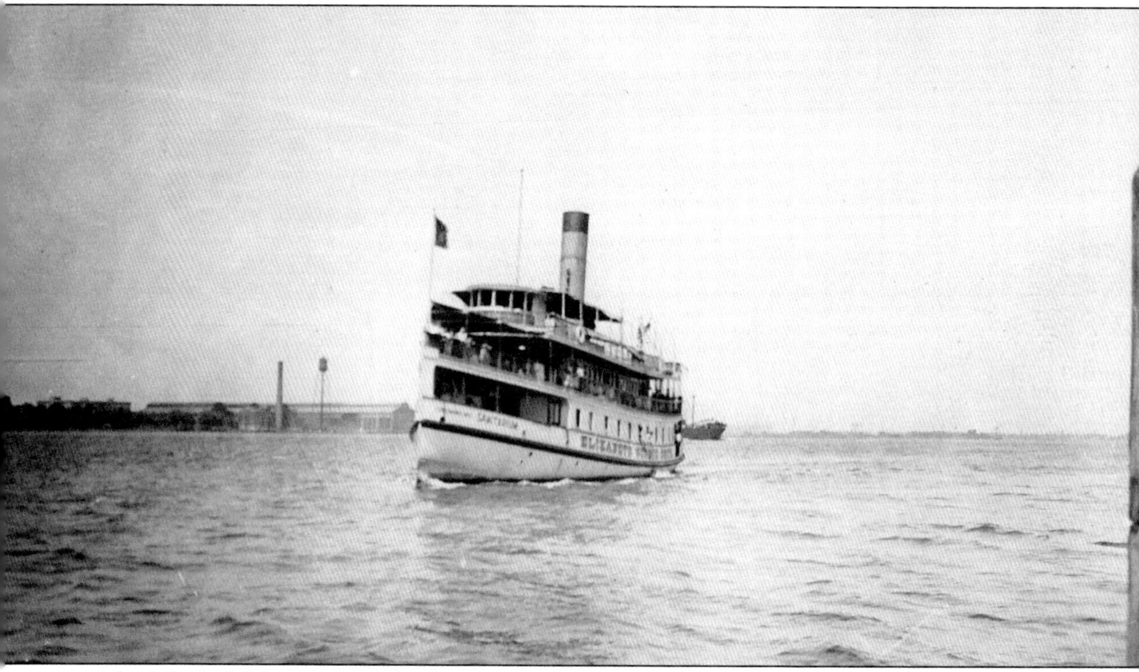

The *Elizabeth Monroe Smith* ("Lizzie") was one of the ferries that transported children between Soupy Island and Philadelphia. The boat was named after Elizabeth Monroe Smith, a distinguished contributor to the charity. When a need for a second boat arose, the *John F. Smith*, named for her husband, was built. (Courtesy of the Bornmann family.)

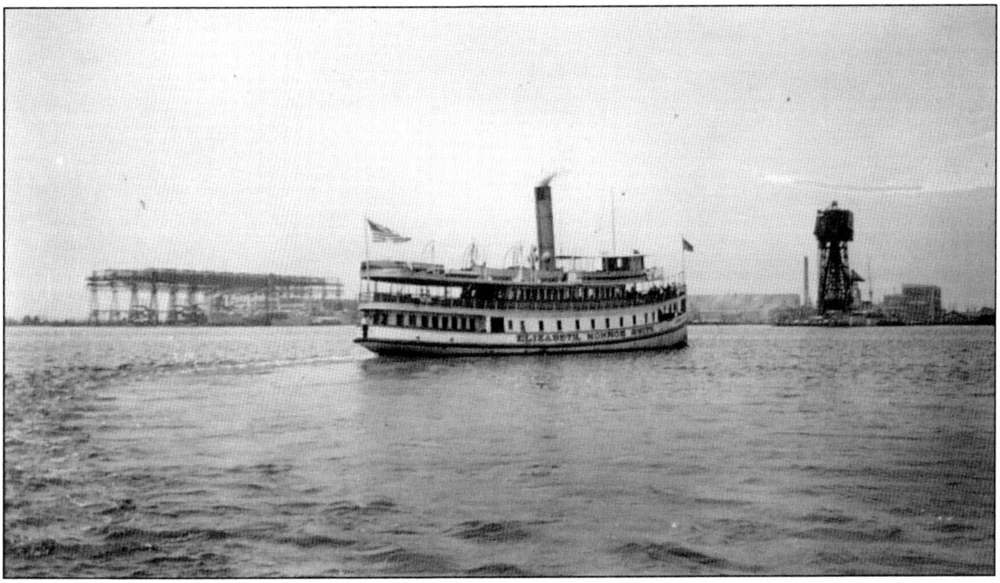

Soupy Island had its own dock to accommodate the children arriving from the city. Employees and lifeguards waited for the steamships to arrive so that they could help the children disembark from the ferries. (Both, courtesy of the Bornmann family.)

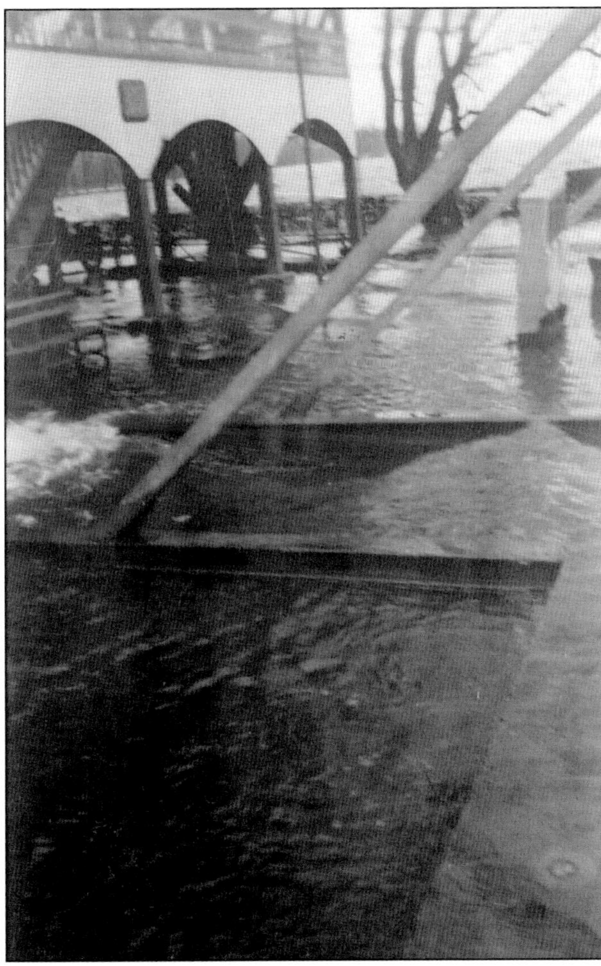

TABLE

Showing Daily Admissions to the Sanitarium and Classification of Ages.

(Compiled by the Superintendent.)

1891.	No. of days.	Notes of Weather.	Adults,	Infants under two years.	Between two and five years.	Between five and ten years.	Over ten years.	Total daily.
June 4 . .	1	Clear.	324	232	153	112	43	864
" 5 . .	2	Cloudy.	45	76	54	48	26	249
" 6 . .	3	"	157	267	225	198	54	901
" 8 . .	4	Clear.	85	171	139	115	47	557
" 9 . .	5	"	209	328	274	234	74	1,119
" 10 . .	6	"	219	326	278	242	65	1,130
" 11 . .	7	"	257	366	318	278	66	1,285
" 12 . .	8	"	338	468	395	363	105	1,669
" 13 . .	9	"	763	881	833	802	202	3,481
" 15 . .	10	"	419	591	566	457	163	2,196
" 16 . .	11	"	509	631	579	543	117	2,379
" 17 . .	12	"	611	773	705	650	149	2,888
" 18 . .	13	Rain.	47	92	77	54	11	281
" 20 . .	14	Cloudy.	272	386	341	313	83	1,395
" 22 . .	15	Clear.	383	516	472	426	123	1,920
" 23 . .	16	"	617	779	722	661	169	2,948
" 24 . .	17	"	621	738	692	659	171	2,881
" 25 . .	18	"	672	804	753	712	189	3,130
" 26 . .	19	"	556	687	638	609	147	2,637
" 27 . .	20	"	521	658	591	544	158	2,472
" 29 . .	21	"	667	813	754	702	177	3,113
" 30 . .	22	"	522	671	609	569	144	2,515
July 1 . .	23	"	264	388	336	279	77	1,344
" 3 . .	24	Rain.	106	175	134	113	41	569
" 6 . .	25	Clear.	622	778	731	644	211	2,986
" 7 . .	26	Cloudy.	395	526	479	427	111	1,938
" 9 . .	27	"	118	215	184	151	72	740
" 10 . .	28	Clear.	274	426	378	322	125	1,525
" 11 . .	29	"	400	531	482	430	132	1,975
" 13 . .	30	"	559	705	639	597	147	2,647
" 14 . .	31	"	266	375	330	290	88	1,349
" 15 . .	32	"	584	734	666	617	163	2,764
" 16 . .	33	"	518	669	608	552	148	2,495
" 17 . .	34	"	466	595	543	497	144	2,245
" 20 . .	35	"	551	662	624	575	157	2,569

A table from the summer of 1891 shows daily admissions to the sanitarium. Careful records were kept by the superintendent and were reported annually to the trustees. (Courtesy of the Bornmann family.)

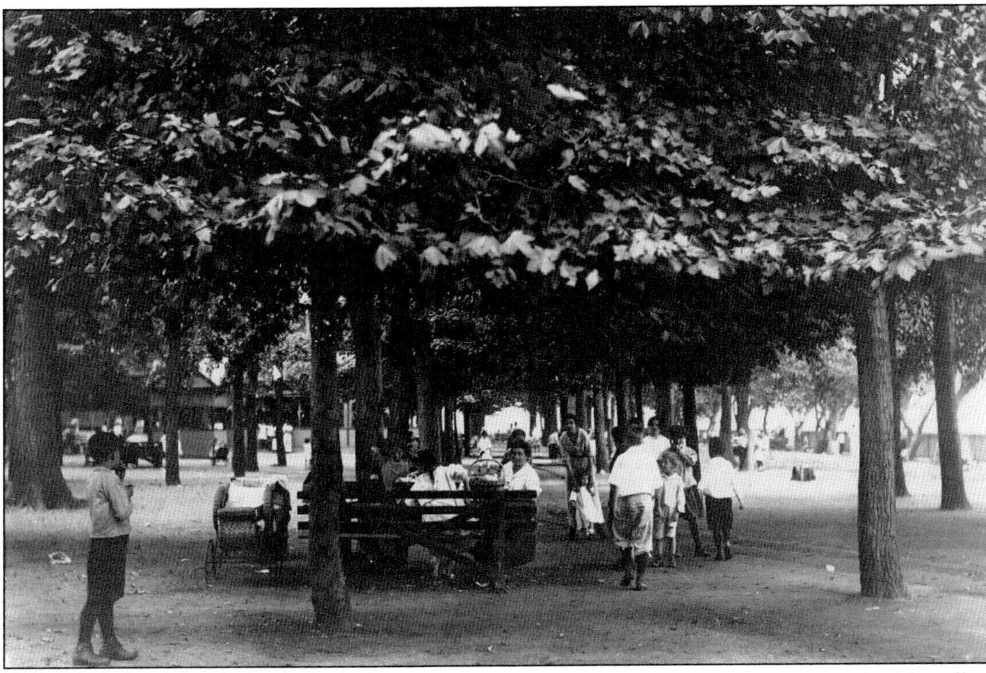

Whether visiting Soupy Island with a family or a larger group, a good time was had by all at Soupy. In the early years, mothers were able to stay at Soupy Island with their sick children. Later, groups of city children were brought to the park for a day of fun in the sun. (Both, courtesy of the Bornmann family.)

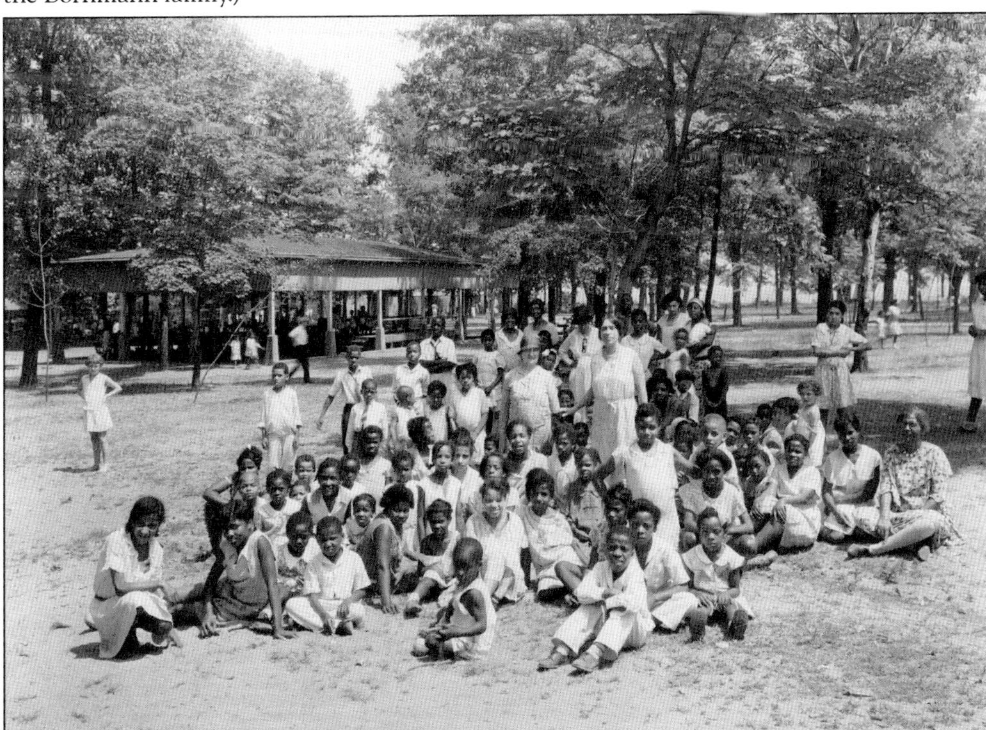

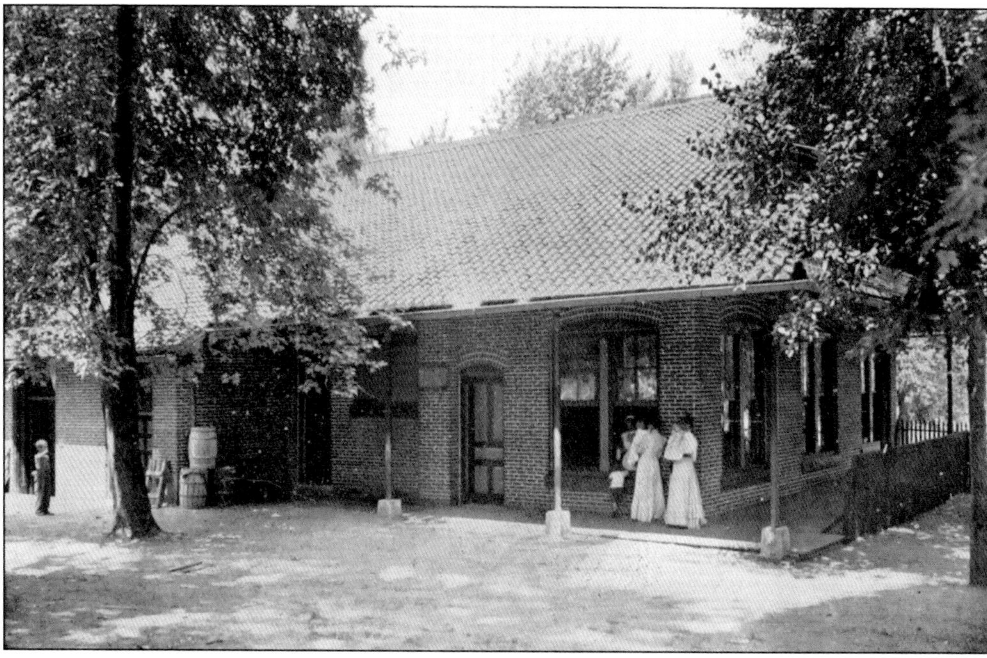

The name Soupy Island was derived from the fact that soup was served every day at noon. This tradition continues today. For many years, choices included chicken noodle, minestrone, or vegetable beef. The soup was heated in 80-gallon stainless steel kettles (shown on the cover picture). Children were allowed as much soup as they would like. Pictured is the Simon Muhr Diet Kitchen, which was where the children lined up daily for a nutritious lunch of soup, crackers, and milk. (Both, courtesy of the Bornmann family.)

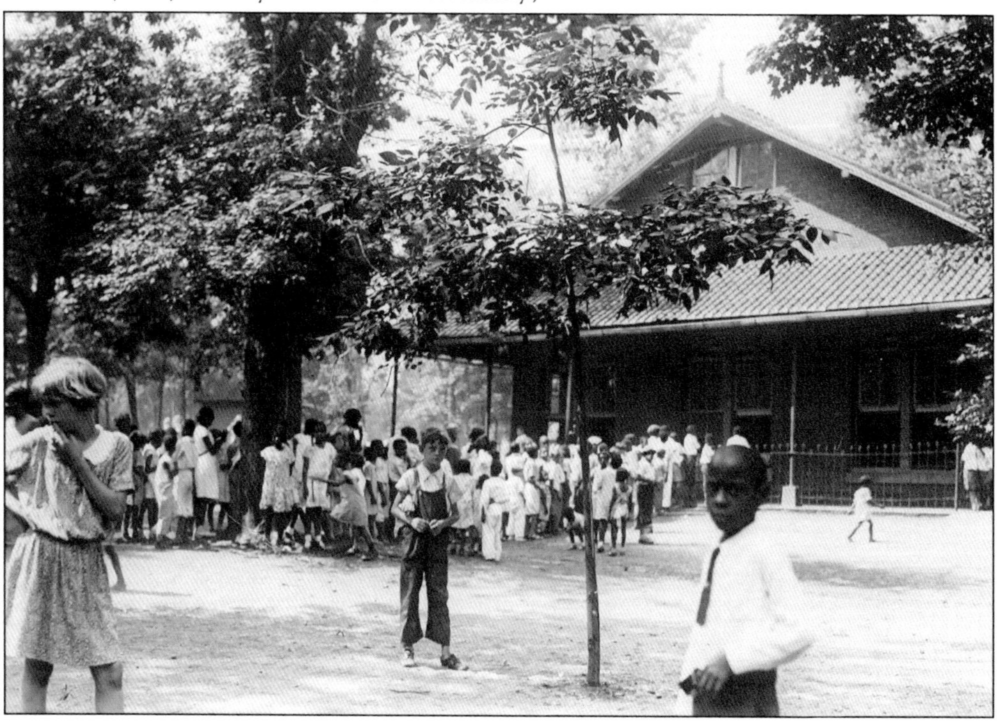

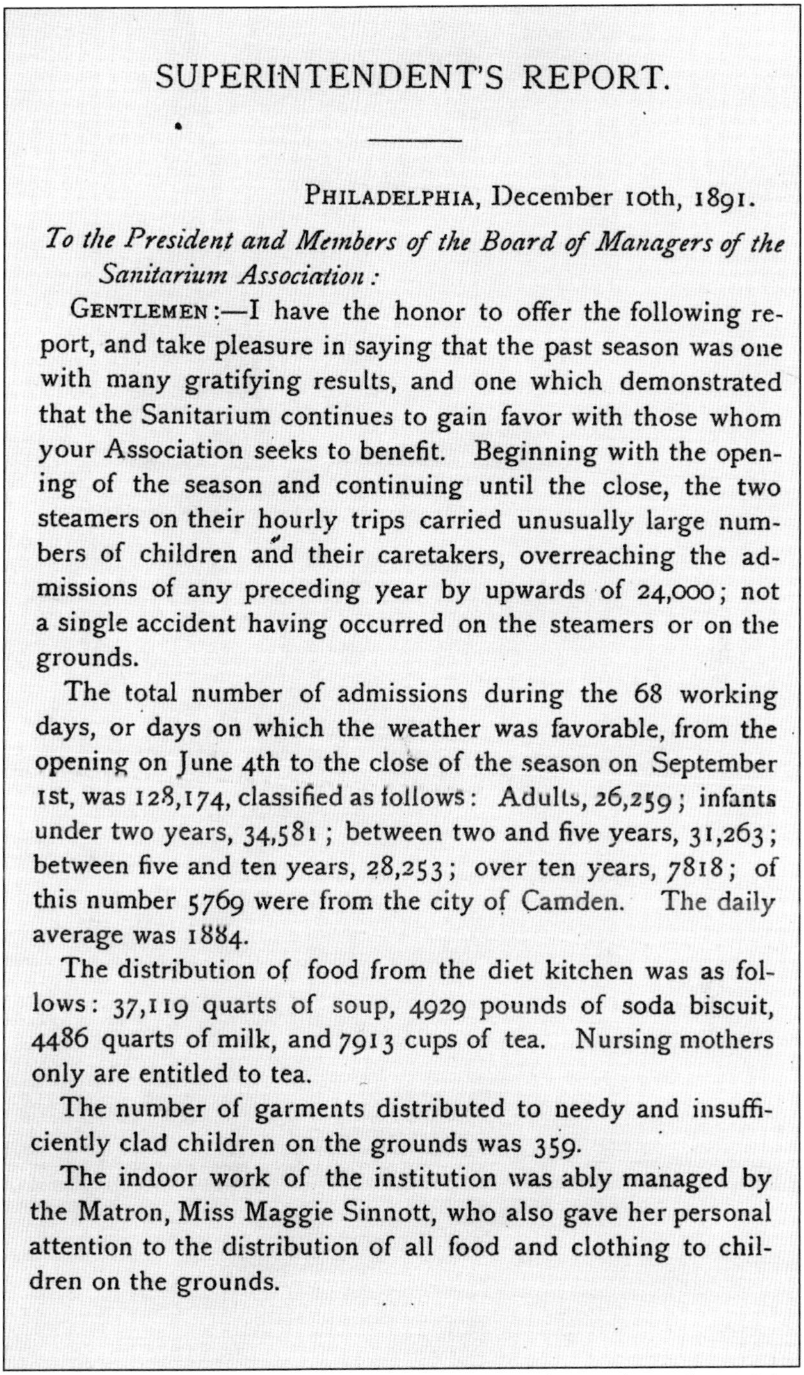

SUPERINTENDENT'S REPORT.

PHILADELPHIA, December 10th, 1891.

To the President and Members of the Board of Managers of the Sanitarium Association:

GENTLEMEN:—I have the honor to offer the following report, and take pleasure in saying that the past season was one with many gratifying results, and one which demonstrated that the Sanitarium continues to gain favor with those whom your Association seeks to benefit. Beginning with the opening of the season and continuing until the close, the two steamers on their hourly trips carried unusually large numbers of children and their caretakers, overreaching the admissions of any preceding year by upwards of 24,000; not a single accident having occurred on the steamers or on the grounds.

The total number of admissions during the 68 working days, or days on which the weather was favorable, from the opening on June 4th to the close of the season on September 1st, was 128,174, classified as follows: Adults, 26,259; infants under two years, 34,581; between two and five years, 31,263; between five and ten years, 28,253; over ten years, 7818; of this number 5769 were from the city of Camden. The daily average was 1884.

The distribution of food from the diet kitchen was as follows: 37,119 quarts of soup, 4929 pounds of soda biscuit, 4486 quarts of milk, and 7913 cups of tea. Nursing mothers only are entitled to tea.

The number of garments distributed to needy and insufficiently clad children on the grounds was 359.

The indoor work of the institution was ably managed by the Matron, Miss Maggie Sinnott, who also gave her personal attention to the distribution of all food and clothing to children on the grounds.

Pictured is a page of the superintendent's report to the president and members of the Board of Managers of the Sanitarium Association of Philadelphia from 1891. It includes how many adults and children were admitted to the playground. It also reported the distribution of food from the diet kitchen. Note that garments were "distributed to needy and insufficiently clad children." Detailed records were essential due to the fact that Soupy Island has always been funded by a trust funded by generous donations of others. (Courtesy of the Bornmann family.)

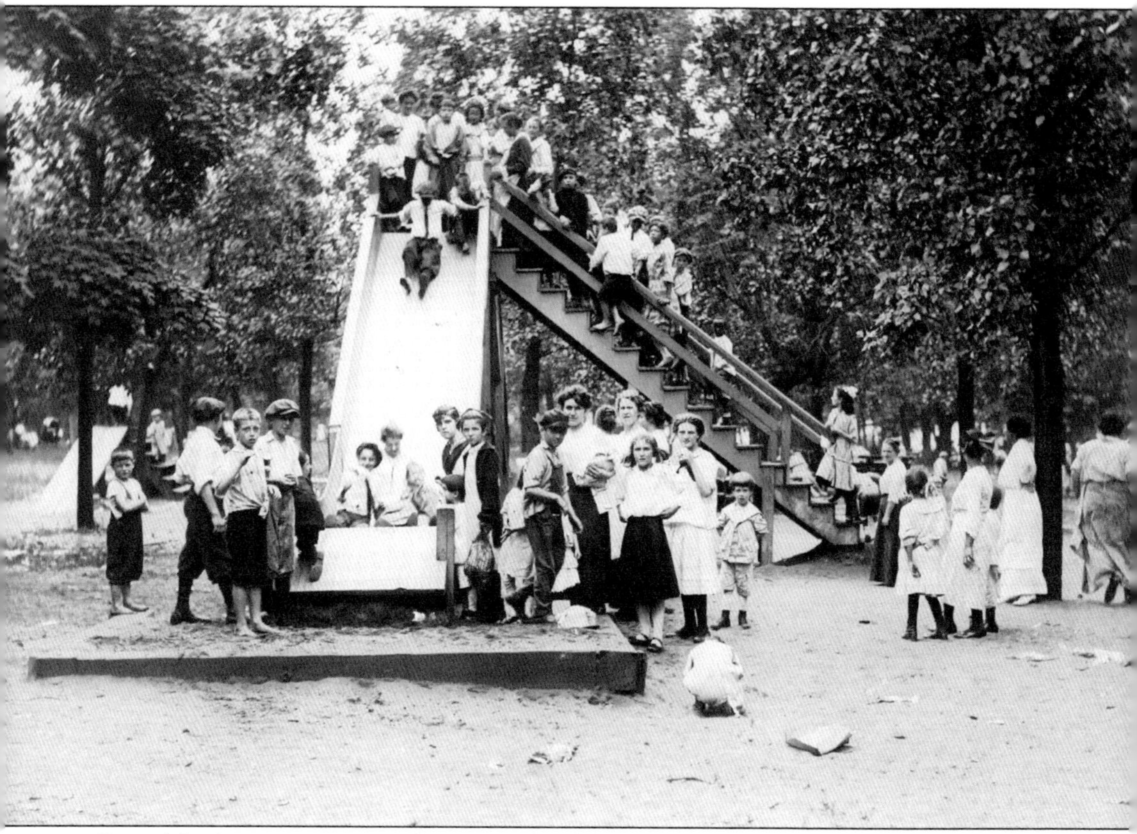

One of the first amusements at Soupy was the sliding board. Pictured are children zooming down the slide around 1931. Today, children bring wax paper for a quick ride down an old favorite. (Courtesy of the Bornmann family.)

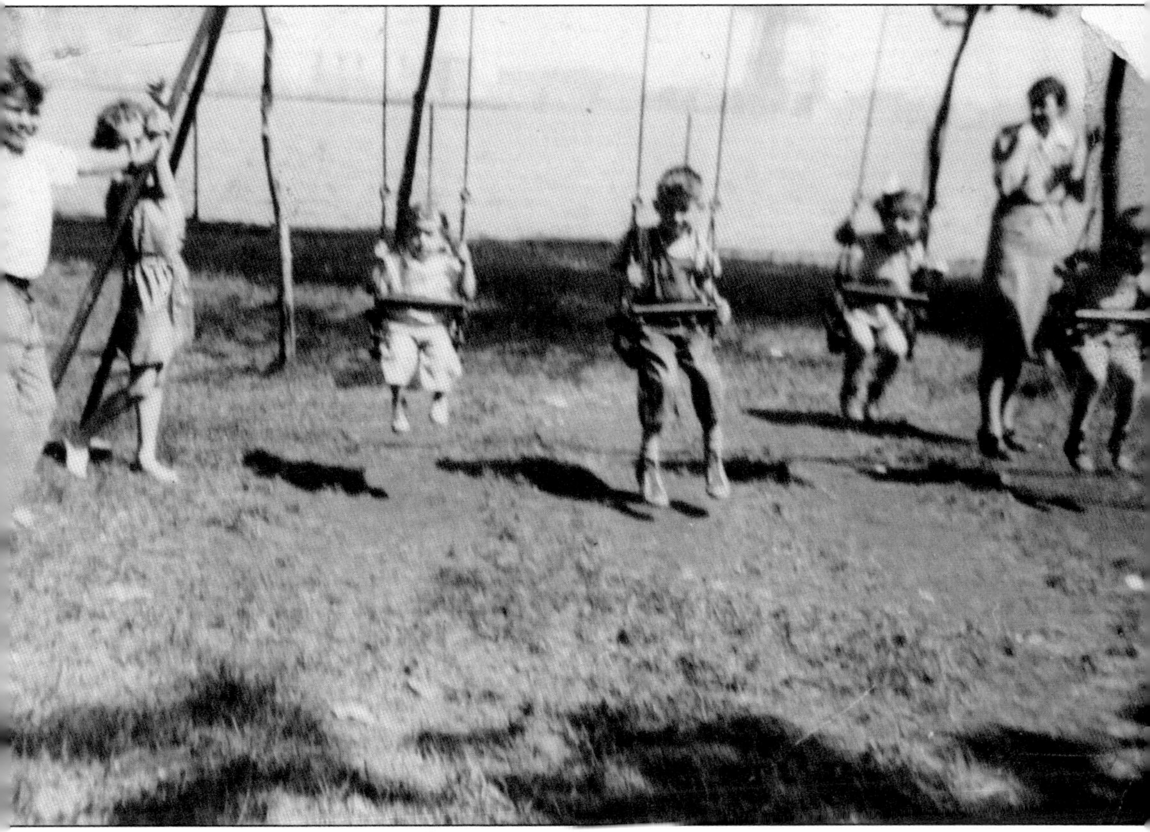

Pictured are children around 1940 on the swings in the grove at Soupy. Seesaws and a tire climb are other amusements that children enjoy when visiting the park. (Courtesy of the Bornmann family.)

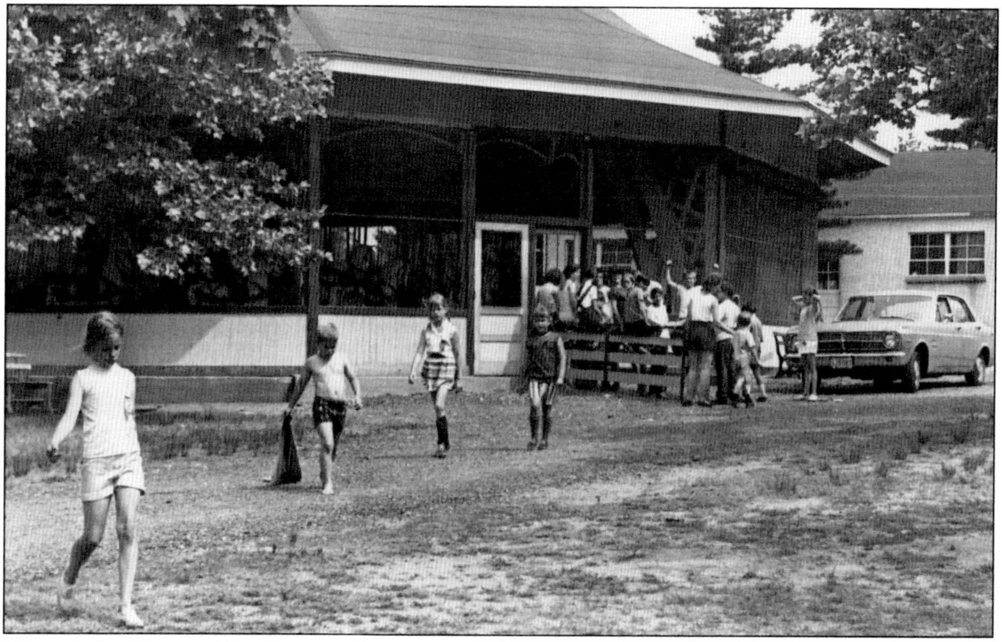

The original Soupy Island steam-driven carousel operated from 1907 until 1941, when it broke down. Being an all-time favorite for both children and adults, it was replaced with a second carousel, which was moved from a North Jersey site. It has 63 wooden horses painted white with red, green, and gold trim and arranged in four concentric circles. All but the outer horses rise and fall as the carousel turns at five revolutions per minute. Taped calliope music, and now CDs, play while it runs. (Both, courtesy of the Bornmann family.)

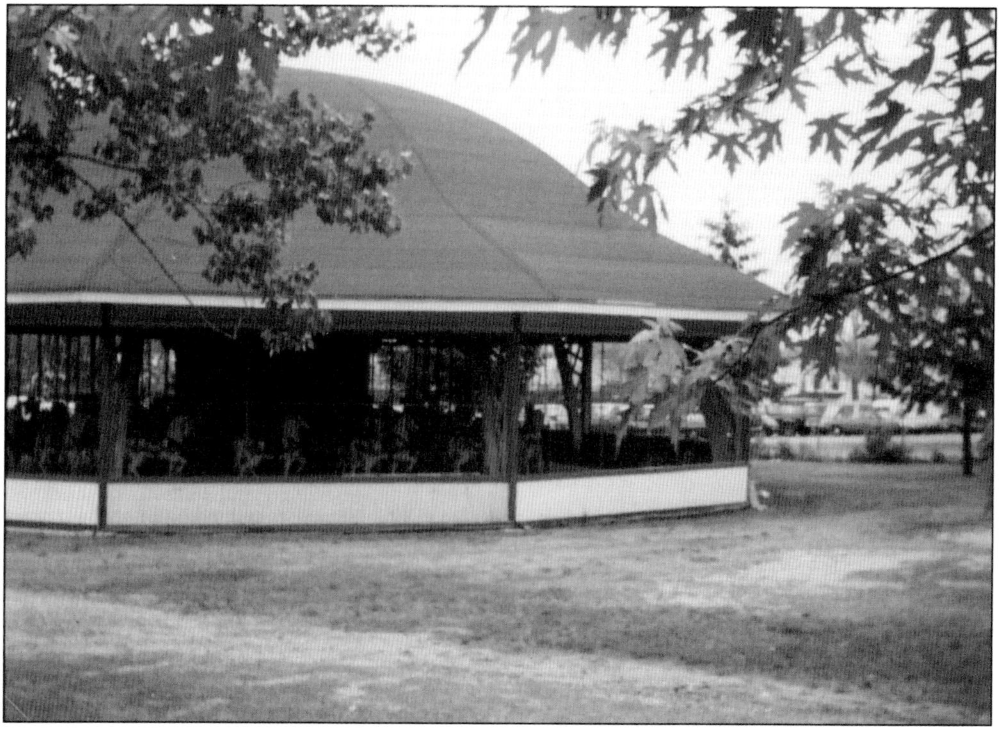

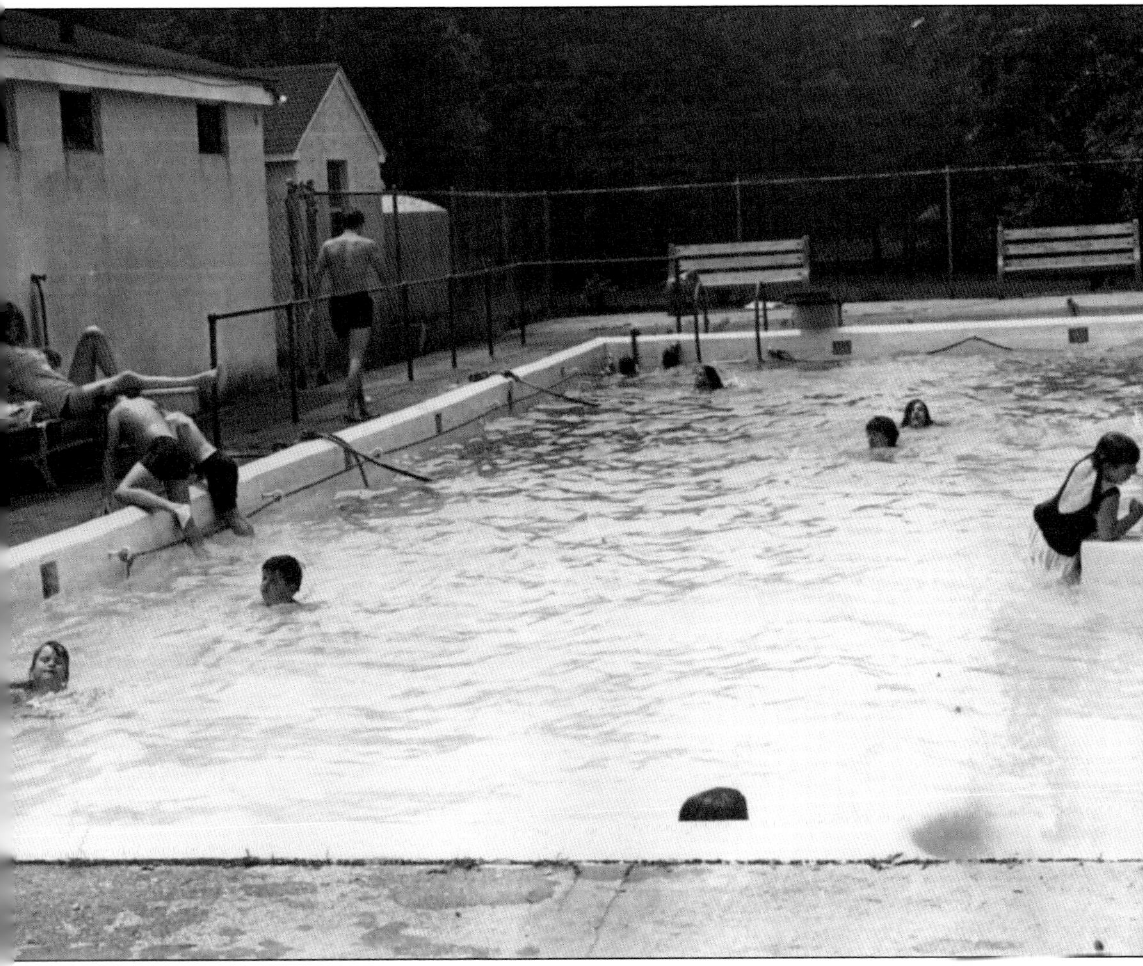

Soupy Island boasts a swimming pool and wading pool for summer guests. The pool stands on the spot that was once occupied by the basement of the sanitarium. (Courtesy of the Bornmann family.)

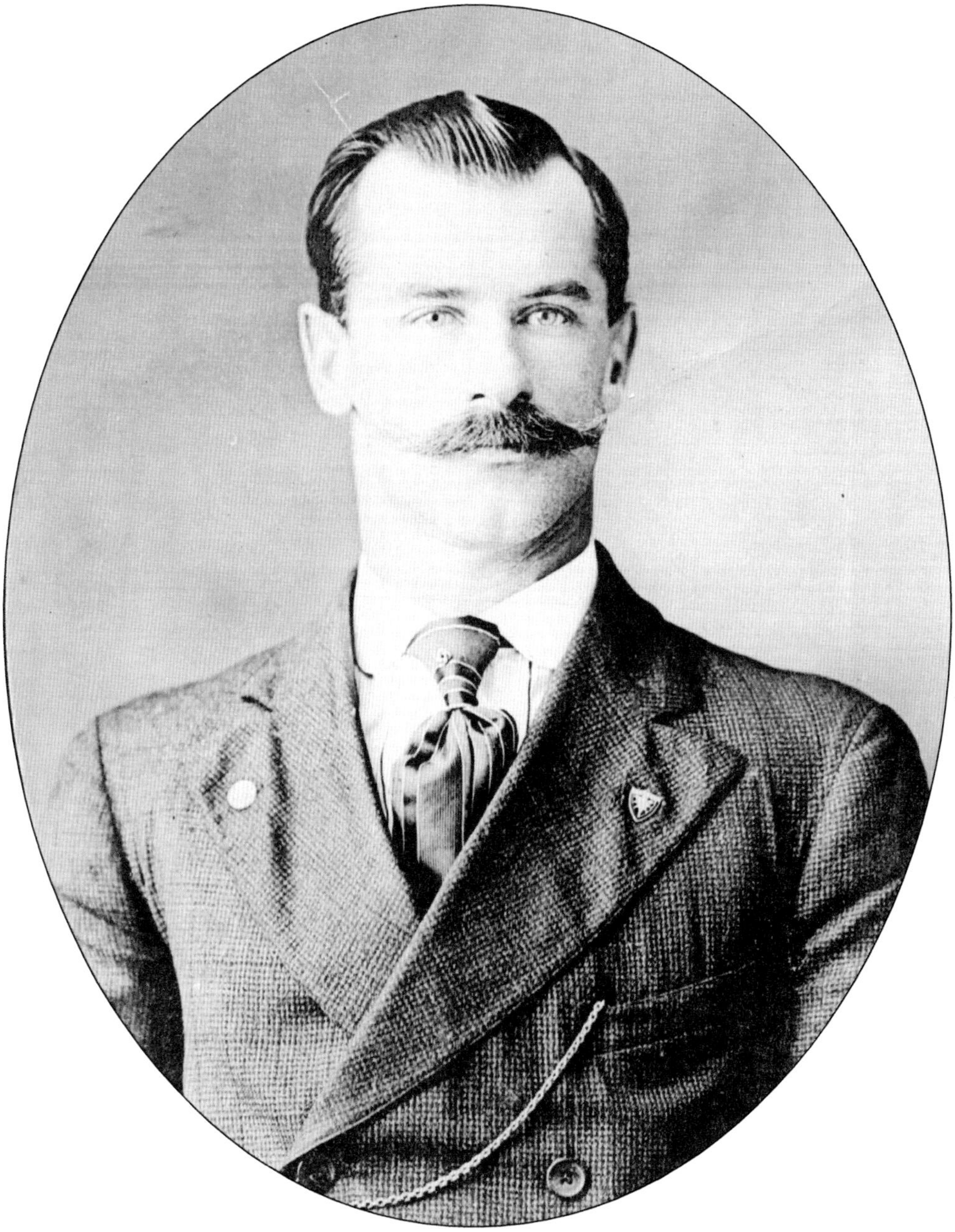

The Nickerson family has been a part of Soupy Island since the late 1800s. It began with Virgil Nickerson (pictured), who was a handyman at Soupy. His son Welden Nickerson was employed at Soupy for over 50.5 years. His daughter Ruth and her husband, Joe Bornmann, carried on the tradition of caring for Soupy until their retirements. Currently, their daughter Denise and her husband, Armond Perez, oversee the management of the park. Superintendents have always been an important part of Soupy Island. They not only kept accurate records to report back to the board of trustees, but they were also responsible for the upkeep of the park. The superintendents of Soupy Island were William Hutt, Henry F. Keyser, William Jackson, Clayton T. Jackson, Bruno Glutch, Tubby Glutch, Bernie Hill, Gene Jeffers, Joseph Bornmann, and Armond Perez. (Courtesy of the Bornmann family.)

Seven
Eagle Point

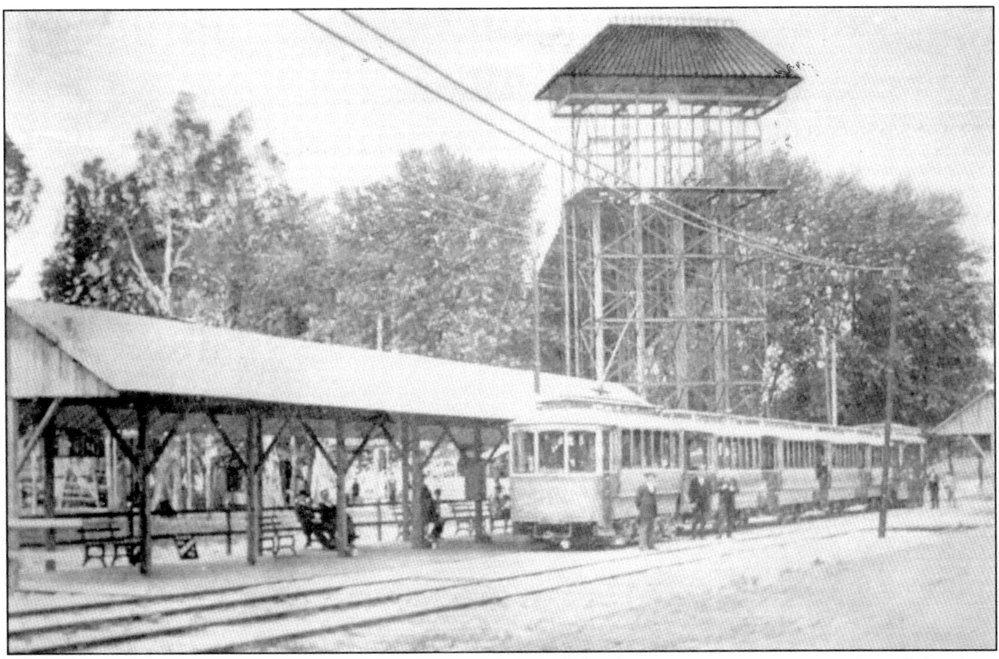

Washington Park on the Delaware River was one of the largest amusement parks of the day. William J. Thompson was a major businessman in Gloucester. His largest venture was a racetrack, from 1892 to 1895. When the racetrack was shut down by state legislation, he had a straw buyer purchase the Eagle Point property in West Deptford with the intent to turn it into a horse farm. Instead, Thompson built what was said to be one of the largest amusement parks in the country. Trolleys, like the one pictured above, brought many families to Washington Park. (Courtesy of the Gloucester County Historical Society.)

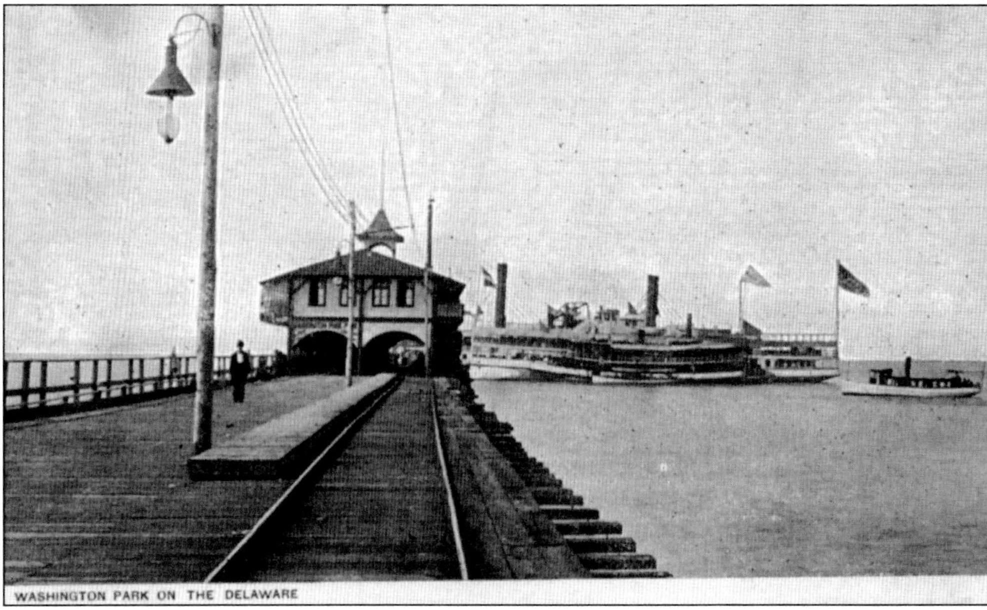

Since it was located on the Delaware River, ferryboats were also used to bring families to the park. Thompson built a 1,800-foot-long pier, which extended far enough into the Delaware River Channel so that his boats had enough water to maneuver in even during low tide. (Courtesy of Lisa Dunne Jackson.)

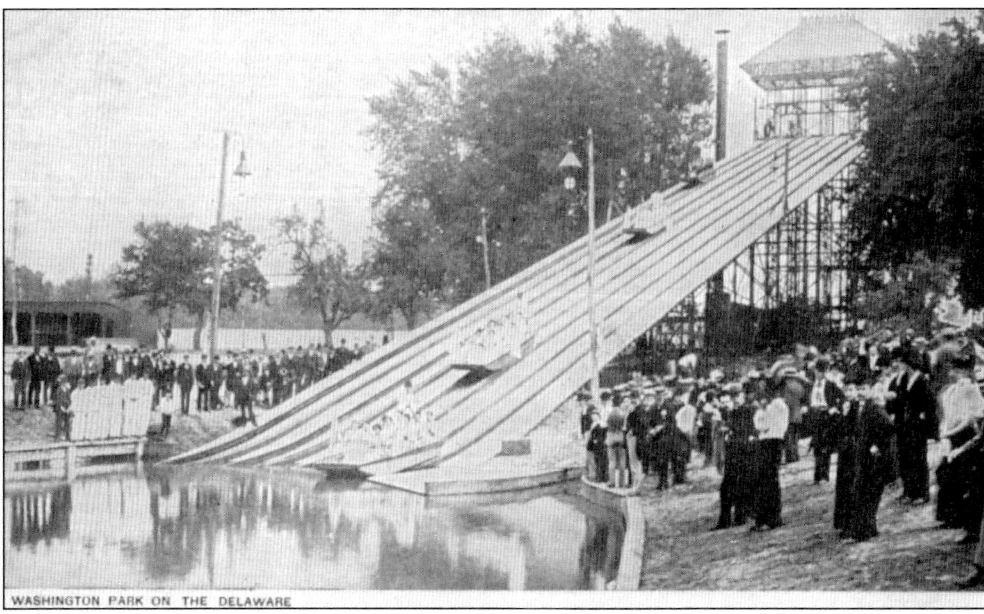

The Shoot-the-Chute was a popular amusement ride in which four boats with 12 passengers each were raised 40 feet and launched down a greased chute, landing in the lake with a tremendous splash. It could be found in West Deptford's famous Washington Park on the Delaware. This 600-acre amusement park opened in 1895 and attracted families from the surrounding communities. Most families visited the park for at least one week of the summer each year. Located along the Delaware River where Sunoco Refinery currently stands, it operated for two decades as the largest and most famous amusement park in the United States. (Courtesy of Lisa Dunne Jackson.)

The Ferris wheel was a popular attraction at Washington Park. It was said to be the largest in the world during this time. (Courtesy of the Gloucester County Historical Society.)

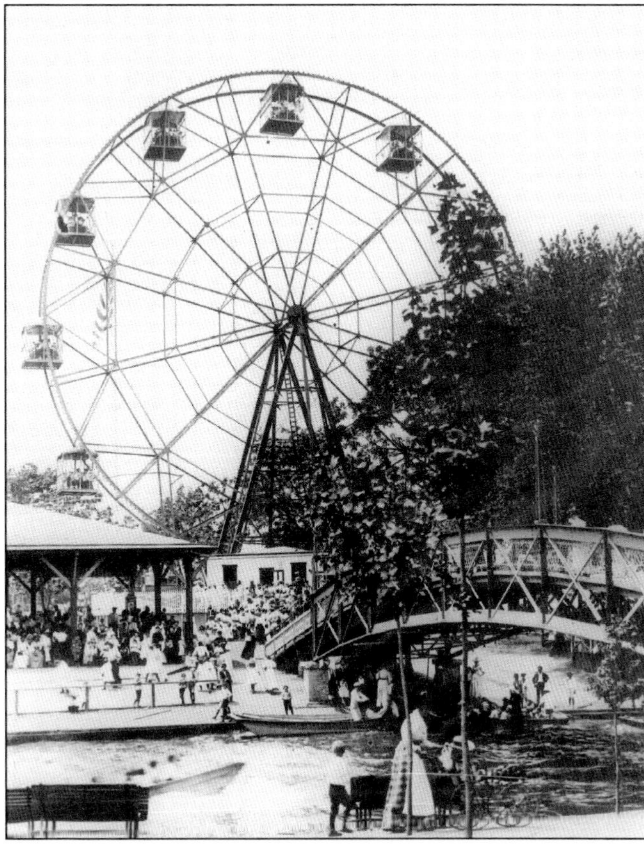

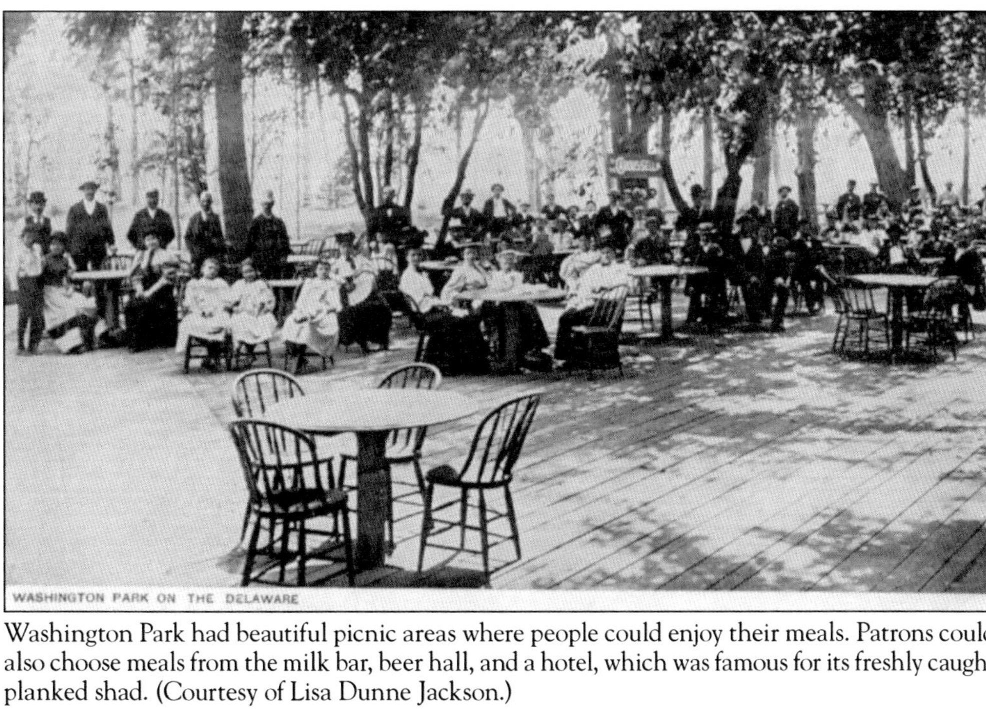

Washington Park had beautiful picnic areas where people could enjoy their meals. Patrons could also choose meals from the milk bar, beer hall, and a hotel, which was famous for its freshly caught planked shad. (Courtesy of Lisa Dunne Jackson.)

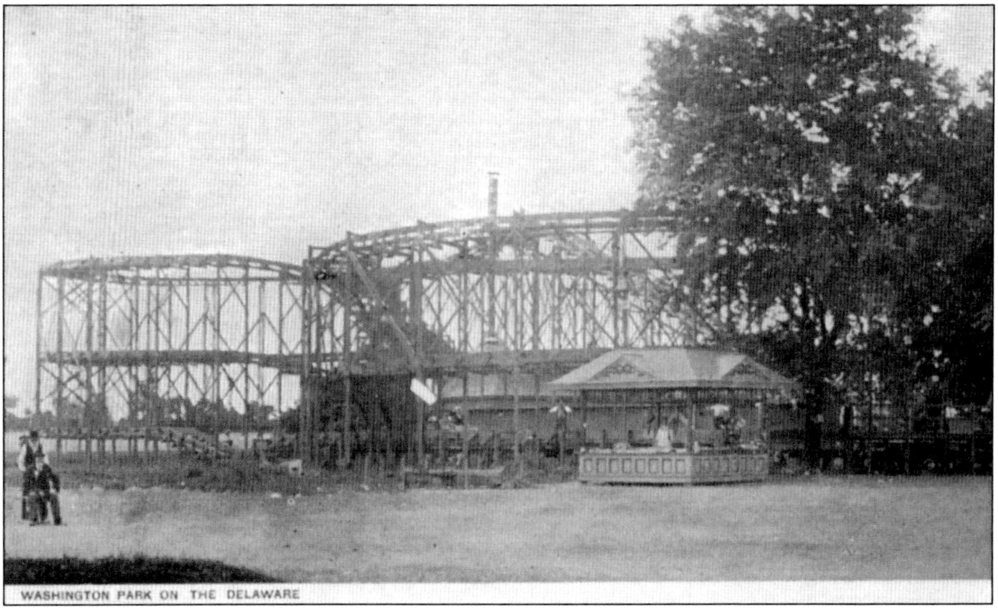

For thrill seekers, Washington Park boasted the Jack Rabbit, a wooden roller coaster. On a big weekend, close to 100,000 people would enjoy the attractions at the park. (Courtesy of Lisa Dunne Jackson.)

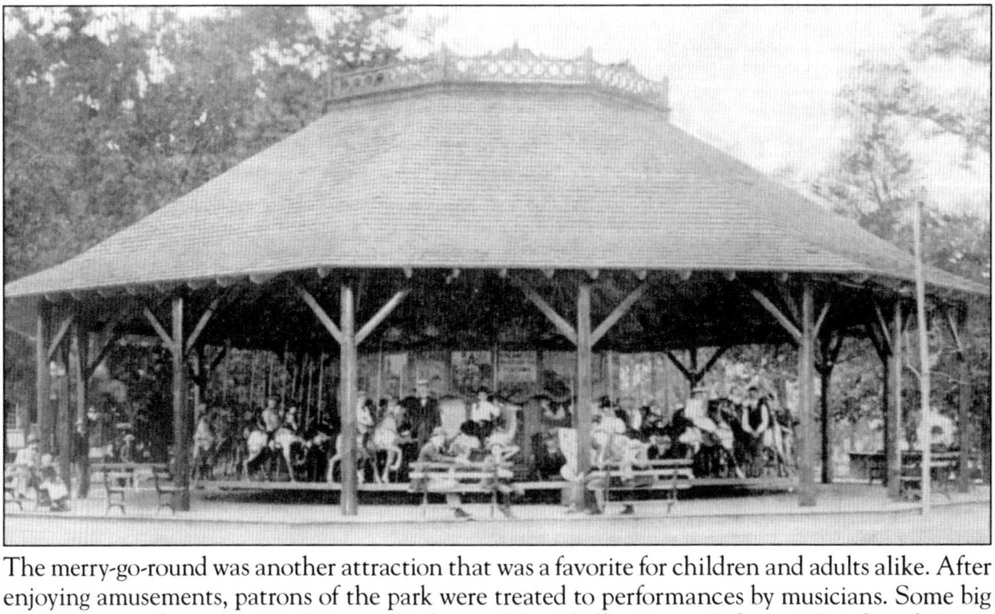

The merry-go-round was another attraction that was a favorite for children and adults alike. After enjoying amusements, patrons of the park were treated to performances by musicians. Some big names that performed in Washington Park were John Phillip Sousa, Gilmore's Band, and Victor Herbert. Sadly, Washington Park was sold at auction in April 1913 and purchased by the Campbell's Soup Company. (Courtesy of the Gloucester County Historical Society.)

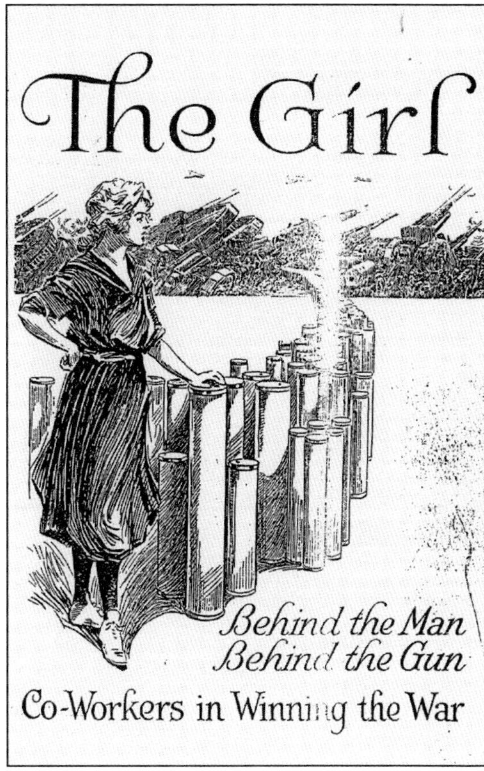

During World War I, Campbell's Soup Company leased the property to the government. The government built the Woodbury Bag Loading Munitions Plant. Advertisements, like these, were created in hopes of attracting young women into the workforce since men were hard to find; they were serving their country.

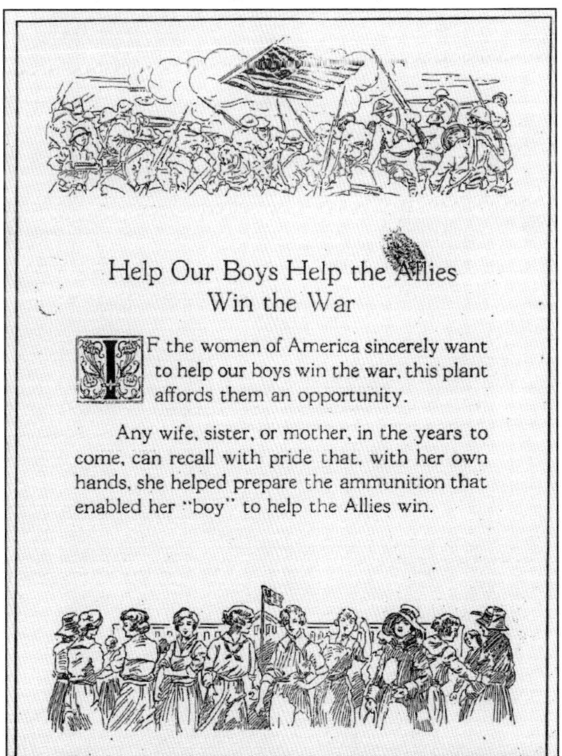

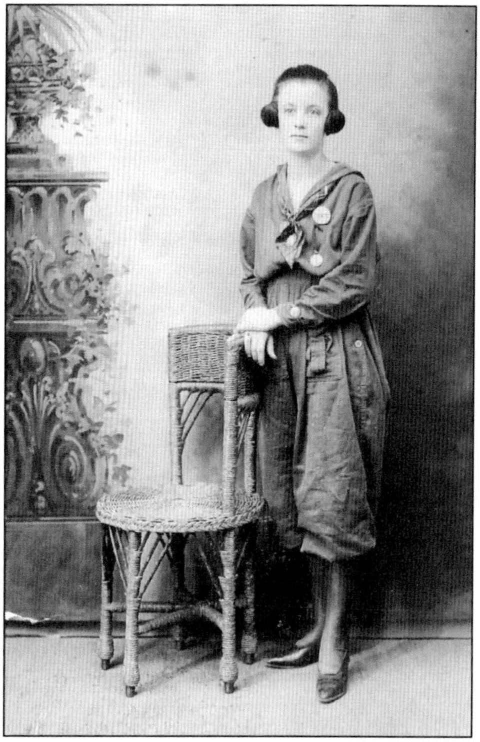

Ella Grant was a secretary in the office of the Woodbury Bag Loading Munitions Plant. The MacArthur Brothers Engineering Company built the plant for the government. Pictured is Ella Grant on July 18, 1918. (Courtesy of O.C. Berry.)

After a long day working in the plant, young women retired to their dorm rooms for the evening. Pictured is a typical matron room in the dormitory at the Woodbury Bag Loading Munitions Plant, which were built on the property. (Courtesy of Harvard Art Museums/Fogg Museum, on deposit from the Carpenter Center for the Visual Arts, Social Museum Collection, 3.2002.2058.1. Copyright: Imaging Department, President and Fellows of Harvard College.)

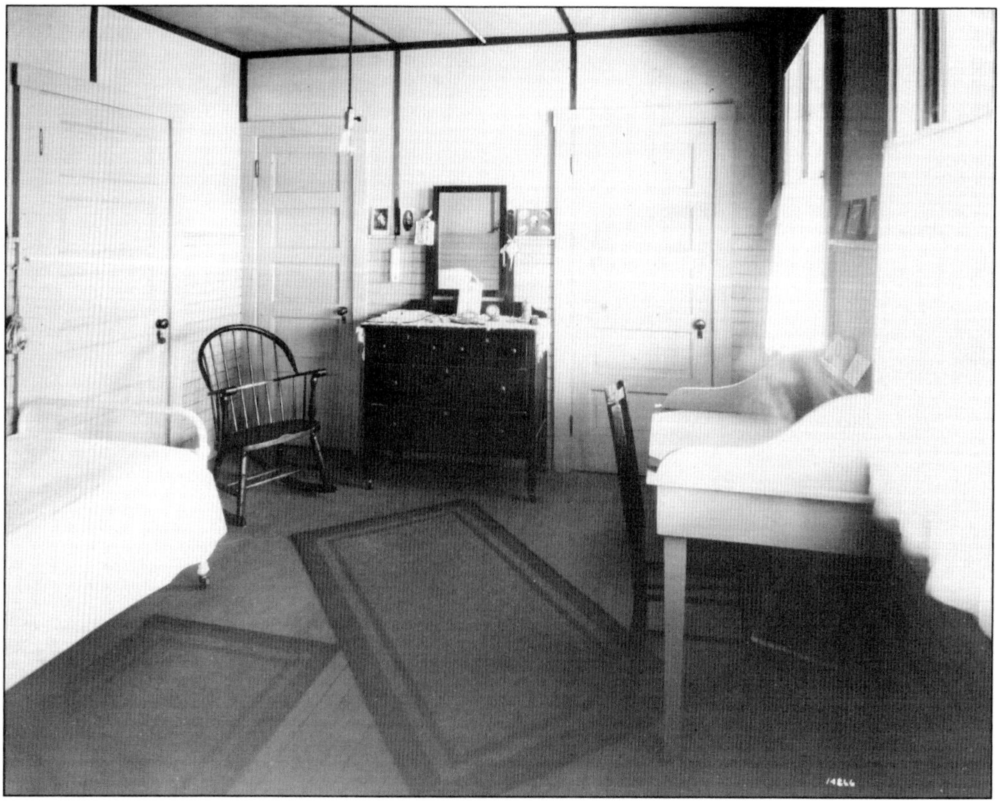

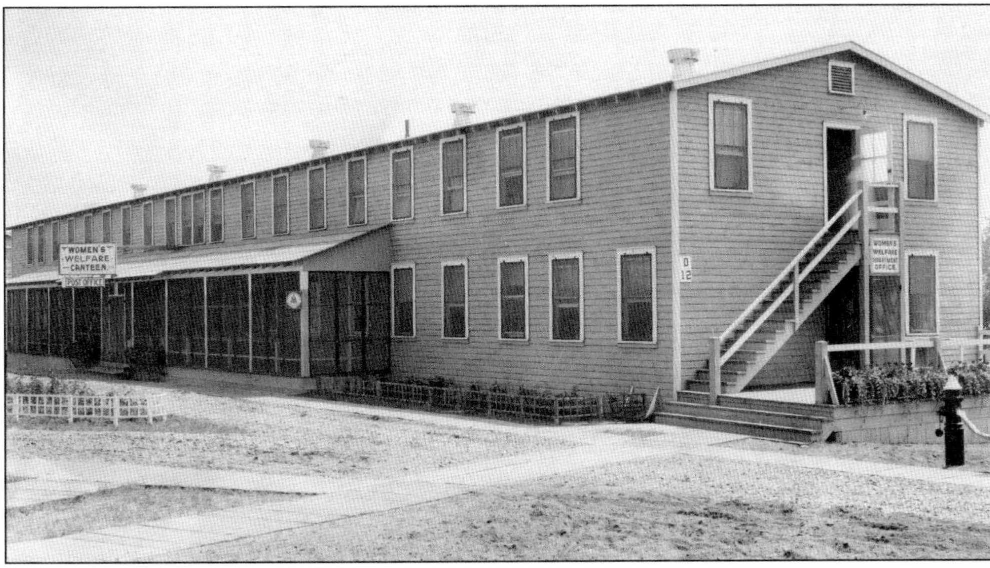

Several dormitories lined the property. Women would stay and sleep in the barracks during the week, only to return home on the weekends. Above is dormitory no. 12, Welfare Office of the Woodbury Bag Loading Munitions Plant. Also shown is the interior view of the cafeteria at the plant where women could enjoy a nice meal. (Courtesy of Harvard Art Museums/Fogg Museum, on deposit from the Carpenter Center for the Visual Arts, Social Museum Collection, 3.2002.2057.2 and 3.2002.2055.2. Copyright: Imaging Department, President and Fellows of Harvard College.)

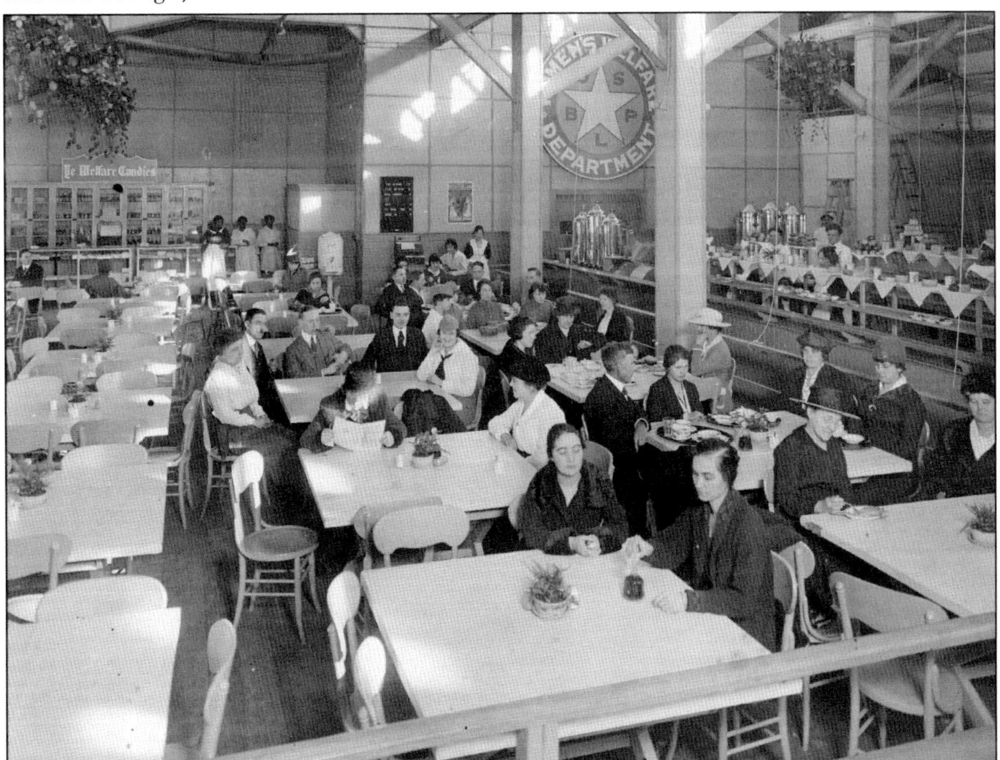

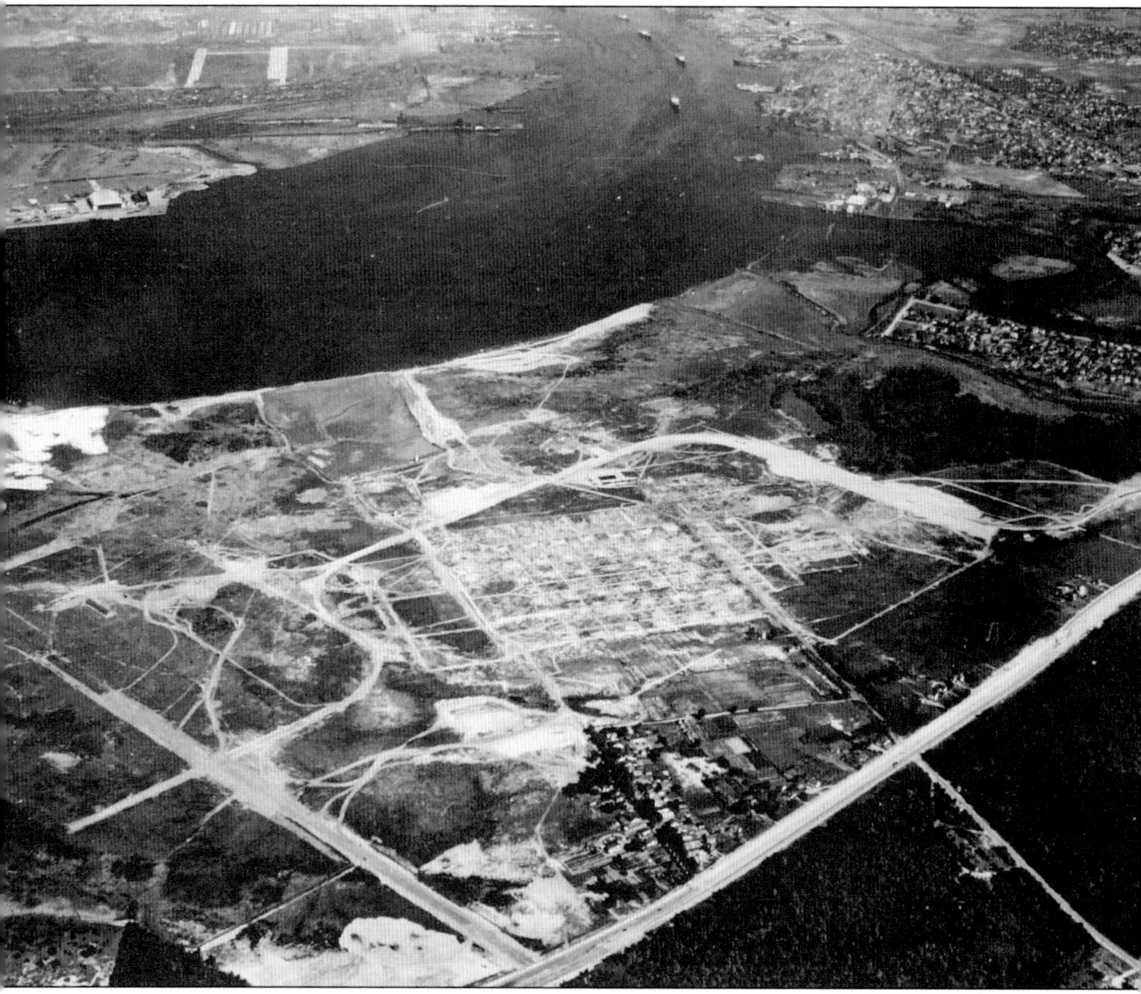

This aerial view of the Eagle Point property was taken in the 1940s. After the munitions plant closed, Campbell's Soup Company sold the Washington Park property to Texaco Company in 1947. Texaco built a refinery on the site. The refinery still stands today.

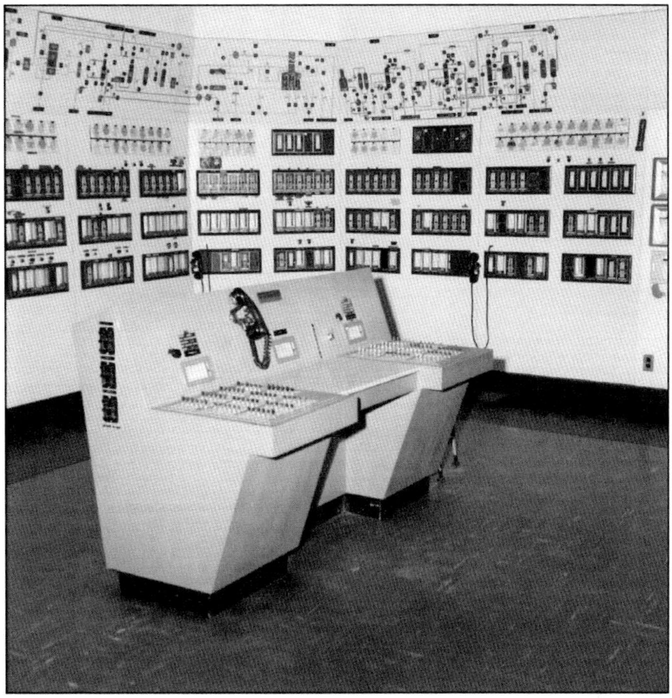

Shown below is the building of the Texaco Eagle Point Oil Refinery in 1947–1948. Buildings, operating units, and tanks were constructed. The control room, pictured at right, represents the technology used to operate a single unit from the late 1960s.

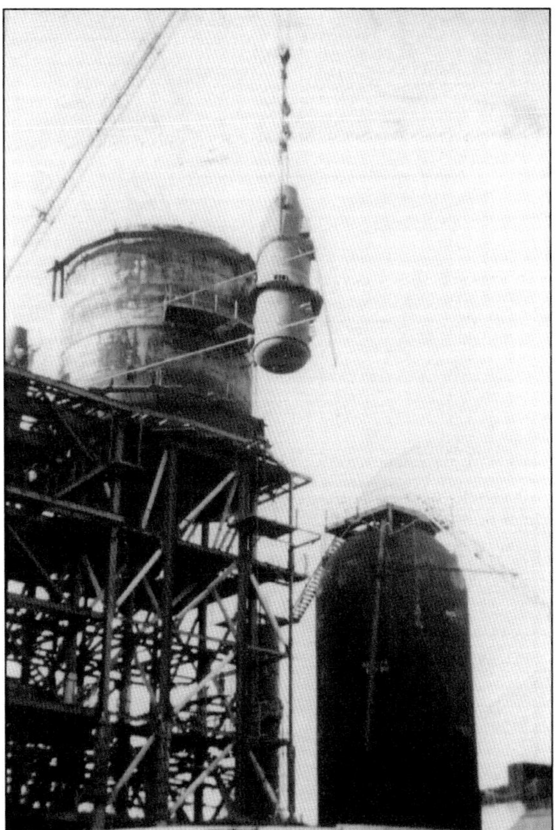

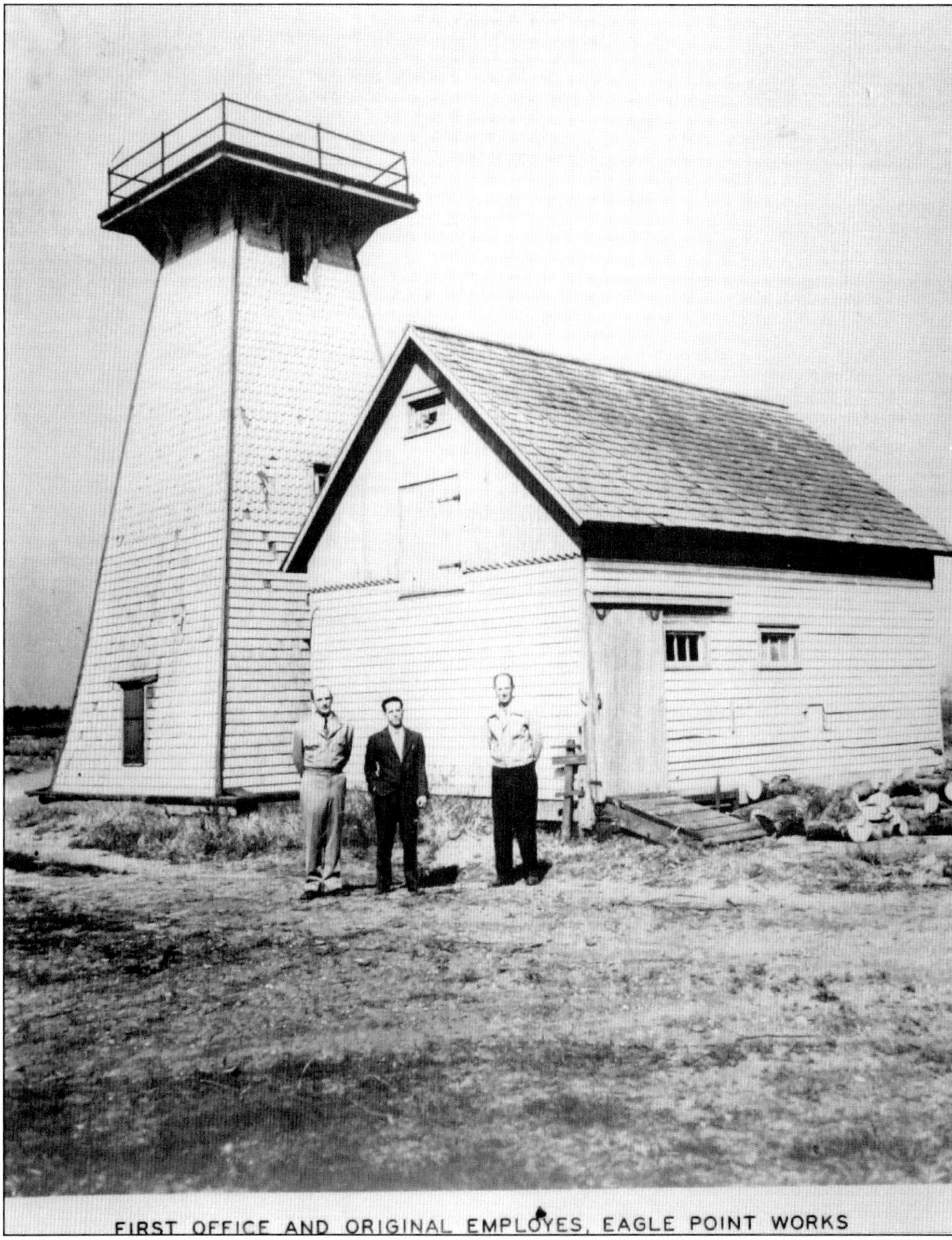

The first offices for Texaco at Eagle Point were located in the Horseshoe Range Light Station. Pictured from left to right are Bob Brumund, Ray Wood, and Preston Creel posing in front of their office.

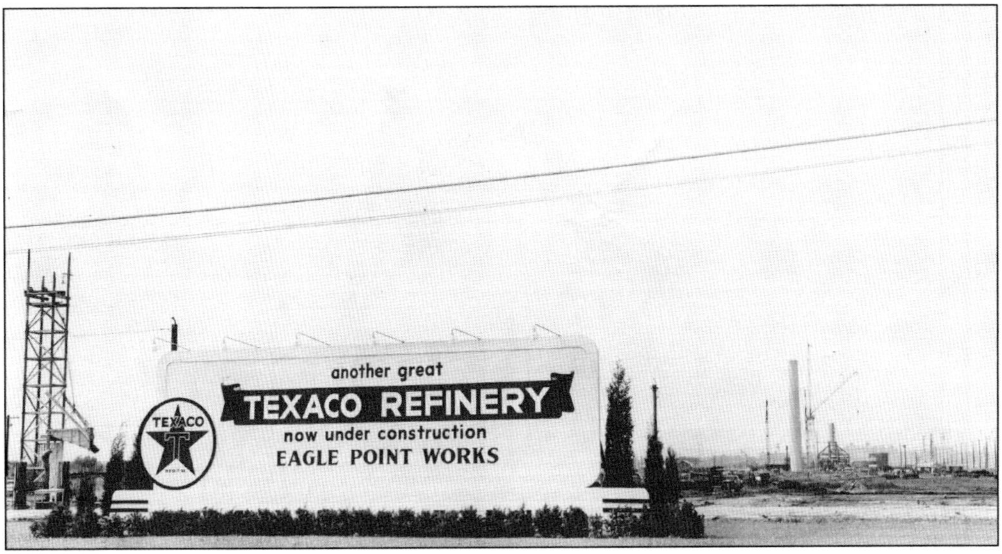

The first advertisement for the new Texaco Refinery sits on the front lawn of the new site, located on Route 130 in West Deptford Township.

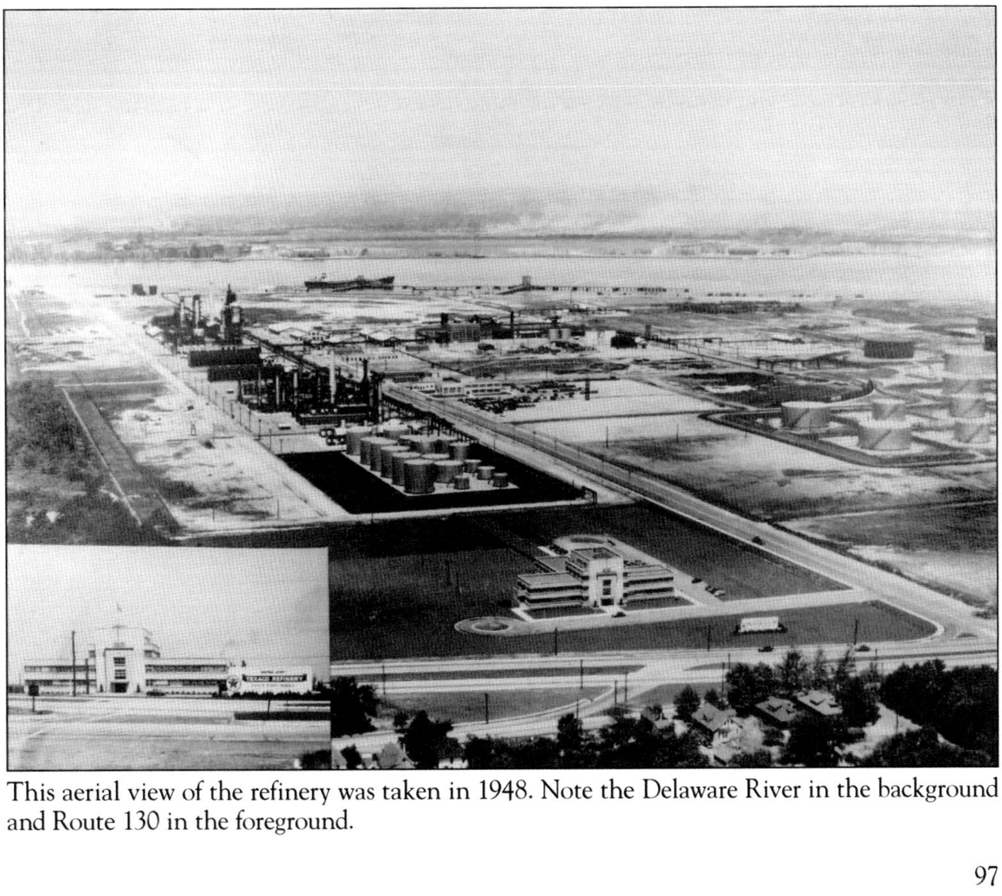

This aerial view of the refinery was taken in 1948. Note the Delaware River in the background and Route 130 in the foreground.

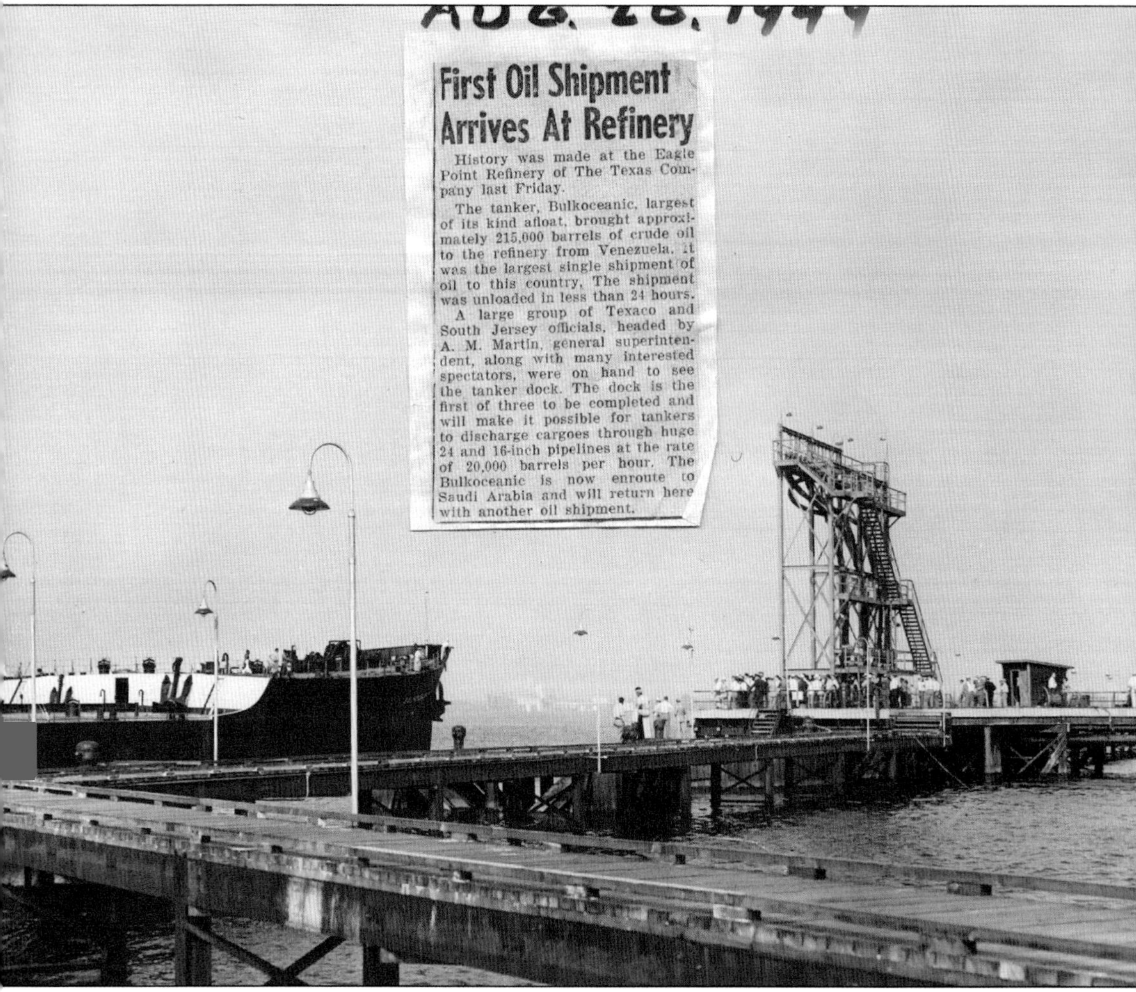

First Oil Shipment Arrives At Refinery

History was made at the Eagle Point Refinery of The Texas Company last Friday.

The tanker, Bulkoceanic, largest of its kind afloat, brought approximately 215,000 barrels of crude oil to the refinery from Venezuela. It was the largest single shipment of oil to this country. The shipment was unloaded in less than 24 hours.

A large group of Texaco and South Jersey officials, headed by A. M. Martin, general superintendent, along with many interested spectators, were on hand to see the tanker dock. The dock is the first of three to be completed and will make it possible for tankers to discharge cargoes through huge 24 and 16-inch pipelines at the rate of 20,000 barrels per hour. The Bulkoceanic is now enroute to Saudi Arabia and will return here with another oil shipment.

Texaco received it first shipment of 215,000 barrels of crude oil on August 26, 1949, from Venezuela.

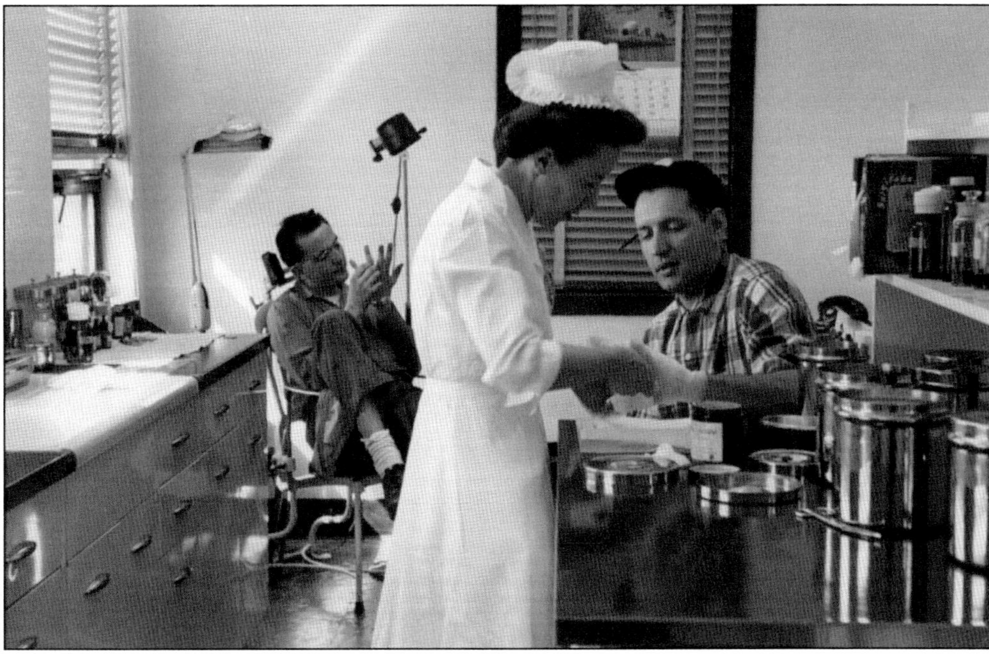

As the Texaco Refinery began operations, its very own health and safety department took care of it many employees. Here, a nurse helps a Texaco employee.

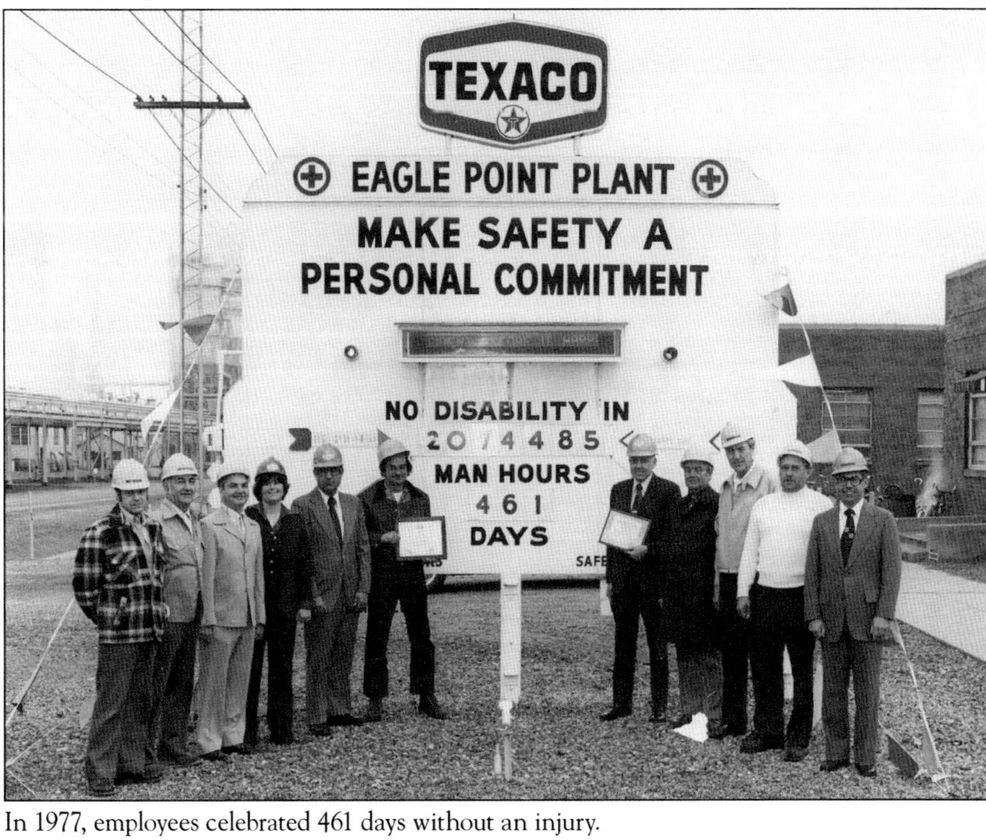

In 1977, employees celebrated 461 days without an injury.

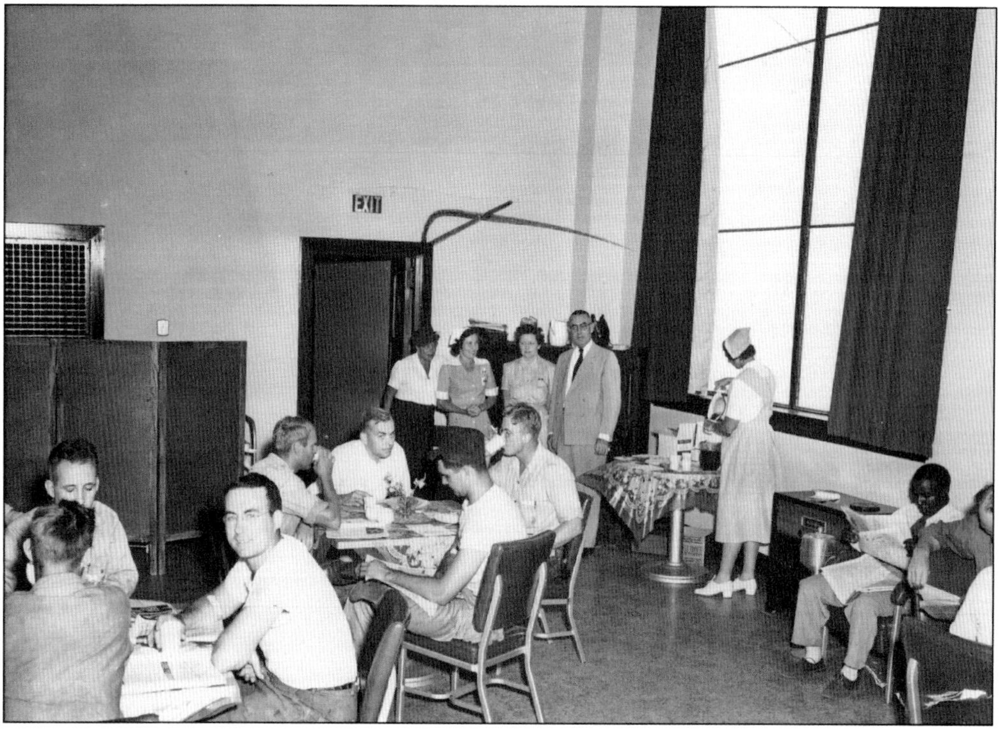

During the late 1940s and early 1950s, employees of the Texaco Refinery take a few moments to help fill the local Red Cross blood bank and play a few innings of baseball. The Texaco Refinery was sold in 1985 to the Coastal Corporation and again in 2001 to the El Paso Corporation. In 2004, it was sold to Sunoco Corporation, which still owns the property today.

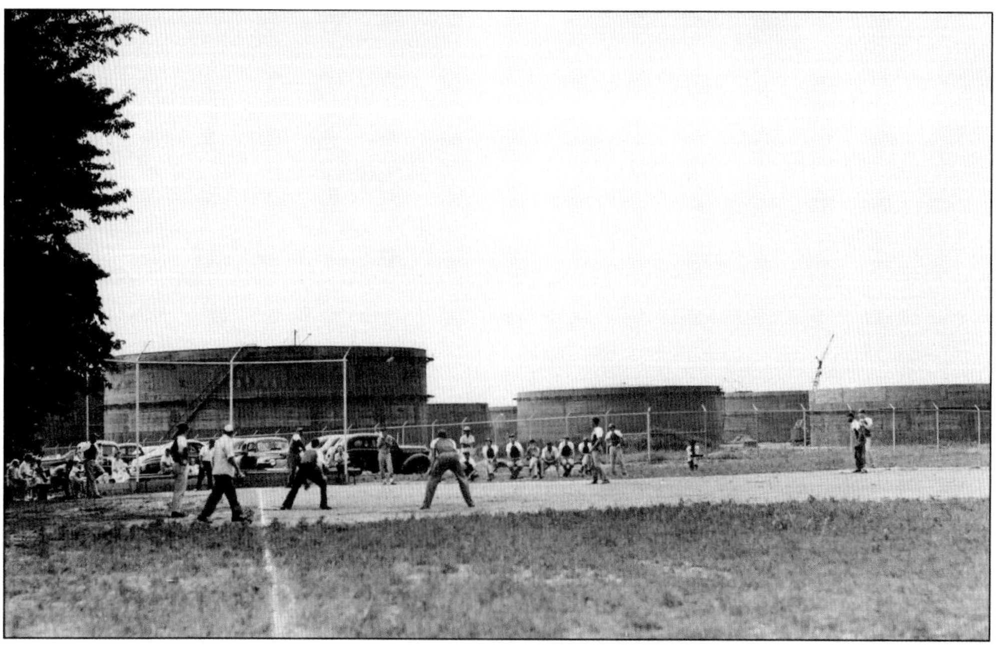

Eight
Houses of Worship

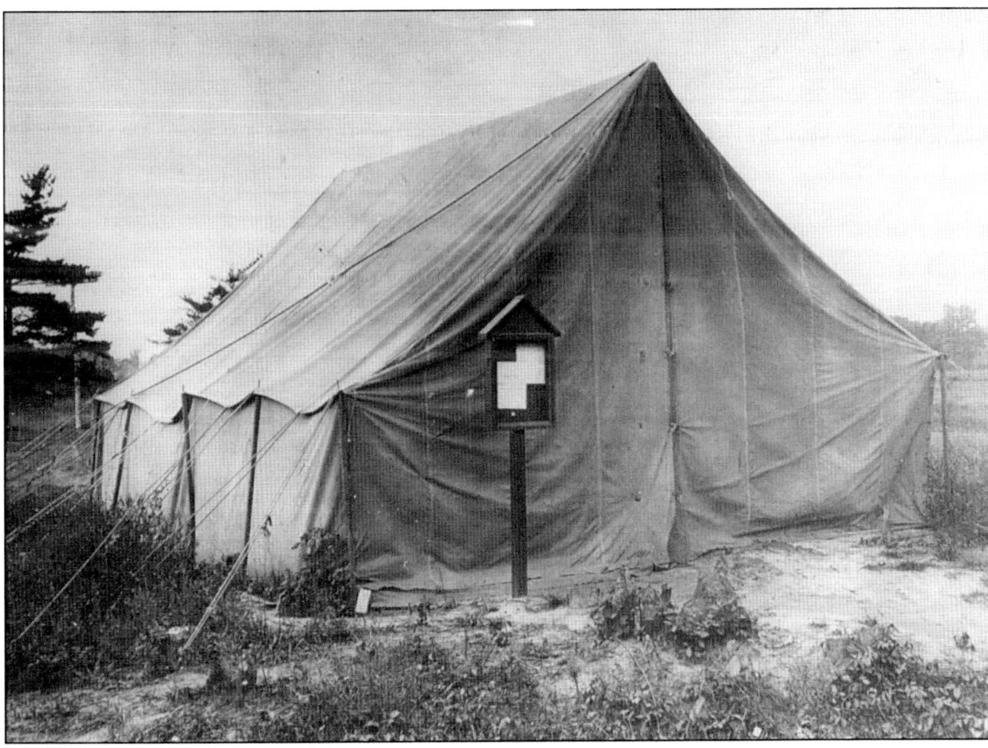

The Verga Welfare United Methodist Church began in July 1917. It had its start when the women of the Woodbury Bag Loading Munitions Plant wanted a place to worship. A tent was erected on the firehouse grounds at Crown Point Road and Hessian Avenue. Shortly after, ground was purchased for a church building on Crown Point Road and Mail Avenue.

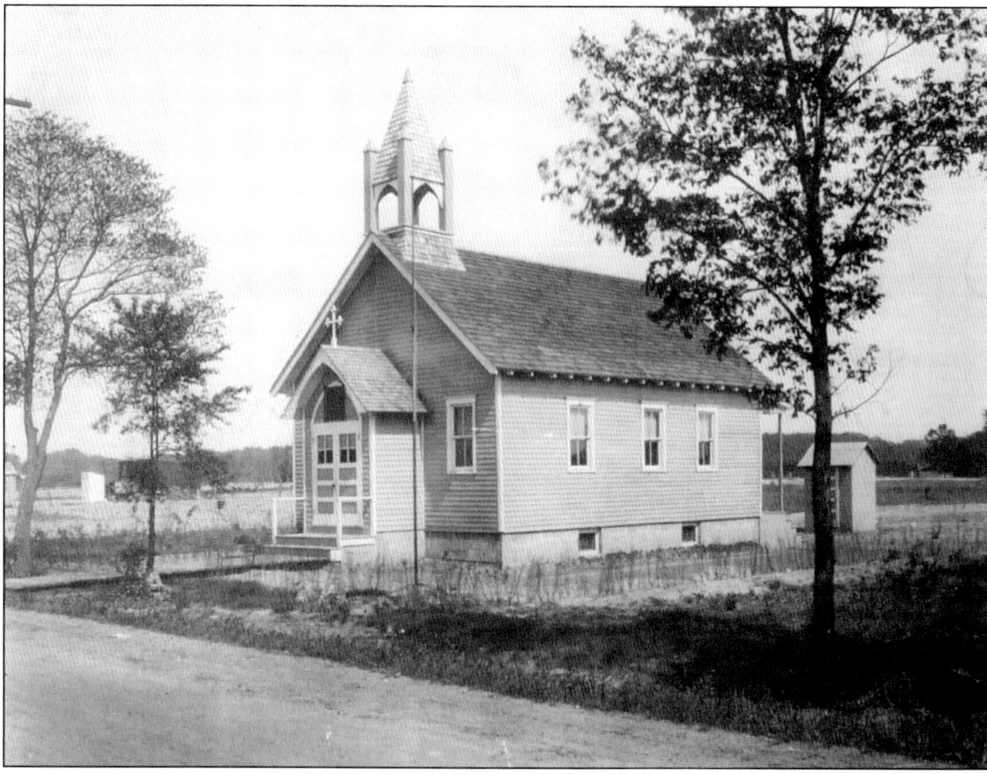

On March 23, 1918, the First Union Welfare Church was opened. The cost to build the church was donated by Arthur F. MacArthur of the Woodbury Bag Loading Munitions Plant and Jane Everett of the Women's Welfare Department. Today, it is known as the Verga Welfare United Methodist Church.

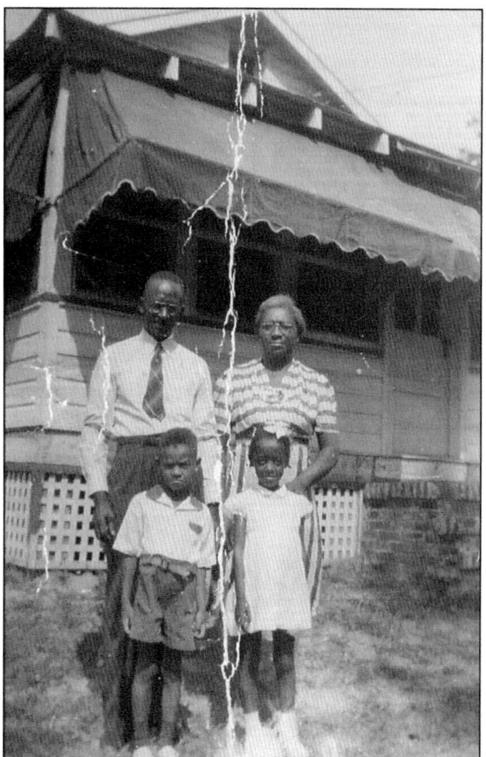

The St. James AME Church began in 1921 when township residents Frances Johnson, William P. Purnell, and William's wife, Della E. Purnell, organized the first Sunday school class. The class was held in the Purnell family home on Salem Avenue in the Thorofare section of town. Pictured outside of their home are William P. Purnell, Della Purnell, grandson Frederick Purnell, and granddaughter Barbara Purnell Green around 1940. (Courtesy of the Purnell family.)

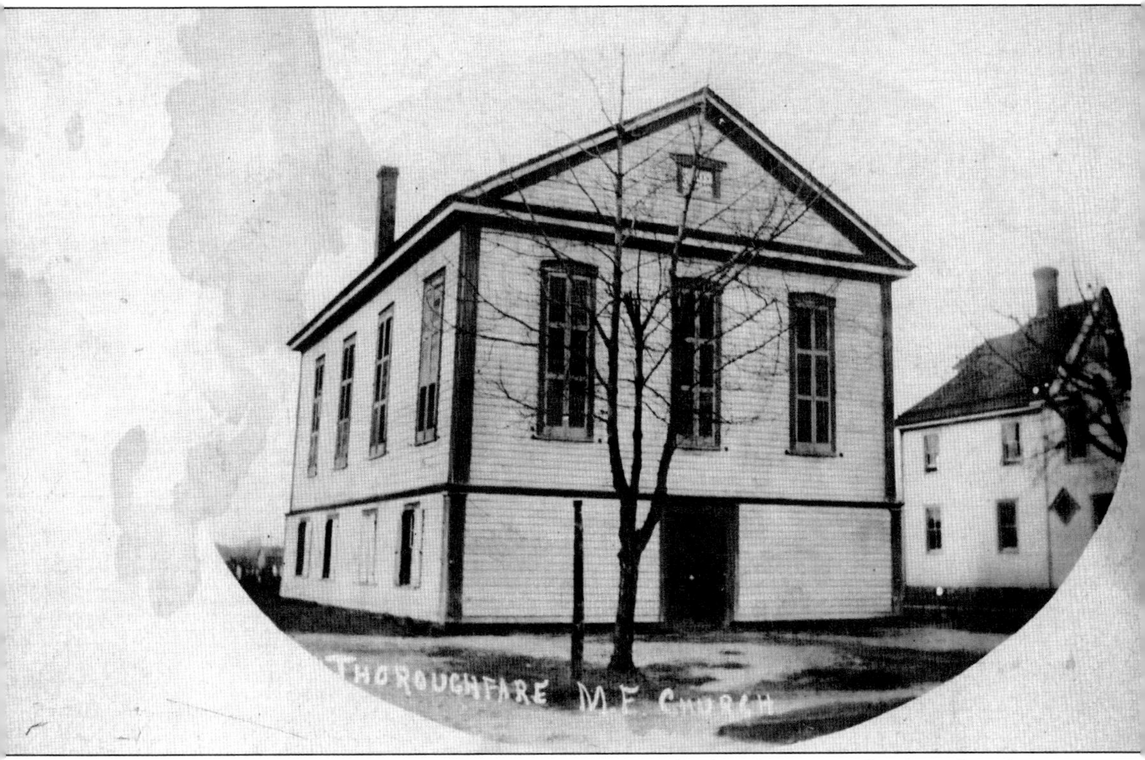

Pictured is the original Thoroughfare Methodist Episcopal Church. It was the first church in West Deptford Township. In 1858, the congregation built its first church on Church Street in the Thorofare section of town. By 1908, the congregation outgrew the original church, and a new building was erected. In 1939, the word Episcopal was dropped, and the church became St. Paul's Methodist Church. In 1968, the name was once again changed to St. Paul's United Methodist Church.

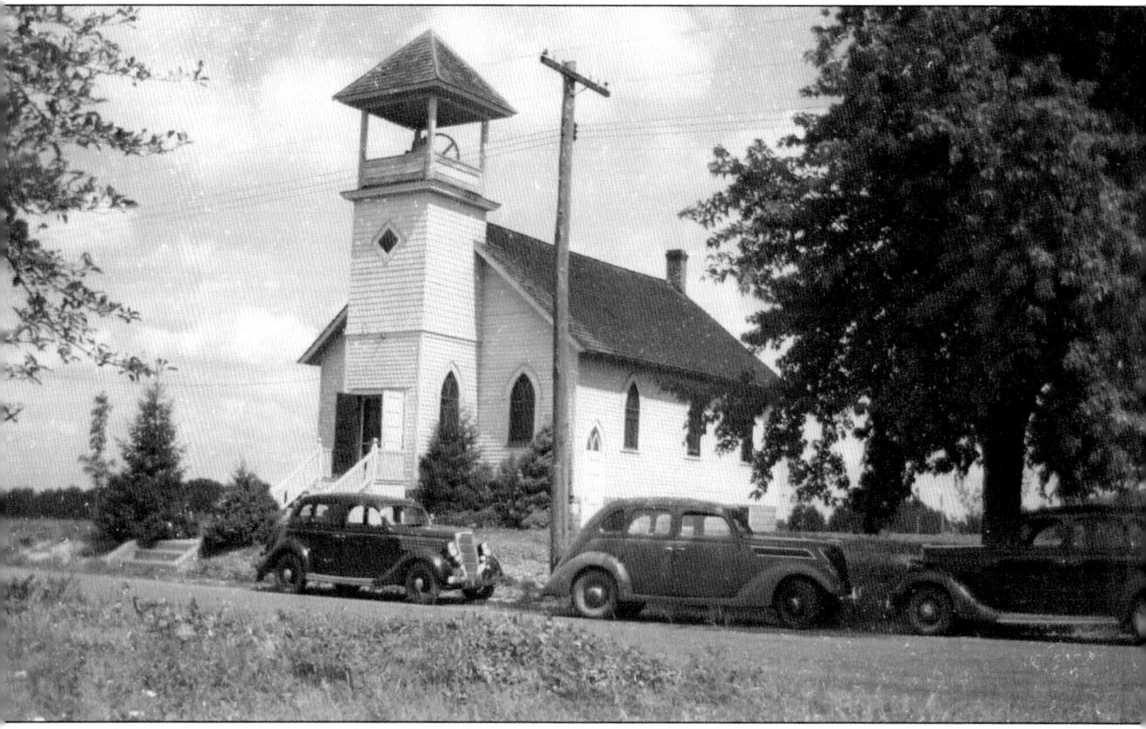

The Mantua Grove Sunday school history dates back to 1870 when meetings were held in the Mantua Grove Schoolhouse. In 1920, John Nolte Sr. donated the land for the church. The chapel was dedicated on April 2, 1922, and the belfry was dedicated in 1926 with John Nolte Sr. ringing the bell, which he had presented to the congregation. Nondenominational services are still held every Sunday and Wednesday.

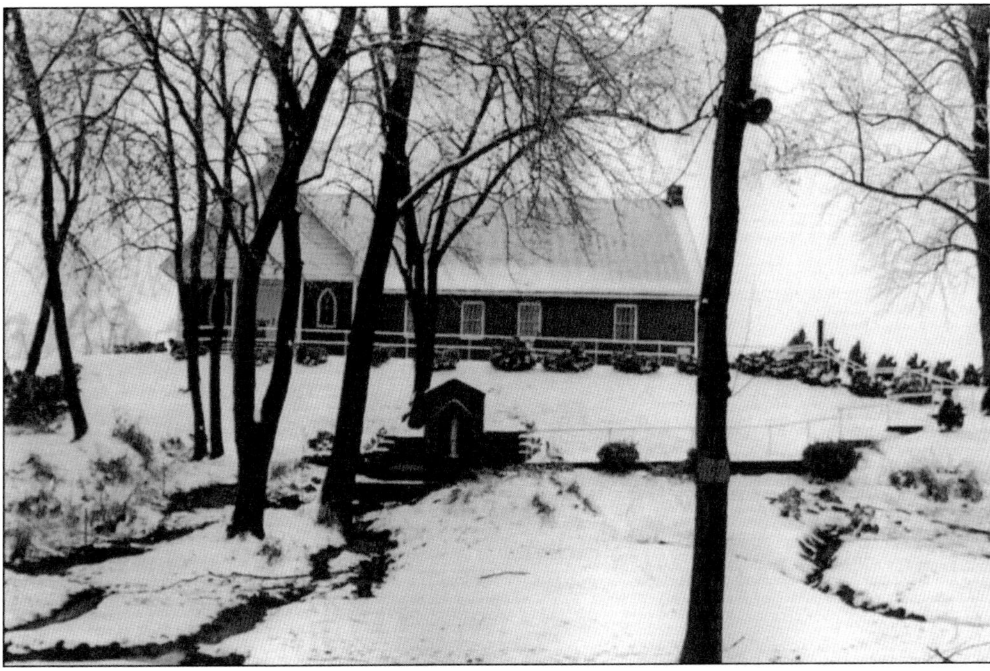

Pictured is the God's House of All Faiths and People, located on the Hangsterfer property. William Hangsterfer, a successful, international industrialist, built a nondenominational house of worship on his West Deptford property. He wanted to get people of various religions together where they could put their actions into deeds regardless of their religious affiliation. For years, religious organizations and individuals used the chapel for weddings and christenings. The building is currently closed to the public, but the family continues to maintain the chapel in honor of William Hangsterfer. (Both, courtesy of Hangsterfer and Jones family.)

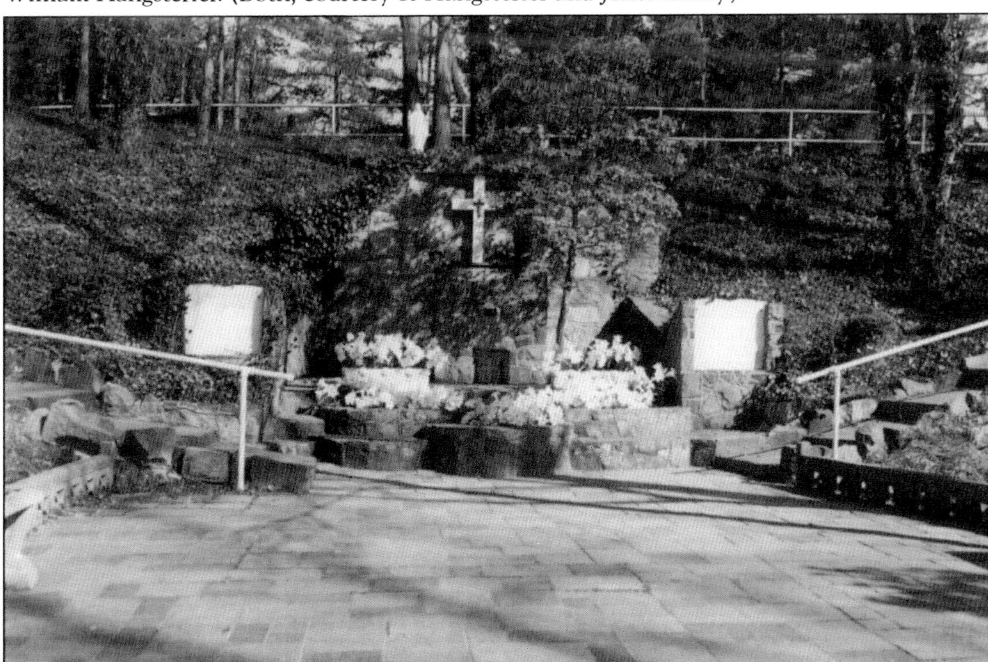

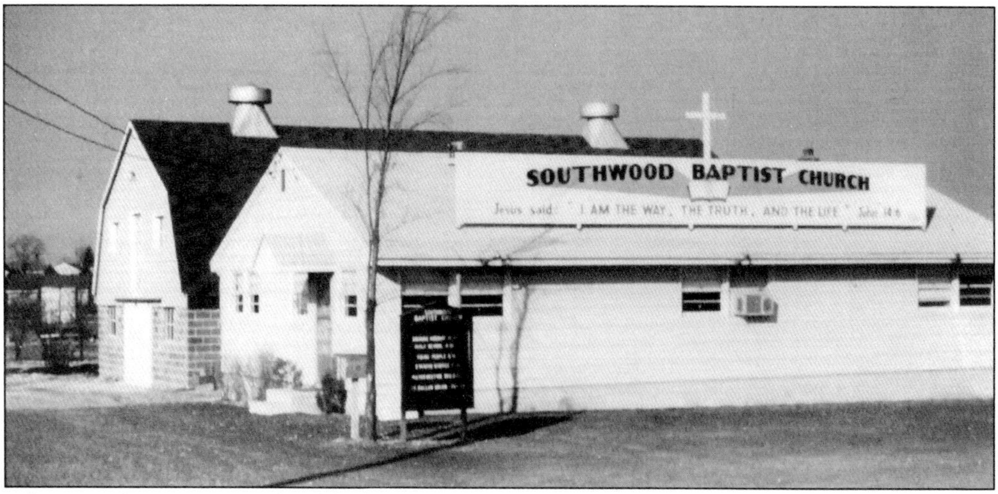

After initially meeting in a local firehouse, the newly formed Southwood Baptist Church purchased land on Biscayne Boulevard in Green-Fields Heights that had served as the storage shed and office for Greenfield Village's developer. Services were held in the barn from 1957 until 1965, when a new location was found.

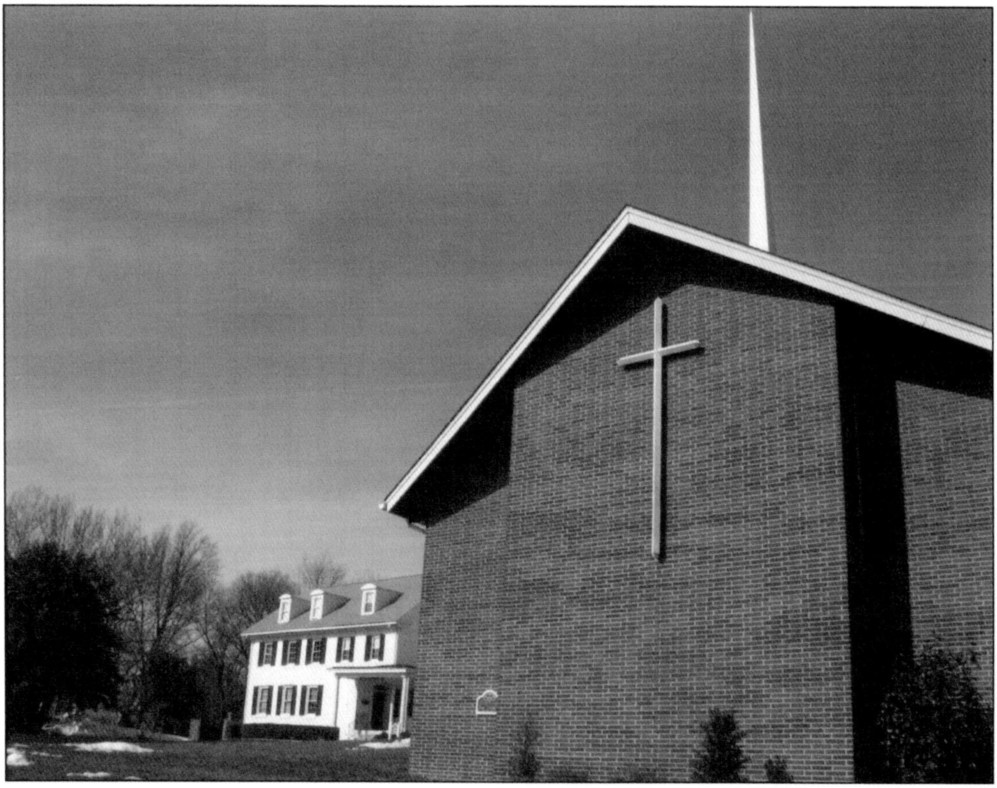

In 1965, the Southwood Baptist congregation purchased the historic Griscom Homestead with two additional acres on Griscom Lane in Greenfields Village. Services were first held in 1970. The Griscom Homestead still stands and is used as the church's administration building. Note that the famous Griscom holly tree sits in the background. It is one of the oldest holly trees in the state of New Jersey.

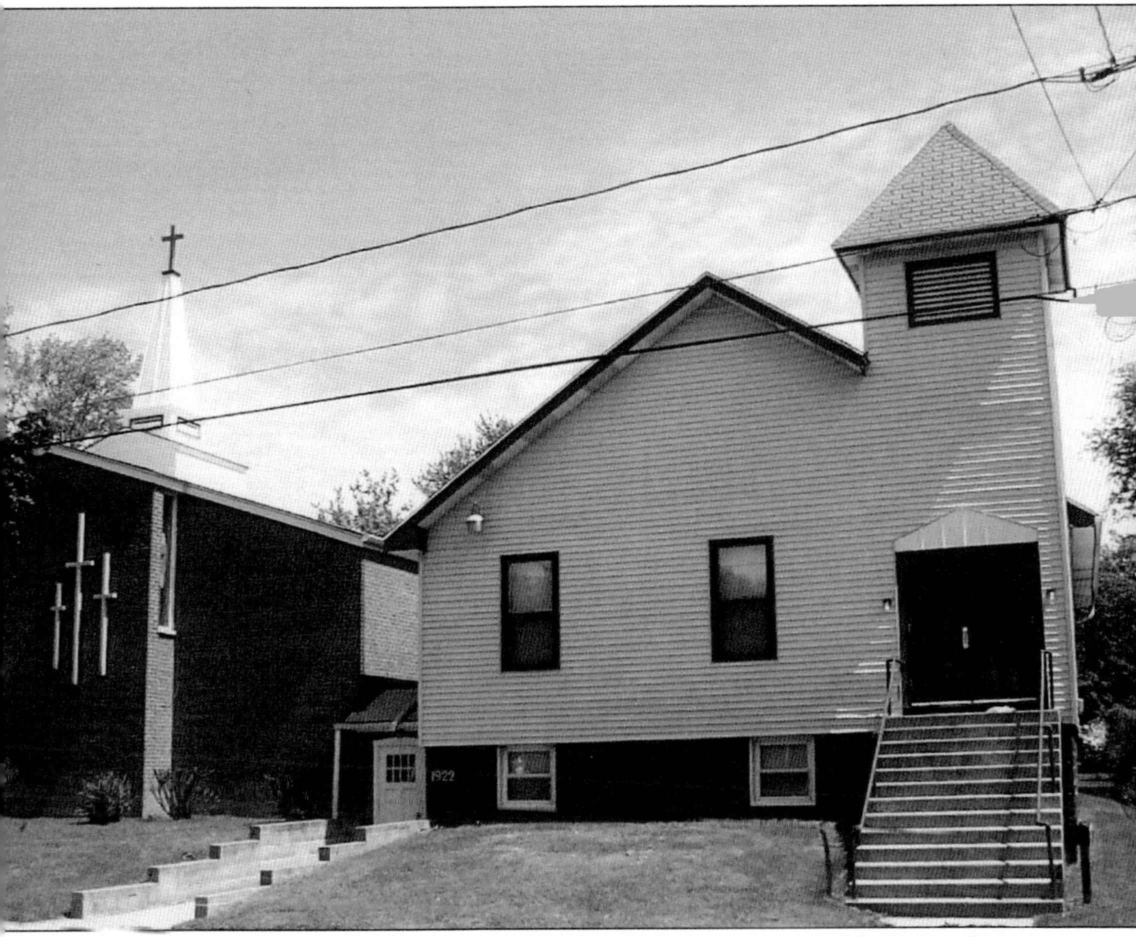

Colonial United Methodist Church began in June 1922 and was first known as the Colonial Manor Methodist Episcopal Church. The original building, which is still in use today, was constructed with volunteer laborers on land donated by the Colonial Land Company, which sold lots to new residents in the Colonial Manor section of town.

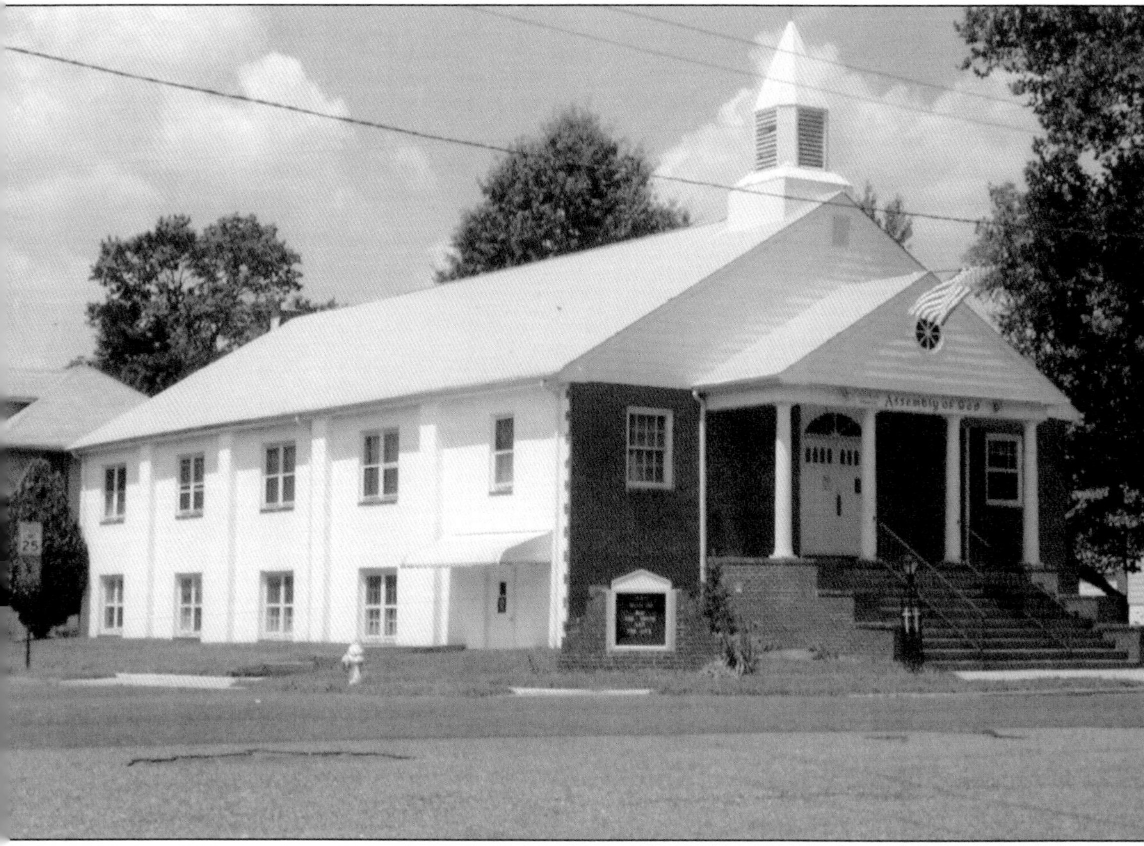

Colonial Manor Assembly of God was incorporated on May 12, 1955, as Woodbury Full Gospel Church. In June 1955, the church was affiliated with the General Council of the Assemblies of God. On March 28, 1956, the church purchased property on Colonial Avenue for the bargain price of $1. By 1957, the basement was finished and services were held there. Services were moved upstairs when the upper level was completed in 1961.

Nine
Sites and Landmarks

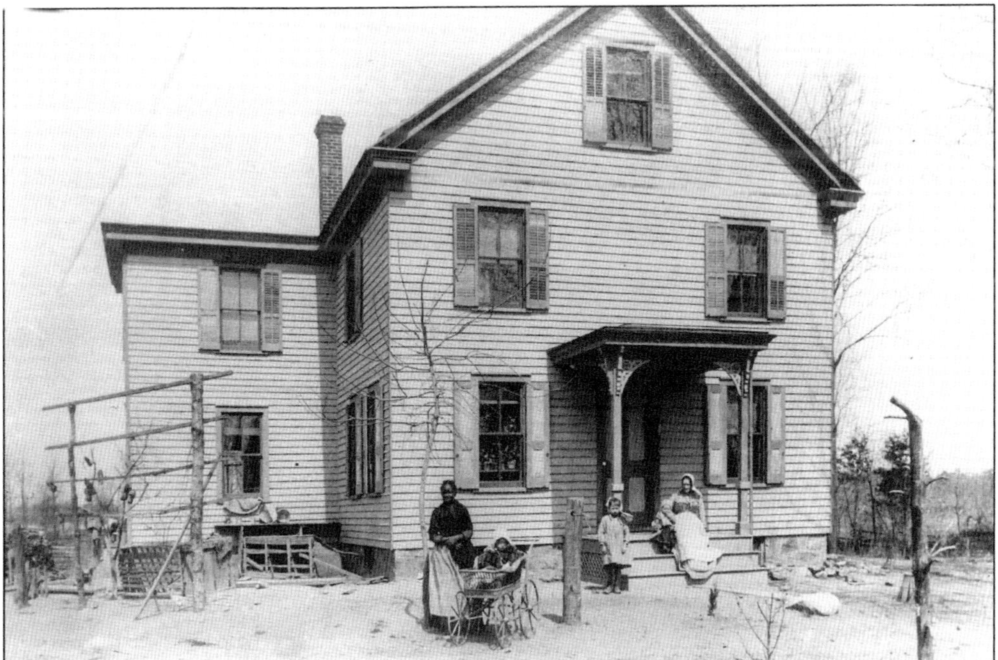

Pictured is the Budd farmhouse. Andes and Emma Budd lived with their family on Hessian Avenue. Emma Budd is sitting on the porch, while the nanny stands by a Budd child in the carriage. (Courtesy of the Gloucester County Historical Society.)

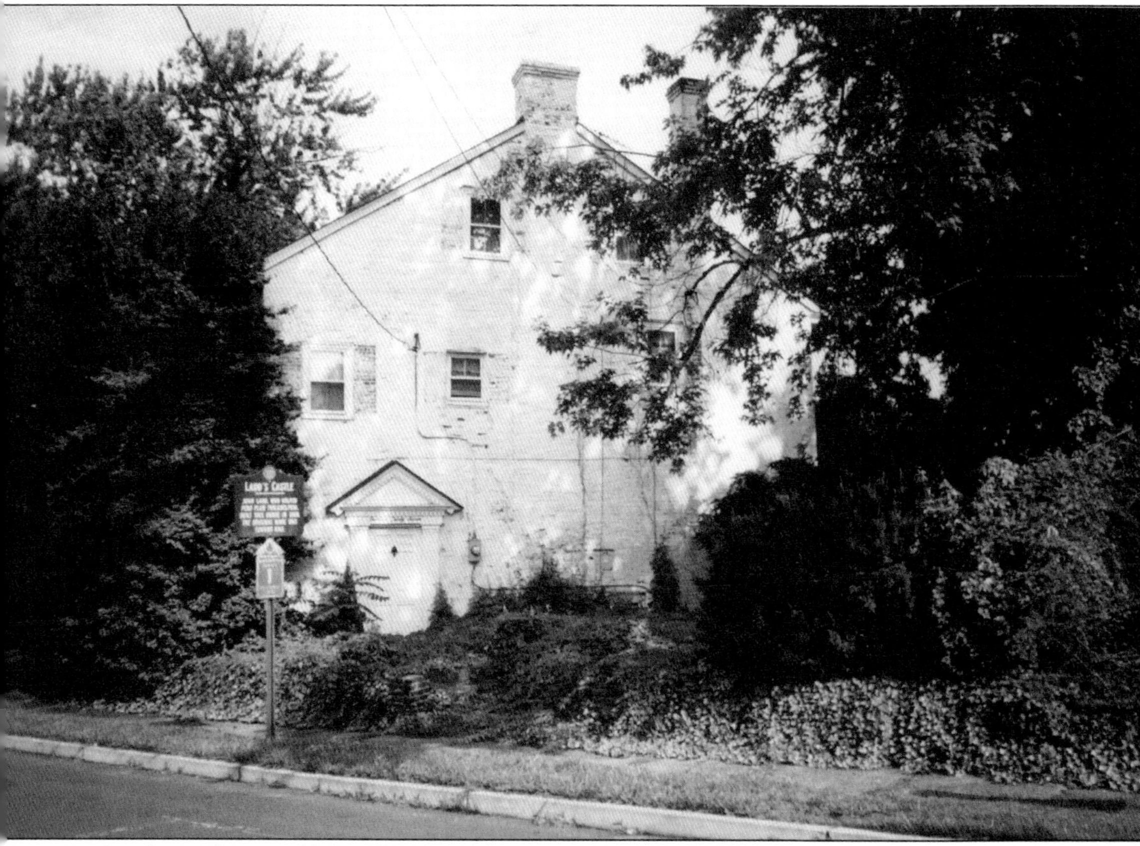

Candor Hall, or Ladd's Castle, was the home of John Ladd. He was contracted by William Penn to lay out the city of Philadelphia. In 1688, he acquired 7,000 acres of land on which he built a brick home with log wings on each side. He lived there until his death in 1743. (Courtesy of Ted Trowbridge.)

Located on Broad Street in West Deptford Township, J.J. Magee Original General Machinist and Automobiles Repaired and Stored was a family-owned business. Today, the company is known as Magee Locksmith. (Courtesy of the Gloucester County Historical Society.)

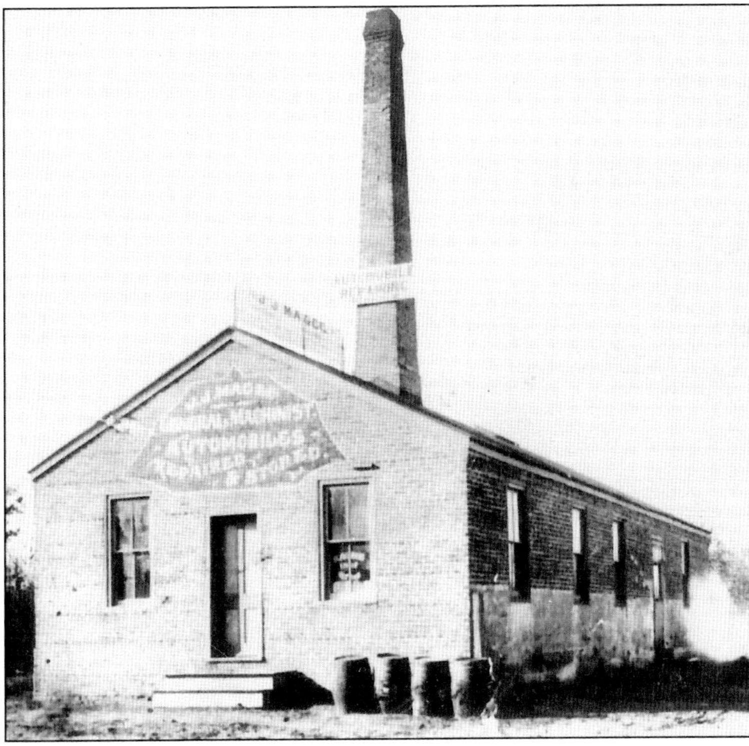

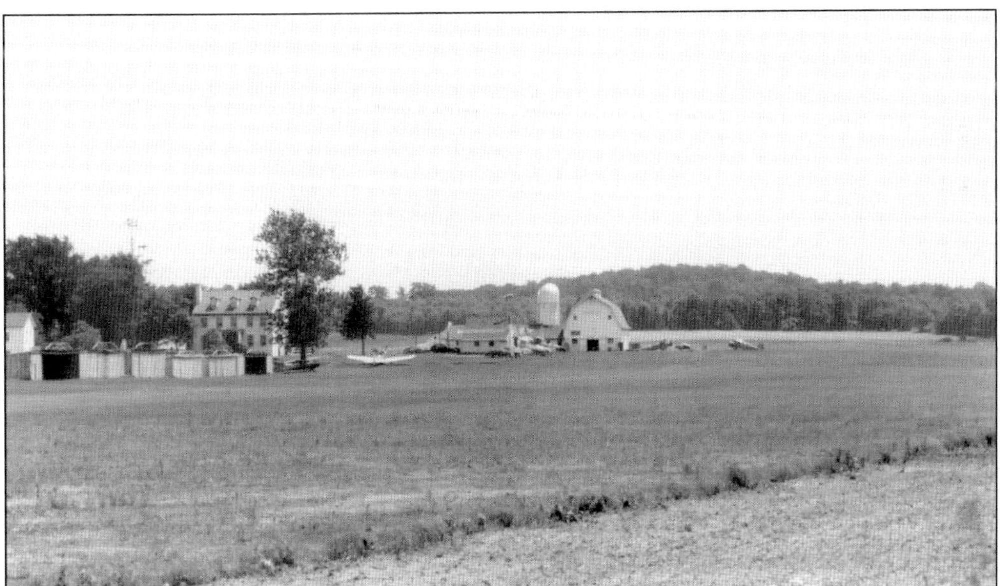

The Hill Airport was located in the Greenfields section of the township. It was located on the site of the Reeves homestead. The property housed three airstrips. (Courtesy of the Gloucester County Historical Society.)

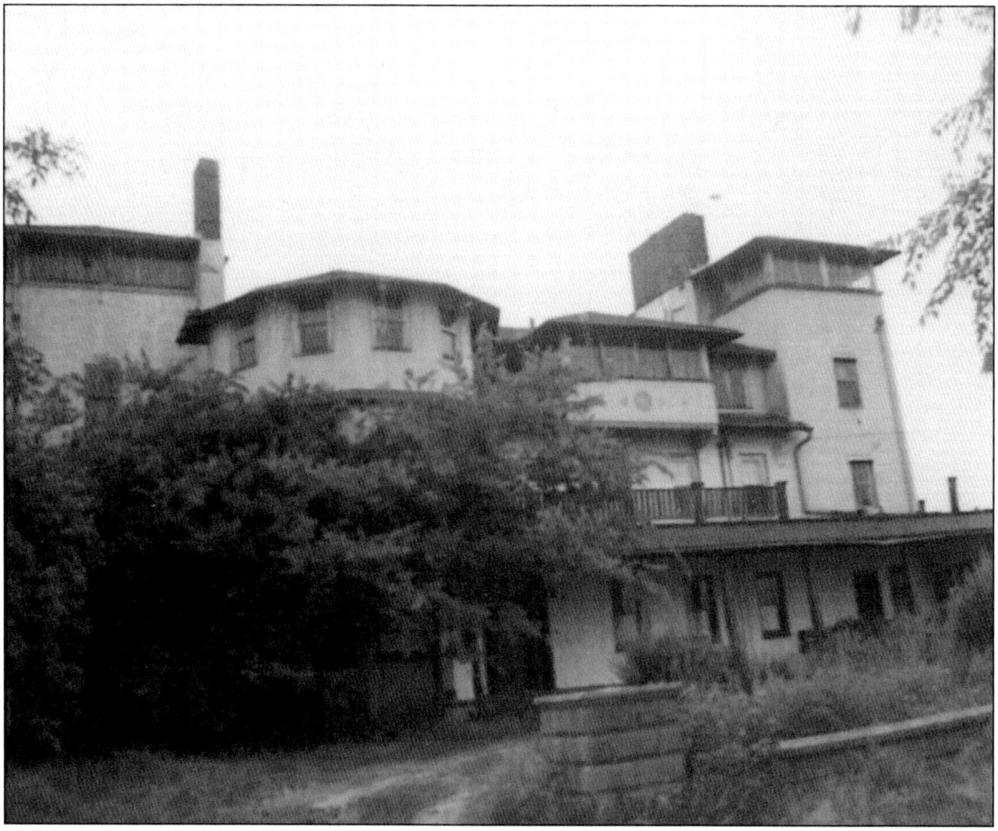

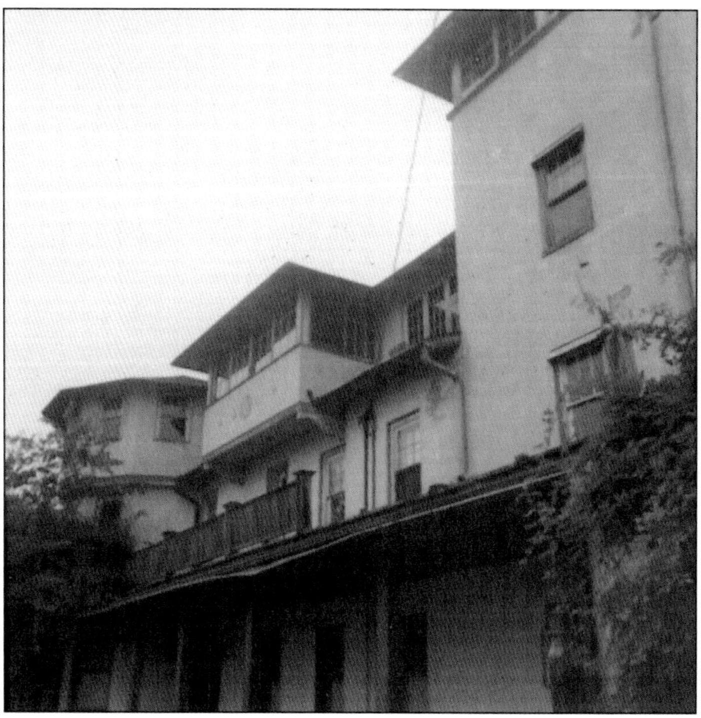

The Isidore Strittmatter home was located on Leonard's Lane near the Delaware River. Doctor Strittmatter was a physician in Philadelphia and the former president of the Philadelphia Medical Society. He purchased the property in 1914 at a cost of $125,000 from Wilson Fitzgerald. The home was originally two houses from the Revolutionary period. It is said that during the Revolutionary War, the homes were used as hospitals. (Both, courtesy of Charles Leonard Jr.)

During the Korean War, antiaircraft bases were established in two locations in West Deptford. One was located on the Texaco Refinery property, and the second was on Paradise Road heading into Paulsboro. C-Battery, or Charlie Battery, was to defend the air corridor for Philadelphia and the refineries. D-Battery, or Dog Battery, was to defend Philadelphia's airport. The camps came to the area in 1952. Construction of the barracks for D-Battery is shown at right. Pictured below is the camp. (Both, courtesy of Joan Wilson.)

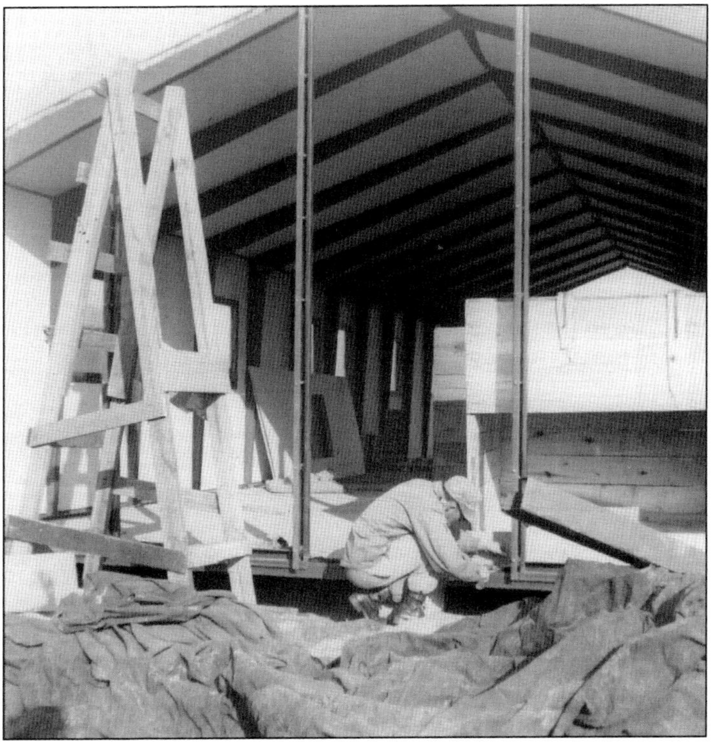

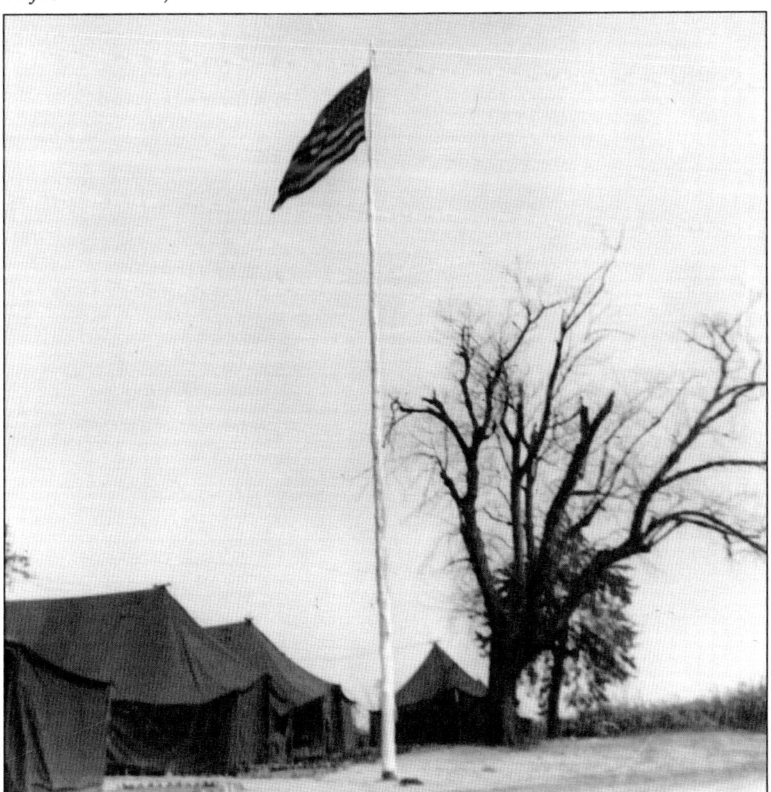

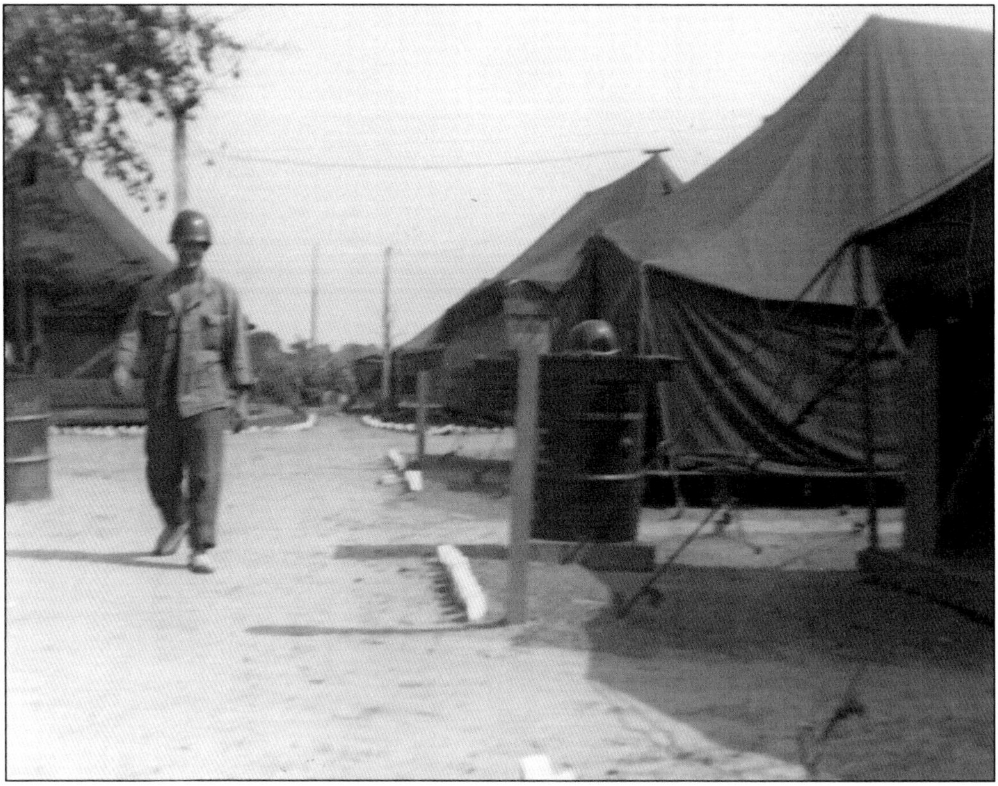

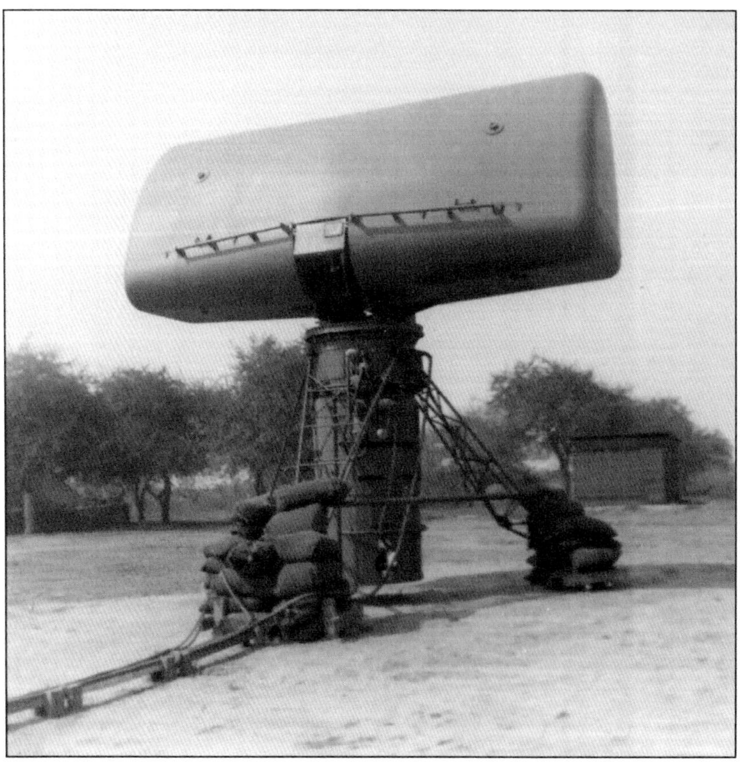

Pictured above is a lone soldier patrolling the camp located in West Deptford. Pictured below is the radar unit that was used to track aircraft. (Both, courtesy of Joan Wilson.)

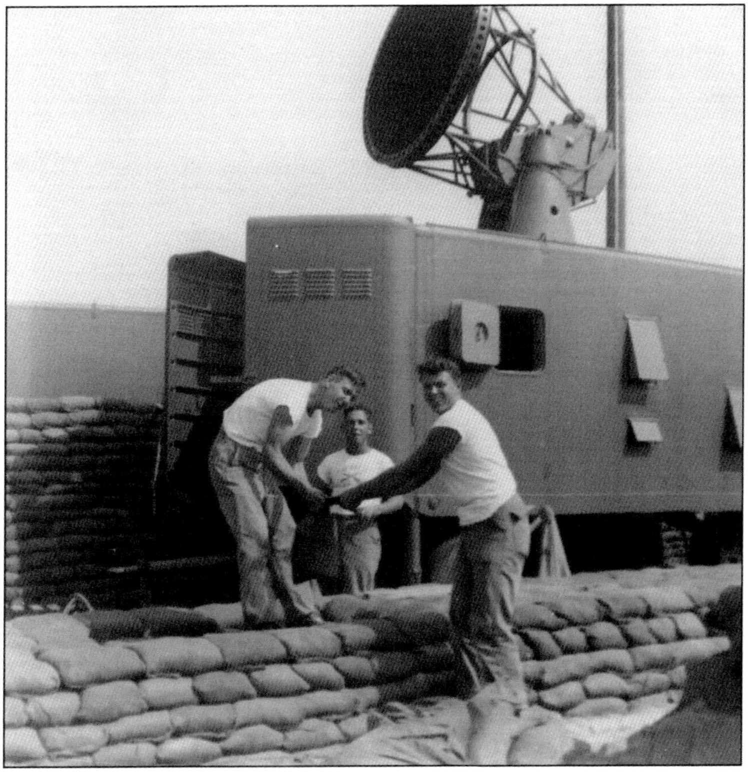

Soldiers build a sandbag barrier around the radar unit. Pictured below is the rear of the radar unit with the sand barrier in place. (Both, courtesy of Joan Wilson.)

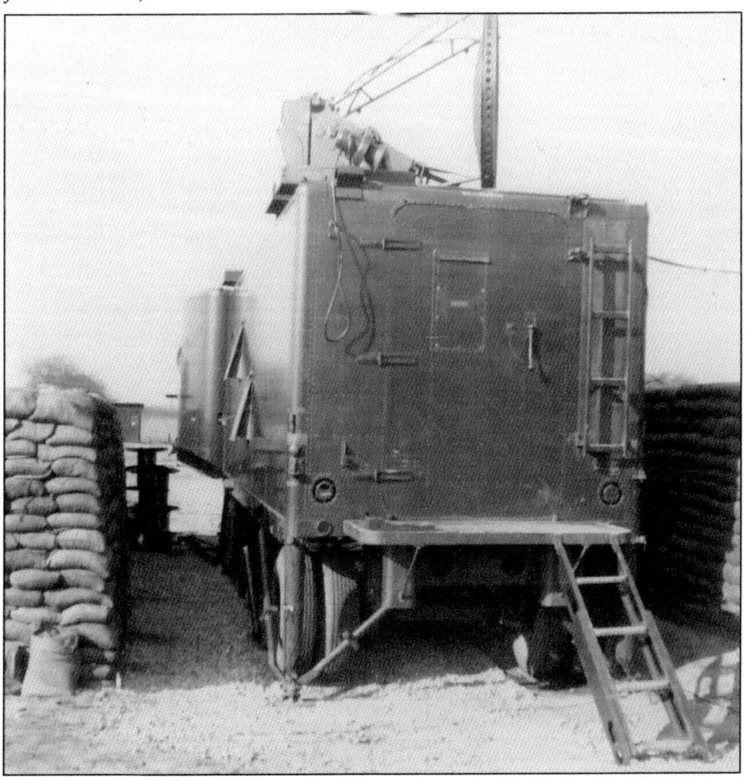

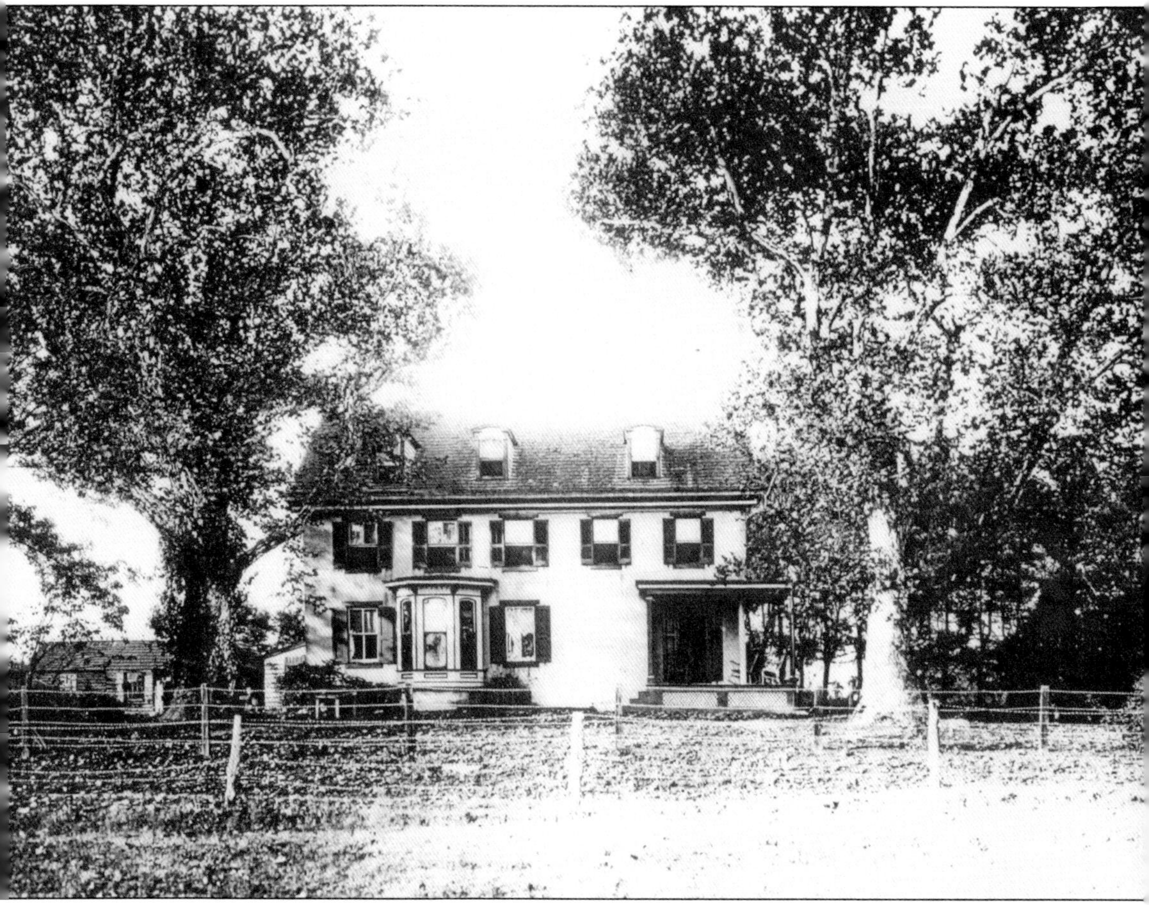

Located in the Greenfields section of West Deptford, the Griscom House stands as a reminder of West Deptford's role during Colonial times. Ann Cooper, widow of John Cooper, purchased the property in 1731; the farm consisted of 231 acres. It was deeded through the families for generations. It is said that, during her childhood, Betsy Griscom Ross spent summers at the "Green-Fields Farm." (Courtesy of the Gloucester County Historical Society.)

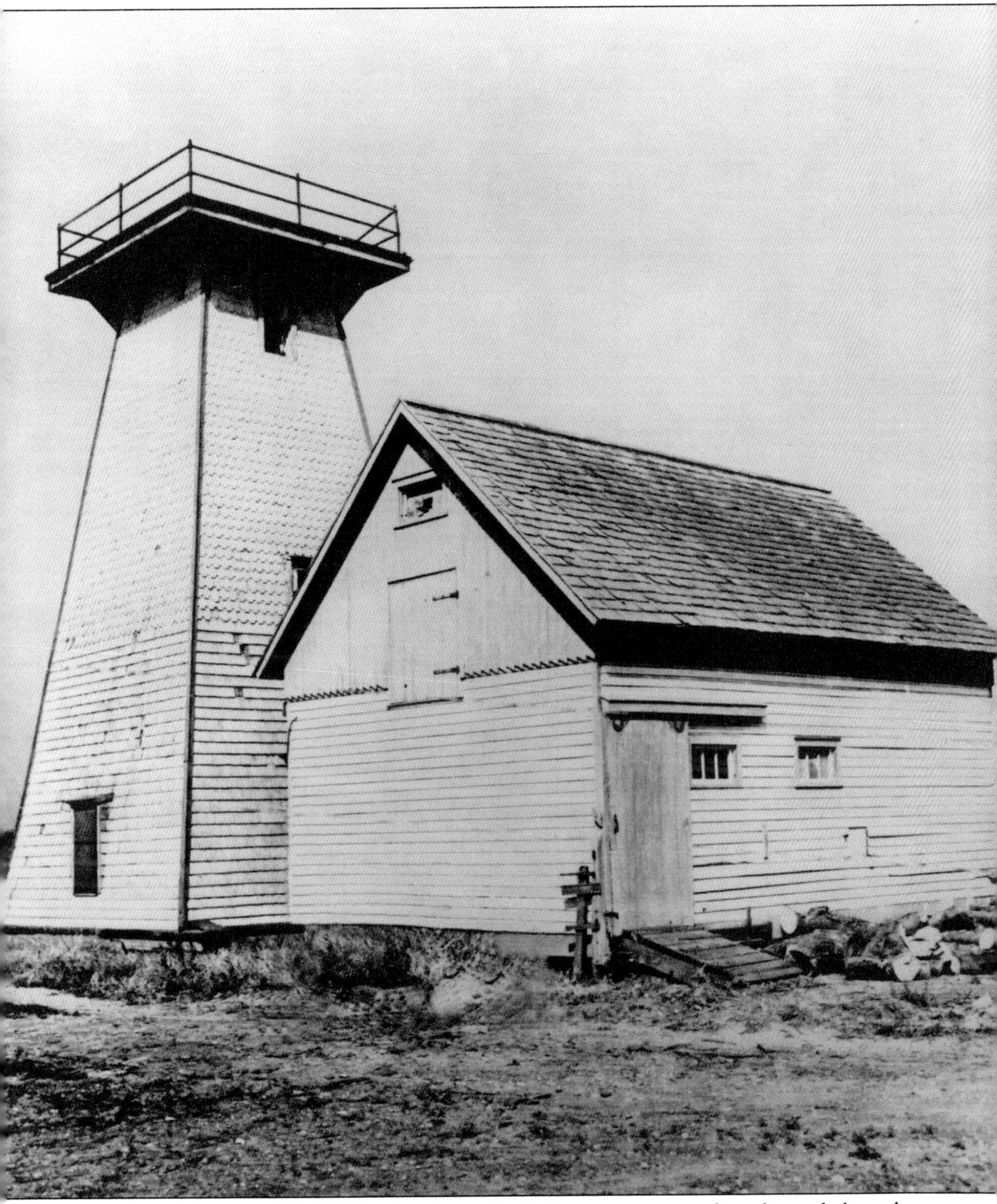

The Horseshoe Range, East Group, Rear Range Light Station was one of two located along the Delaware River. The West Group Light Station was located on Fort Mifflin Military Reservation in Pennsylvania. The Horseshoe Light Station lit up the night sky for the first time on October 1, 1881. The ranges were built to help ships safely pass the Horseshoe Shoal and navigate Horseshoe Bend on the Delaware River.

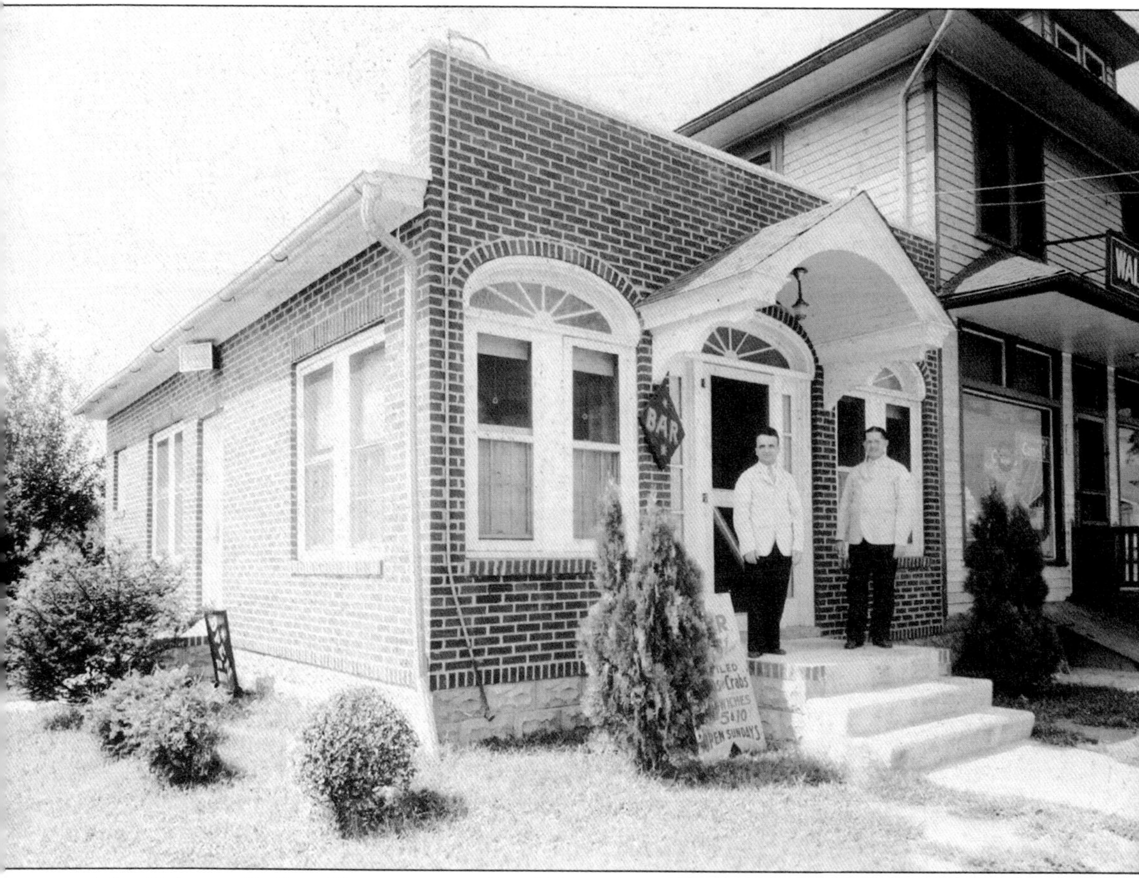

The Colonial Café and Bar was opened in 1934 and was attached to the Walt Whitman Grocery Store. It was located on Colonial Avenue in the Colonial Manor section of the township. (Courtesy of Mike Bittner.)

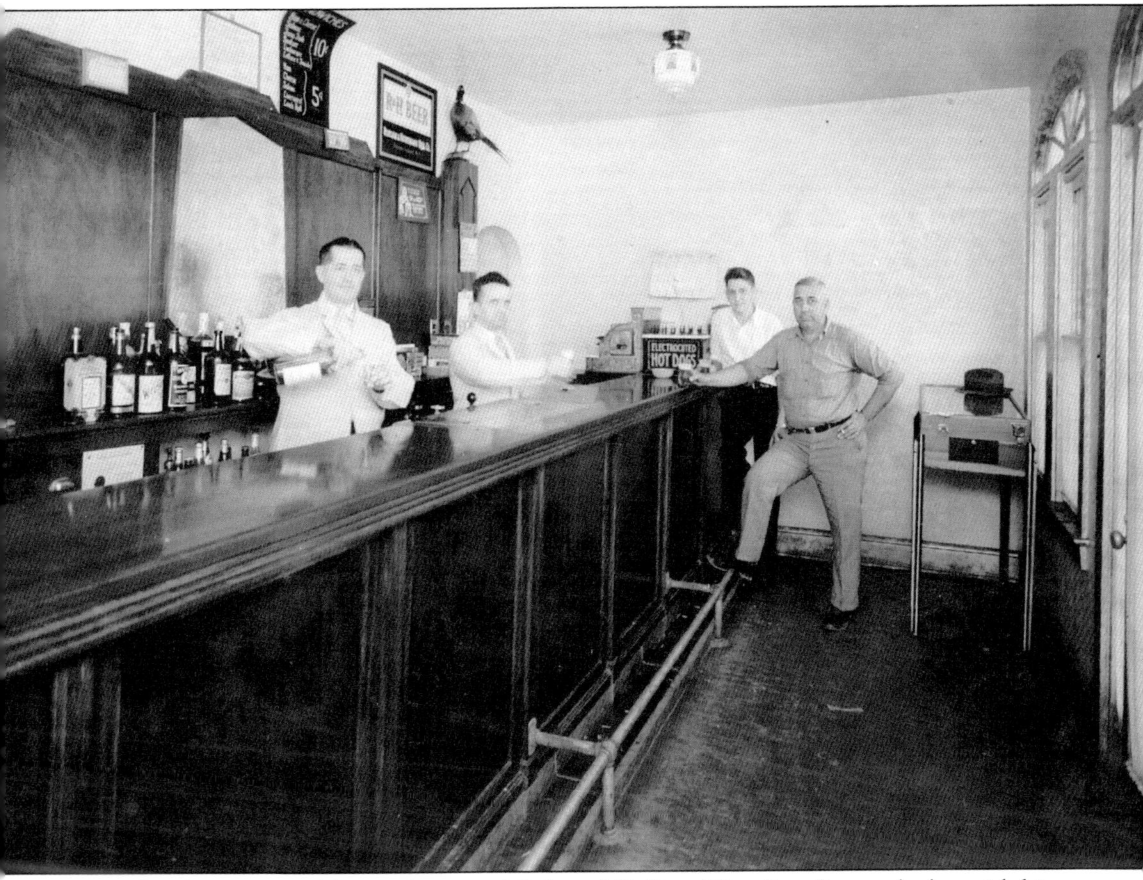

Pictured is the interior of the newly opened Colonial Café and Bar. Standing at the bar with his leg on the rail is customer Phil Barnes. The Colonial Café and Bar continues to operate today. (Courtesy of Mike Bittner.)

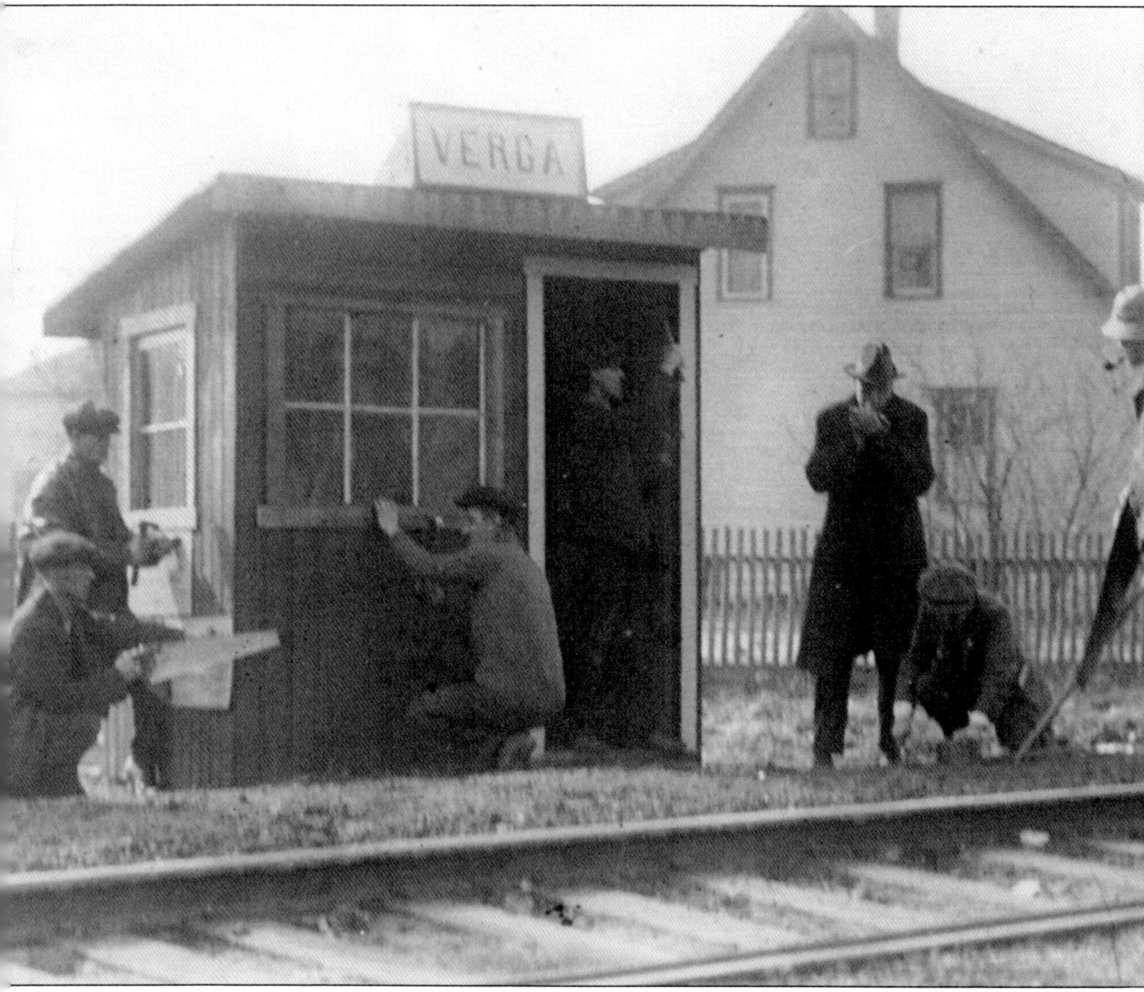

During the early 1900s, people depended on the train system to ship goods. Pictured is a train depot in the Verga section of the township. (Courtesy of Verga Volunteer Fire Company No. 1.)

Ten

RECREATION

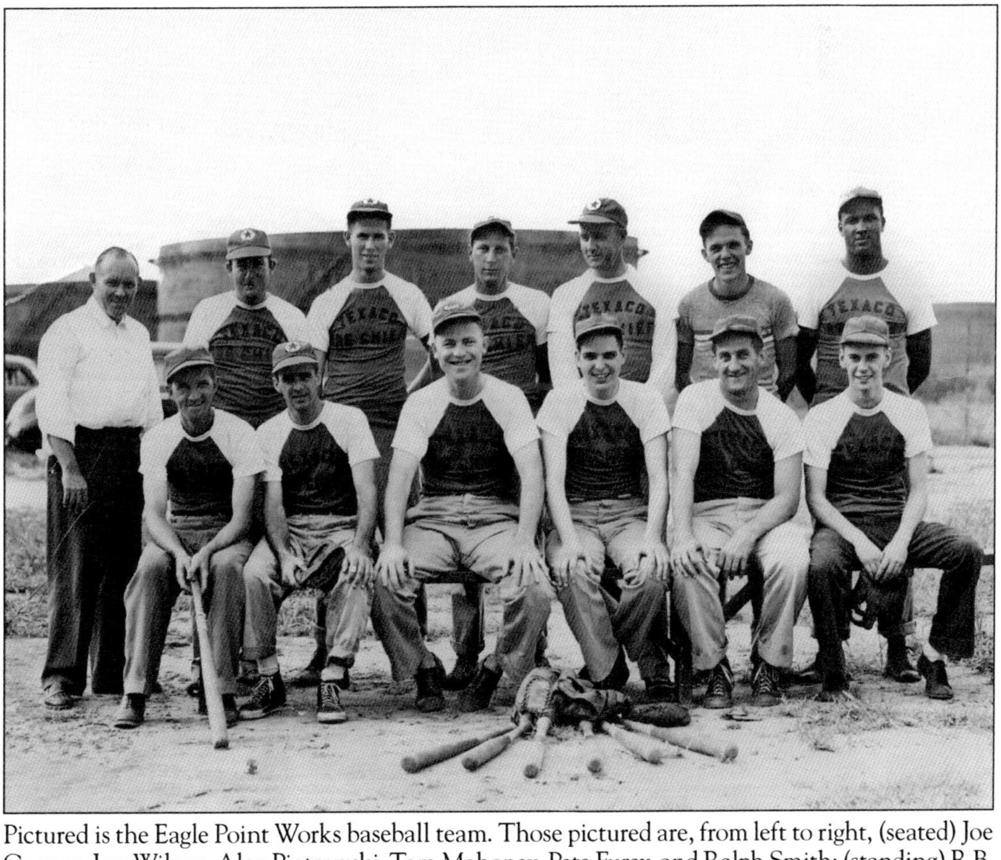

Pictured is the Eagle Point Works baseball team. Those pictured are, from left to right, (seated) Joe Cooney, Jess Wilson, Alex Piotrowski, Tom Mahoney, Pete Furey, and Ralph Smith; (standing) R.B. Johnson, Ed Cobb, Jim Scott, Howard Morrissey, M.B. Burks, Bob Densten, and Jay Frisbey.

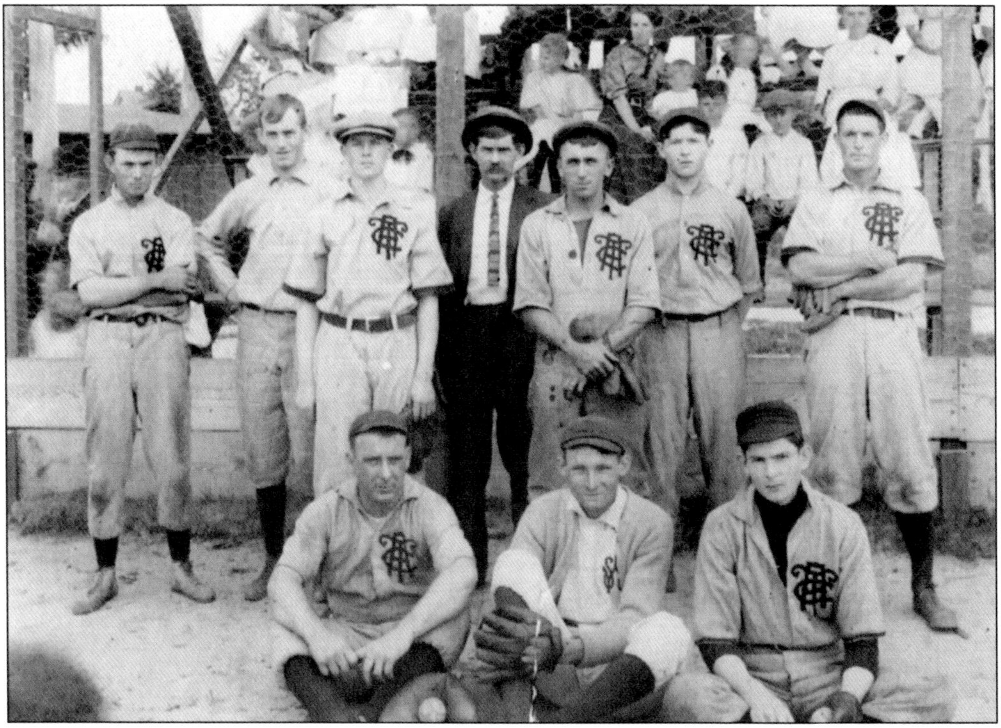

Pictured is a baseball team around 1910. Those pictured are, from left to right, (seated) Edward Morris, Alex Bonsack, and Frank Rambo; (standing) Charles Leonard, unidentified, Elwood Rambo, Warren Rambo, manager Isaac Bowers, Herbert Rambo, and Walter Marpole. (Courtesy of Charles Leonard.)

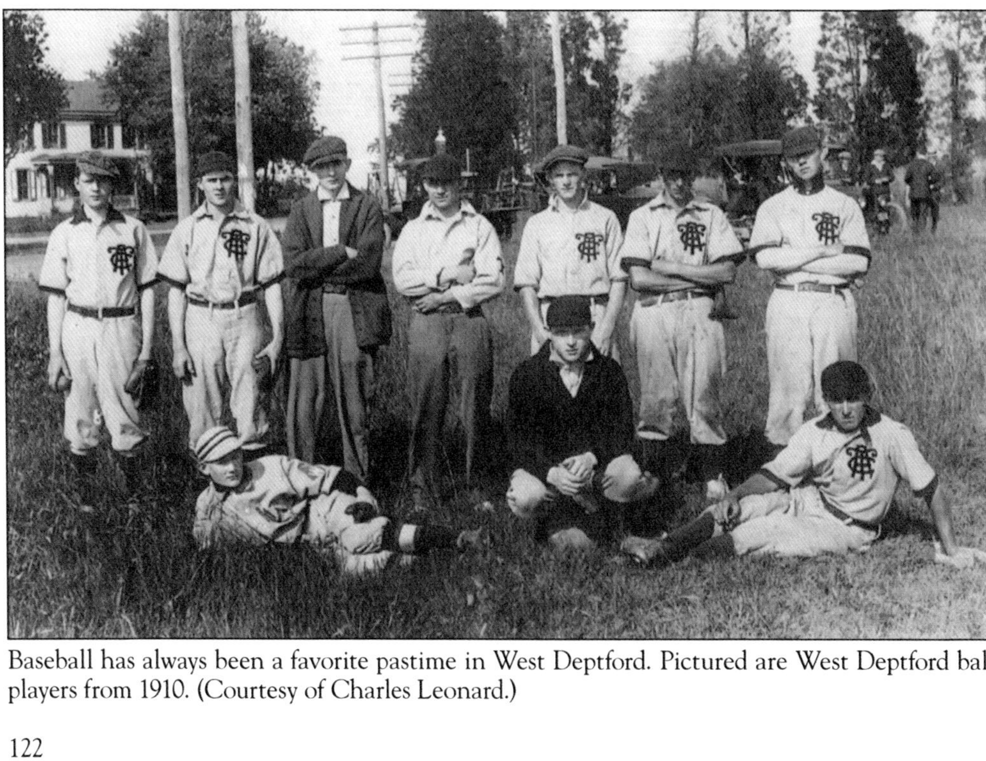

Baseball has always been a favorite pastime in West Deptford. Pictured are West Deptford ball players from 1910. (Courtesy of Charles Leonard.)

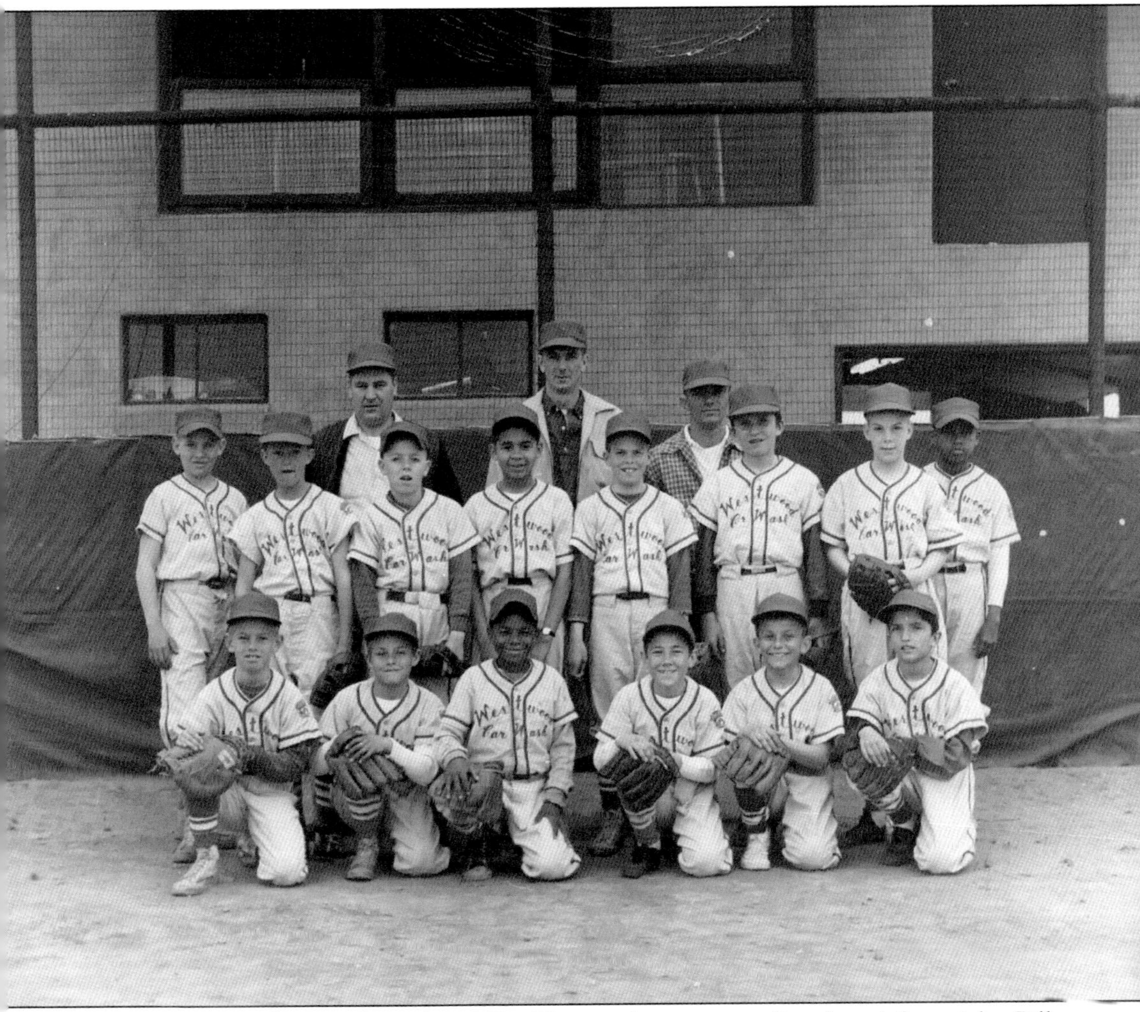

Pictured is a baseball team from the 1960s. The coaches are, standing from left to right, Bill Sampson, Andy Campbell, and Frank Stinger. (Courtesy of Andy Campbell.)

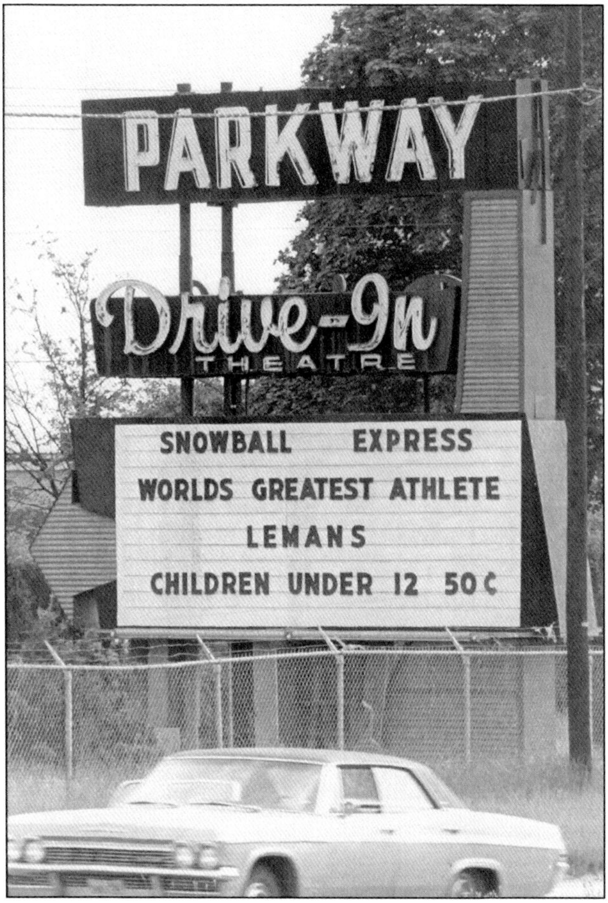

The Parkway Drive-in Theatre was located on Route 130 in West Deptford Township. Patrons were attracted by the large marquee located along the highway. Pictured below is a ticket good for one adult admission to the drive-in. (Both, courtesy of the Gloucester County Historical Society.)

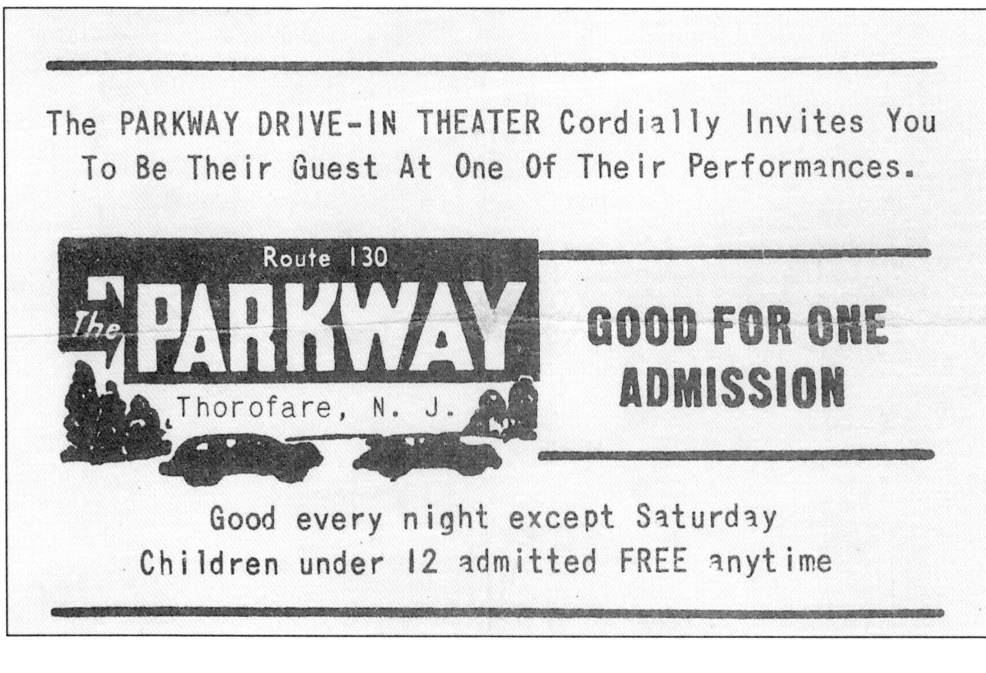

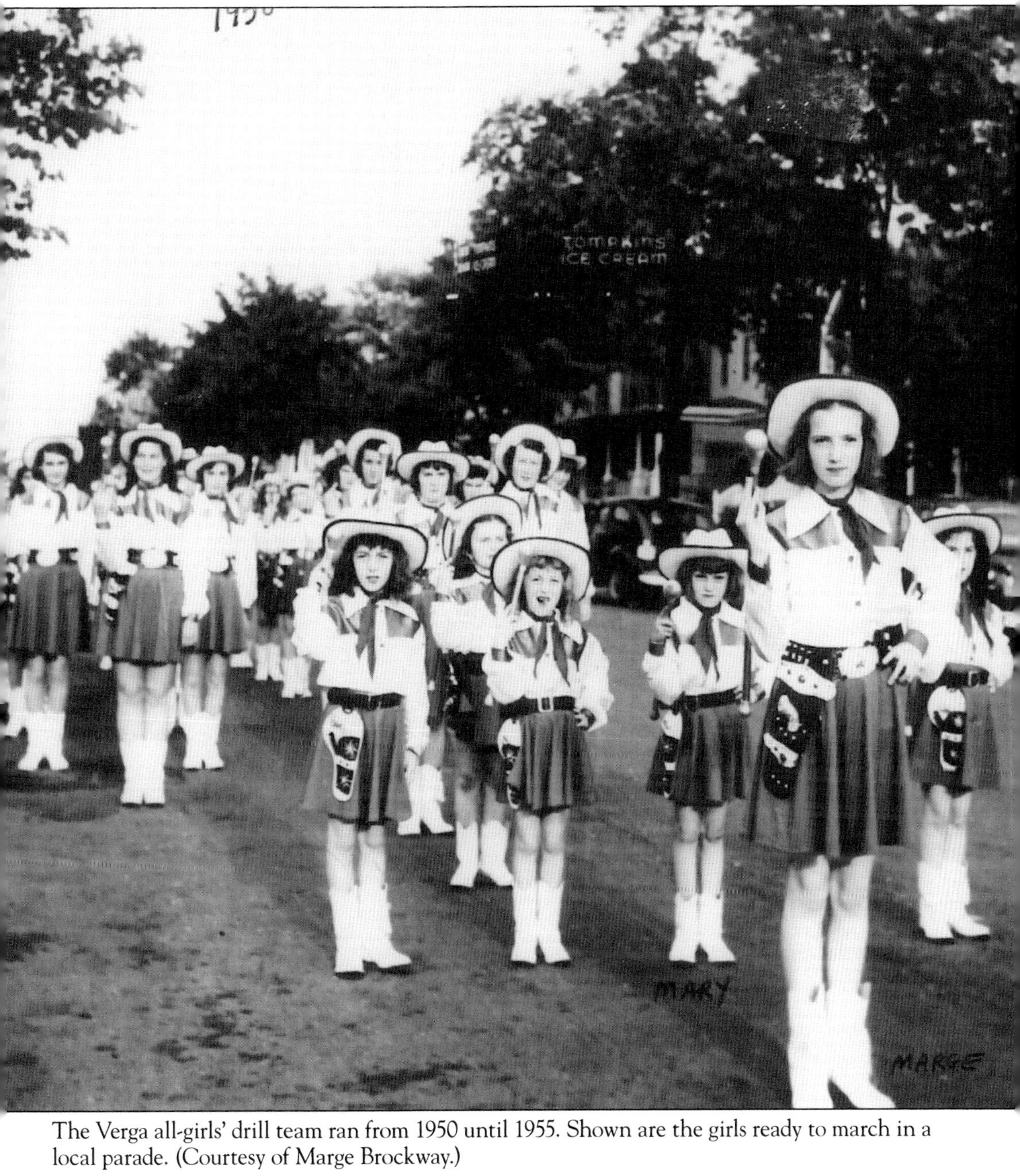

The Verga all-girls' drill team ran from 1950 until 1955. Shown are the girls ready to march in a local parade. (Courtesy of Marge Brockway.)

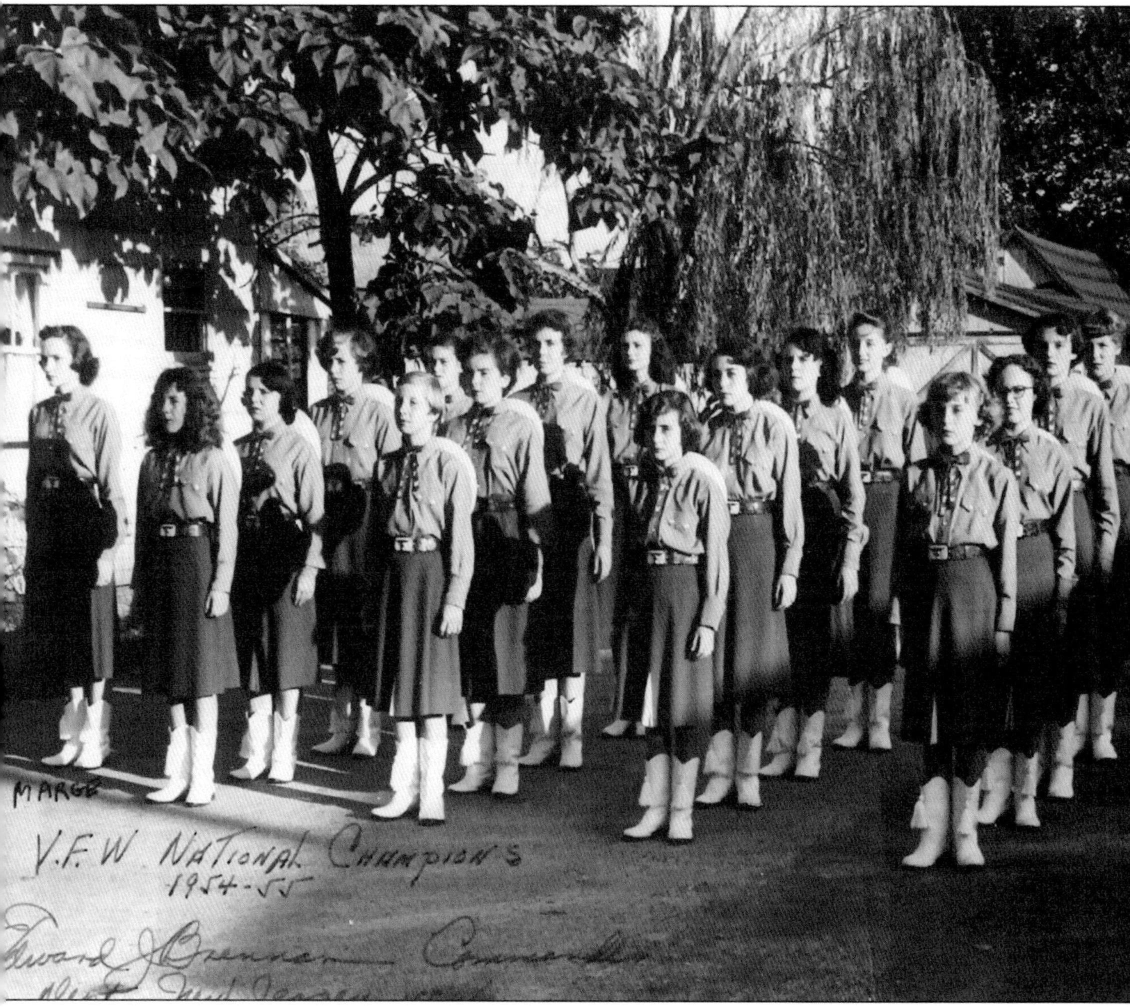

The Verga VFW Post 7125 all-girls' drill team was National Champions in 1954–1955. (Courtesy of Marge Brockway.)

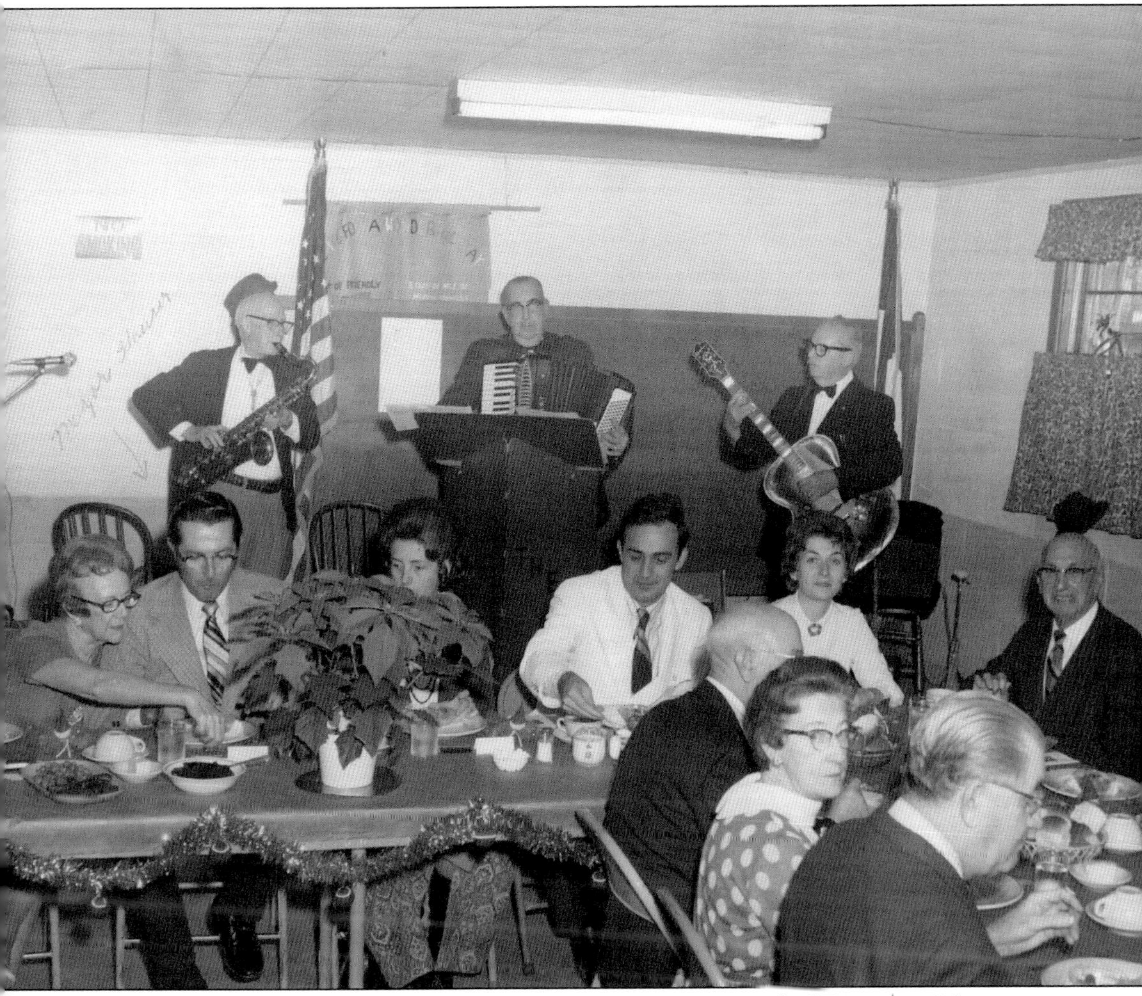

Youths were not the only ones with organized activities in West Deptford Township. The senior citizens also participated in many activities. Above, they are celebrating the holiday season at their annual Christmas party around 1973.